# AN INTRODUCTION TO THE
# PHONETICS
## OF
# AMERICAN ENGLISH

CHARLES KENNETH THOMAS, Ph. D.

PROFESSOR OF SPEECH, UNIVERSITY OF FLORIDA

*Second Edition*

THE RONALD PRESS COMPANY · NEW YORK

PE1135
T5
1958

16MP

Library of Congress Catalog Card Number: 58–5837
PRINTED IN THE UNITED STATES OF AMERICA

# Preface

This book deals with the pronunciation of English in the United States, and is designed primarily for elementary courses in phonetics. It should also be useful in courses dealing with the improvement or correction of voice and speech. Chapters 21 to 23 should be useful in an advanced course in linguistic geography.

Two principles underlie the presentation of the subject matter. One is that the distinctive sound unit, or *phoneme*, as discussed in Chapter 1, is basic to our understanding of speech. English, like any other language, rests on basic phonemic patterns, but not all varieties of English use exactly the same pattern.

On the other hand, the phoneme is not the whole story. In the actual production of speech the phoneme may be thought of as an abstraction or as a target. No two individuals pronounce the same words in exactly the same way, and no individual says the same word twice in exactly the same way. The individual units in the sequence of actual sounds are known as *allophones*. The allophones represent the phonemes, but include nondistinctive as well as distinctive features in their makeup. If the speaker speaks intelligibly, his allophonic variations will be interpreted by the listener in terms of whatever phonemic pattern the speaker and the listener both understand.

iii

Some of these allophonic variations are characteristic of individual speakers; with a large enough sampling of a particular kind of speech they tend to cancel out. Some variations are regional; the variations in the vowel quality in a word like *yarn* are quite different in Missouri from what they are in Minnesota, though both sets may represent the same vowel phoneme. When the laboratory phonetician makes mechanical or electronic analyses of the sound waves used in speech, he analyzes the particular allophones used by a particular speaker at a particular time. Ordinarily he does not indicate whether the speaker comes from Missouri, Minnesota, or elsewhere. Nor can he indicate how these particular allophonic details fit into the speaker's over all pattern of phonemes and allophones. Such laboratory analyses represent a valid and useful line of investigation which has yielded important results in recent years, but for the practical phonetician engaged in investigating either phonemic or regional patterns, laboratory methods are largely irrelevant. The student of phonemics wants to know what sounds contrast meaningfully with what other sounds. The student of regional patterns wants to know what characteristics in one type of speech may be set up in contrast with other characteristics in other types of speech. Both need to know something about the speech background of the particular user of the particular set of allophones that the laboratory phonetician has analyzed, and both need to know the extent to which the speaker represents one or another of the various types of English.

Both phonemes and the variable allophones which represent them in actual speech are relevant to our study. A good many investigators mark the distinction between phonemes and allophones rigidly, usually by enclosing symbols which refer to phonemes between diagonal bars, and symbols which refer to allophones between square brackets. There are, however, many occasions in which it makes no difference whether we refer to the phoneme or the allophone, for instance in referring to the first sound in *me*. Where the distinction is important, for instance between the first and last sounds in *taught*, there is generally a need for explanation beyond the mere symbolization. I have therefore used square brackets for both phonemes and allophones, with additional explanation where it seems needed. Students find this system less confusing than an insistence on keeping the distinction whether that distinction is relevant or not.

The other principle which underlies the presentation of the material is that speech is one aspect of the unity-in-variety that characterizes American life. We do not expect the American scene to remain monotonous from Sandy Hook to San Diego. We should lose some of the savor of American life if Boston, Minneapolis, Kansas City, San Francisco, and New Orleans became mere echoes of one another. The objective student of American English soon recognizes that there are differences, sometimes obvious, sometimes subtle, in the patterns of speech that predominate in these five cities and in other parts of the country. I have sought to make those patterns somewhat clearer.

The arrangement of the subject matter has been designed to present a series of graded units, each of which may serve as a single assignment or a small group of assignments. The order in which the sound units and their phonetic symbolization occur in Chapters 4 through 15, though apparently haphazard, has a pedagogical purpose. These chapters introduce the student first to a group of simple, familiar sounds, then to more difficult sounds, a few at a time, so that he may be neither unduly bored at first nor unduly discouraged later. Sometimes there is a natural grouping; in Chapter 8, for example, [æ] and [ɑ] are introduced together because their common use of the spelling *a* makes it desirable to keep them differentiated from the outset;

[r] is introduced at the same time because of the frequency of the sequence [ɑr]. Both the order of presentation and the rate at which the symbols are introduced have worked well in my teaching.

Some sounds, however, notably those discussed in Chapters 9 and 12, will necessarily be difficult for the student to grasp, since they represent variations that do not occur in all types of American English. Though the student need not, except for special purposes, add such new sounds to the stock he himself uses in everyday speech, a certain familiarity with them will be valuable to him, if only for the sake of minimizing the provinciality with which he, like the rest of us, starts out. Pronunciations which differ from those which predominate in the student's home town are not necessarily quaint. If the phonetics class is fortunate enough to include students from various parts of the country, a wholesale comparison of pronunciations can add light and interest to these two chapters.

Wherever it has seemed desirable, I have included exercises designed to enable the student (and the teacher) to test progress in understanding. These exercises are numerous and varied enough to give the instructor some leeway in choosing exercises if he does not wish to assign them all. For an elementary course, I recommend the first fifteen chapters, plus Chapter 24. Should more time be available, other chapters may of course be included, but it is better to cover the indicated chapters thoroughly than the entire book sketchily. Chapters 21 to 23 are, as previously noted, suitable as a foundation for an advanced course in linguistic geography, provided they are accompanied by recordings or "live" samplings of regional speech.

The sources of my material are thirty years and more of phonetic study, the steadily increasing phonetic and linguistic literature that has appeared during much the same period, and detailed analyses of the speech patterns of over fourteen thousand people. I have interviewed about ten thousand of these speakers face to face. Before the second World War, I made on-the-spot notes of their speech; since the war, I have increasingly relied on the tape recorder. I have made recordings of my own, and have also sent reels of recording tape to friends, colleagues, and even total strangers, whenever I found them willing to make local recordings for me. Thanks to their kindness, I have been able to collect data on the speech of four thousand more speakers. The total includes speakers from over 2,500 of the 3,000-odd counties in the United States, and is probably the largest collection of data about individual speakers in any one set of files.

This wide sampling makes possible, I believe, a more accurate analysis of American pronunciation, especially in its regional variations, than has hitherto been possible. As a result, the large area shown on many speech maps as "General American" (a term which I have myself used) is now broken up into smaller areas. The uniformity implied in the term "General American" simply does not exist. The boundaries between regional types indicated in this book represent my interpretation of the data gathered from fourteen thousand speakers and plotted on many maps. I have no doubt that the accumulation of additional data will require some modification of the boundaries, which usually represent not lines of sharp changes in pronunciation but rather the middle of transitional areas of varying widths.

No one who has seriously studied the language of the United States in the past generation can have failed to be influenced by Professor John S. Kenyon of Hiram College, Professor Charles C. Fries and Professor Hans Kurath of the University of Michigan, Professor William Cabell Greet of Columbia, or the late Professor Leonard Bloomfield of Yale University. Though I have not always seen eye to eye with them (nor they with one another, for that matter), my indebtedness to them is none the less great. I owe a special debt of gratitude to Professor Daniel Jones of the University of London, under whose guidance I made my first systematic phonetic study. To Professors J. M. Cowan, W. G. Moulton, R. A. Hall Jr., C. F. Hockett, F. B. Agard, and G. H. Fairbanks, all of the Division of Modern Languages at Cornell, I owe a continuously mounting debt for the stimulation of innumerable discussions, formal and informal, of linguistics and other subjects. Finally, to the members of my family—Ruth, Arthur, and Andrew—I express my gratitude for the help, suggestions, and editorial criticism which have helped make the writing of this book possible. For the shortcomings and defects, I alone must take the blame.

C. K. THOMAS

ITHACA, NEW YORK

JANUARY, 1958

# Contents

AN INTRODUCTION TO THE

# PHONETICS

OF

# AMERICAN ENGLISH

# CHAPTER 1

# Introduction

As we start out, it will be useful to ask ourselves where we're going, and with what purpose. Our daily practical routine depends on oral communication. All day long we make noises and listen to noises, and these noises help in getting the day's work done. If we've always spoken English, we don't pay much attention to it, but take it for granted. There are times, however, when it's useful to analyze the language and see how it works. Although most of us think we know English, because we use it more or less efficiently, few of us know it scientifically. Many of us fall into the booby traps of English spelling. Some of us run into conflicting opinions about what is good pronunciation and what is bad, and have no way of settling the conflict. Since our understanding of English is likely to be loaded with misconceptions, let's start afresh.

Let's say, for instance, that we hear a particular sequence of vocal noises that we have come to associate with a particular kind of small animal. As literate people we have also come to associate these noises with a particular set of written or printed symbols which we call the word *cat*. Notice two things: The sounds we make to identify the animal are arbitrary and conventional. There is no necessary connection between them and the animal they symbolize. A Frenchman, a Brazilian, or a Japanese would use quite different sound patterns as symbols. Second, there is no necessary connection between the printed symbols and either the animal itself or the sounds we use to identify it. The French symbols, printed *chat*, look like a quite different word, and the French spoken symbols sound quite different from either English *cat* or *chat*. The Japanese symbols, either spoken or printed, are meaningless to those of us who do not understand Japanese. Animal, sound, and spelling are associated arbitrarily, and only arbitrarily. The study of written or printed symbols, as used in English and most of the languages of western civilization, is known as *orthography*. The study of oral sounds used in communication is known as *phonetics*.

Now compare *cat* and *hat*. By changing the first, or initial, letter you have symbolized a quite different object, and by changing the initial sound you may do the same thing orally. By making similar changes, in speaking and writing, you get such words as *rat*, *pat*, *bat*, *fat*, *mat*, and *sat*. For *that* and *gnat* you have again produced new words by changing the initial sound, but have to resort to a more cumbersome spelling to change the printed symbolization. Pronounce *that* and *gnat* aloud; compare them with *fat* and *mat*, until you've convinced yourself that the double letters at the beginning of *that* and *gnat* represent single sounds.

Now put your mind on the middle part of *cat*. By changing the middle letter you get *cot* or *cut*. With each new spelling you associate a new sound, and a new meaning for the whole word. If you change the middle sound again you may get *kite*, or *caught*, or *curt*. Here the change in spelling is less obvious, and the relationship between sound and spelling more complex and cumbersome. But you can always test the substitution by comparing the sounds of the words.

If we change the final part of *cat* we get such words as *cap*, *cab*, *can*, and *cash*. In each change we associate a new spelling with a new sound and a new meaning for the word as a whole. Thus our analysis shows that *cat* consists of three orthographic elements, or letters, corresponding to three phonetic elements, or sounds, and that these elements are distinctive. They are distinctive in the sense that a change in any one of them is associated with a change in the meaning of the entire word. Sometimes, of course, a random change produces a combination of symbols for which there is no corresponding conventional meaning, as in the spellings *cet* or *cxt* or the pronunciation of the imaginary word *jat*. It is from this reservoir of pronounceable but hitherto unused short syllables that new names for detergents and breakfast foods are usually drawn.

Keep the word *distinctive* in mind. In phonetics, a distinctive sound is one which may distinguish one word from another, as the final sound of *cat* distinguishes it from *cap*, and the medial sound from *cut*. A nondistinctive sound, or sound change, is one that does not alter the meaning of the word. In *cat*, for instance, we have all heard nondistinctive variations in the quality or length of the medial sound, the vowel. We recognized the reference to the small animal, even though the pronunciation, by our own standards, seemed a bit quaint.

In fact, every pronunciation of every English sound contains both distinctive and nondistinctive components. My pronunciation of the vowel in *cat* will differ from yours in musical pitch, in absolute duration, in tone quality, even perhaps slightly in what might be called its vowel quality, and neither you nor I can say the word a second time without changing some of these elements somewhat; electronic analysis will show the sound waves to be different. If we change only the nondistinctive elements we are in no danger of being misunderstood. If we change the distinctive elements, then the word may be interpreted as *cot* or *cap* or be missed entirely.

For the distinctive features of a speech sound we use the term *phoneme*; for the nondistinctive, the term *allophone*. Specifically, we hear allophones, and interpret the phonemes if we are well enough acquainted with the language in which they occur. If we listen to a language whose phonemes are not known to us, all we hear is a confusing sequence of strange allophones with no evident patterning. In English we can distinguish separate *t* allophones in *till* and *still*, the first *t* a somewhat more energetic articulation than the second. Ordinarily we pay no attention to the difference. In Chinese, however, these two differently articulated *t*'s constitute separate phonemes, and it becomes important to listen for the differences. English *cat* has three phonemes, but any number of allophones depending on slight individual differences in the pronunciation of the word.

Corresponding to the nouns *phoneme* and *allophone* are the adjectives *phonemic* and *allophonic*. Accent the first syllable of *phoneme*, and rhyme the second syllable with *seem*. *Phonemic* rhymes with *anemic*; accent the second syllable. *Allophone* has the rhythm of *telephone*, but the first syllable rhymes with *pal* and *shall*. *Allophonic* has the rhythm of *telephonic* or *transatlantic*. Be sure you understand these technical terms; they will occur from now on.

If all English words involved as simple a relationship between spellings and phonemes as *cat*, the analysis of English sounds would be relatively easy, and spelling would be a useful guide. We have already seen, however, that the spelling of such words as *that*, *cash*, and *caught* introduces cumbersome complexities. As a matter of fact, English spelling is notoriously wayward, and the relationship between sound and spelling may be confused in many ways. A letter may represent any one of several phonemes, and a single phoneme may be represented by any one of several letters or combinations of letters.

To illustrate, the letter *a* represents a different phoneme in each of the following: *name, calm, cat, all, any,* and *above.* In words with less stable pronunciations, variation in allophones, or even in phonemes, may be completely hidden by a standardized spelling. The vowel sound represented by the letter *a* in *cottage* may be an allophone of the vowel represented by *a* in *above* or a weaker allophone of the vowel represented by *i* in *ridge.* The vowel of *ask* may be an allophone of the vowel phoneme of *cat,* or of the vowel phoneme of *calm,* or it may fall acoustically somewhere between these extremes. Some people pronounce the first syllable of *forest* like *for,* others like *far.*

On the other hand, the stressed vowel phoneme of *be, bee, beach, niece, receive, people, Cæsar, subpoena,* and *machine* is the same, though spelled differently in each word, and with differing allophones dependent on the differing quality of the neighboring sounds. We can readily see, therefore, that the simple one-to-one relationship between spelling and sound in *cat* gives us little help in analyzing English sounds, and that the familiar literary alphabet is too complicated and inaccurate for analytical study of the sounds of English.

If chemical symbols were as inconsistent and unreliable as this, chemical formulas would be virtually impossible to construct. The chemist's practice is to use one symbol, and only one, for each chemical element. The phonetician's must be to use one symbol, and only one, for each phoneme, each phonetic element. Thus we obviously need unit symbols to differentiate *cat* from *that, cat* from *cash,* and *cat* from *caught.* The spelling fails to show these differentiations, partly because it uses double symbols for single sounds: *th* in *that, sh* in *cash, au* in *caught;* partly because it uses letters where no sounds occur: *gh* in *caught.* Later we shall have to modify this strict rule somewhat, since allophonic variations are sometimes important clues to regional types of speech.  The vowel phonemes of *road* and *log*, for example, produce some highly variable regional allophones.  For the present, however, be content to identify the phonemes.

How did the present unsatisfactory state of spelling come about? It is well known that various forms of pictorial representation preceded writing.  Inevitably the pictorial representation of common objects and common ideas became simplified and conventionalized.  The pictograph or ideograph eventually came to be a purely formal and conventional representation of the thing or idea represented.  It suggested neither the appearance of the thing nor the sound of the spoken word.  In Chinese writing the conventionalized ideograph survives to this day.  So, in our own culture, does the pointing hand which invites us to go or look in the direction shown by the index finger.  The dollar sign and various mathematical symbols are other familiar ideographs which conventionally represent specific ideas.

In one ideographic system, however, the conventionalizing of the symbols reached the stage at which particular sounds and combinations of sounds began to be associated with particular symbols.  When we speak of the invention of the alphabet we mean that this stage in the visual representation of ideas had arrived, and that writing had shifted from an ideographic to a phonetic basis.  Though the details are obscure, we know that such a true alphabet had been developed in western Asia by the beginning of the first millenium before the Christian era, that it was probably developed by the Phoenicians, and that it was the ancestor of the Hebrew, Arabic, Greek, and Latin alphabets.[1]

[1] See E. H. Sturtevant, *Linguistic Change* (Chicago: University of Chicago Press, 1917); B. L. Ullman, *Ancient Writing and its Influence* (New York: Longmans, Green & Co., Inc., 1932); A. C. Moorhouse, *The Triumph of the Alphabet* (New York: Henry Schuman, Inc., 1953).

But the phonetic basis of writing was incomplete. The Phoenicians symbolized the consonants, but left the vowels to be inferred in much the same way that a present-day stenographer fills in the gaps in her shorthand notes. When the Greeks acquired the Phoenician alphabet they needed fewer consonant symbols than the Phoenicians had provided. Hence they hit on the device of using the left-over symbols for vowels, which, in Greek, could not be left to inference. The Romans adapted parts of both the Greek and Phoenician alphabets. Western Europe adapted the Roman alphabet to languages, including English, with quite different phonetic structures from that of Latin. English added some symbols of its own, but they fell into disuse when type fonts without the special English symbols were brought to England from continental Europe.

Thus phonetic inaccuracies were bound to develop and increase. Written symbols have a permanence which sharply contrasts with the changeableness of speech sounds. There is an inevitable lag between changes in speech which proceed slowly and imperceptibly and changes in writing. The word *knight* was at one time spelled *cniht*, and each of its five letters represented a phoneme. Our present spelling includes three letters, *k*, *g*, and *h*, for which there are no corresponding phonemes. The simple vowel represented by *i* in *cniht* has developed into a diphthong. Only *n* and *t* remain substantially unchanged.

With the invention of printing, spelling became almost static. We can read Shakespeare without difficulty because spelling has changed little since his time. But we should have great difficulty in understanding the spoken language of Shakespeare's time, since the sounds have changed slowly but continually since then.[2]

[2] For fuller details see Wilhelm Viëtor, *Shakespeare's Pronunciation*, Marburg, 1906; A. H. Marckwardt, *Introduction to the English Language* (New York: Oxford University Press, 1942), especially chap. iv; Helge Kökeritz, *Shakespeare's Pronunciation* (New Haven: Yale University Press, 1953).

The discrepancy between sound and spelling has produced two sorts of attempts to narrow the gap and bring about a simple one-to-one relationship like that in *cat*. One is to make the spelling conform more closely to the sound; the other, to make the sound conform more closely to the spelling. With the former we are not concerned. Systems of simplified spelling come and go, and the phonetician generally finds them haphazard and inadequate.

Attempts to make the sound conform more closely to the spelling are, however, of concern to the phonetician, since actual changes in pronunciation may result. Such attempts are of comparatively recent development, since they are one of the by-products of minimal literacy. For example, the *th* of *author* was formerly pronounced like the *t* of *orator*. Analogy with the *th* of *thin* and *both* seems to have produced the change. In British English, *Anthony* is pronounced exactly like *Antony;* in American English, the pronunciation with the *th* of *anthem* has developed.

In our own day we can see how such spelling pronunciations begin. Many people pronounce the *t* of *often* because they see it in the spelling, and because they pronounce *t* in such words as *after* and *crafty*. Thus they reverse the historical process by which *t* was eliminated from the pronunciation of *often, soften, whistle*, and *listen*, without realizing that the changes they have made are hit-or-miss, chancy affairs; they have not yet tried to restore the *t* of *whistle*. Some of them have restored the *l* of *palm*, but not of *walk*. It is hard to avoid the suspicion that spelling pronunciations originate with those people who are not quite at ease in their literacy. Neither the illiterate nor the highly literate are likely to place so high a value on the authority of spelling.

Yet we are all subject to the tendency. With rare exceptions we are visually minded; we rely more on our eyes than on our ears. We feel uncertain about an unfamiliar word till we can visualize its spelling, however odd that spelling may be. Our dictionary makers encourage this visual tendency, else we should not have so many symbols in all but the most recent dictionaries for the unstressed vowel common to *account, soda, silent, April, connect,* and *circus.* So strong is the influence of visible spelling that beginning students of phonetics will find it difficult, at least for a while, to think in terms of sounds. They will think of the *a* in *many* and the *e* in *penny* as separate sounds, rather than as separate spellings for the same phoneme.

The first objective, then, should be to acquire the habit of listening for the sounds which distinguish words from other words: *cat* from *caught, night* from *knife, bud* from *bird, woman* from *women, many* from *penny.* If you close your eyes and repeat these words aloud, you will begin to notice differences which are not apparent to the eye. Put on your mental dark glasses, and start gouging the mental wax out of your ears.

## EXERCISES

1. Read the following words aloud, and pick out all the letters except *a, e, i, o,* and *u* for which there are no corresponding sounds. Results will not necessarily be the same for all readers, since not all pronounce the words in the same way:

listen, knot, write, doubt, corps, aisle, half, whole, pneumonia, weight, mortgage, column, design, thumb, sword, psalm, subtle, Lincoln, plumber, walk, whose, honest, cupboard. (Did you test *r*?)

2. Read the following groups aloud and pick out the stressed vowel sound in each group that differs from the stressed vowel

of the other three words. The stressed vowel is the vowel in the syllable which has the greater emphasis or energy.

> any, many, penny, Danny
> crow, cow, flow, snow
> mood, food, wood, moon
> machine, building, women, England

3. Read the following groups aloud and pick out the initial, or beginning, consonant sound which differs from the initial consonant sound of the other three words in the group:

> pneumatic, knight, gnat, ptomaine
> where, who, what, when
> though, thought, think, thin
> chorus, kite, key, cheese

4. In each of the following groups pick out the two words that differ from each other by a change of only one sound:

> tin, skin, shin, spin
> bowl, owl, whole, scowl
> thank, tank, drank, shrank
> fight, fright, fry, height
> steak, slate, snake, weight

5. Pick from each group the pair of words with identical vowel phonemes:

> eat, ate, great, rat
> hear, chair, char, pear
> vice, voice, choir, vault
> paid, said, aisle, shed
> warm, worn, worm, woke

# CHAPTER 2

# The Mechanism of Speech

In the first chapter we discovered that human speech consists of a succession of distinctive sound units, or phonemes. These sound units are produced by the bodily mechanism and are conventionally represented, in English, by combinations of letters. Some combinations represent the sound units with conventional adequacy: the three letters of *cat* show a simple one-to-one relationship to the three phonemes which compose the word. Other spellings are less adequate: the seven letters of *thought* also represent a succession of three phonemes. Thus we face two problems: (1) an analysis of the physical and physiological processes which produce the sounds, and (2) the development of an adequate system of symbolizing them. The first problem will be the task of this chapter; the second, that of the following.

## Voice Production

For the production of voice, the human vocal apparatus depends, like musical instruments, upon three fundamental factors: a source of energy, a vibrating body, and a resonator. The

13

source of vocal energy is the pressure of the outgoing breath. The vibrating body consists of the vocal bands in the larynx. The resonator consists of the complex and adjustable system of passages leading from the larynx to the outer air. We shall examine these three systems in succession.

## Breathing

The breathing mechanism which supplies the motive power for voice and speech consists of the lungs, the passages which connect the lungs with the outer air, the bones which provide leverage, and the muscles which do the work.

Air may enter the breathing passage through either the mouth or the nose. It then passes into the pharynx, or throat, next into the larynx, sometimes called the voice box, thence into the trachea, or windpipe (*see Figure 1*). At the bottom of the trachea the passage divides, one branch going to the left lung, the other to the right. Each of these smaller tubes continues dividing until an elaborate ramification of small tubes has been formed. At the end of each is a small sac, through the walls of which oxygen and carbon dioxide are diffused in breathing.

The entire structure of the lungs consists of this tree-like formation of tubes, an interlaced system of blood capillaries, and a protective covering. As a whole, the lungs form a soft, spongy mass which completely fills the chest cavity except for the small space occupied by the heart and the esophagus, or food tube. The lungs are passive; they respond to variations in air pressure but do not themselves contain muscular fibers to initiate movement.

The structural base for the whole chest, or thorax, is the vertebral column, or backbone, a system of individual bones, or vertebræ, connected in such a way as to combine strength with

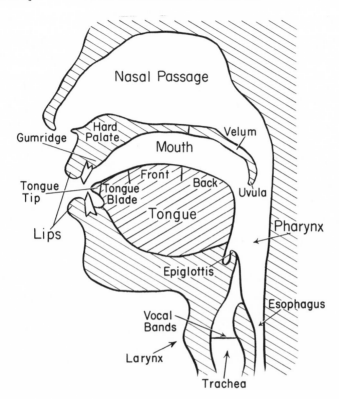

FIGURE 1

Passages of the nose, the mouth, and the throat, through which air passes to the lungs.

moderate flexibility. Extending around to the sides from the vertebral column are the twelve pairs of ribs. As the ribs reach forward they also extend slightly downward, the downward angle being somewhat less for the upper ribs. As they come around to the front of the body, the upper seven pairs of ribs turn upward again, and are attached, by firm but flexible cartilages, to the sternum, or breastbone.

The sternum is a dagger-shaped bone whose upper end can be

felt at the lower edge of the notch of the neck, and whose length can be traced down the midline of the body about half way to the waistline. The eighth, ninth, and tenth pairs of ribs are attached indirectly to the sternum; the cartilage of the eighth rib attaches to that of the seventh, that of the ninth to that of the eighth, and that of the tenth to that of the ninth.

The eighth, ninth, and tenth ribs do not extend as far around to the front as the upper seven. The arch formed by these three pairs and their cartilages can be felt extending diagonally down and back from the lower end of the sternum in the general direction of the hip bones. The eleventh and twelfth pairs, which extend only a short distance from the vertebral column, have no

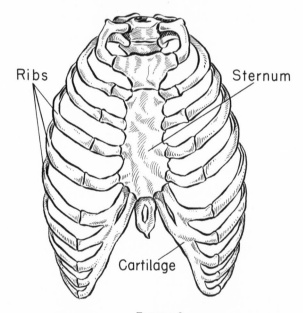

FIGURE 2

The elasticity of the cartilage connecting the ribs with the sternum permits the expansion and contraction necessary in the inhaling and exhaling of air to and from the lungs.

front attachment, and are known as free or floating ribs (*see Figure 2*). You should locate as many of these thoracic bones as possible, by tracing their course with your finger tips.

The bony framework of vertebræ, sternum, and ribs is shaped like a flattened cone, and built like a cage. Between the ribs are muscles which pull the ribs closer together in inhaling, and over the framework is spread a group of larger muscles which enclose the bony structure. Since the upper ribs are more firmly fixed than the lower, the action of the muscles results in the raising of the ribs. Since the ribs lie lower at the sides than at either front or back, raising them necessarily moves them outward at the sides as well. The angle at which the ribs are attached also pivots

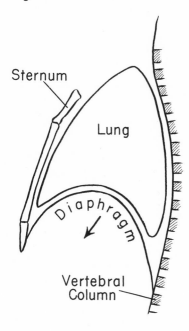

FIGURE 3

The relative position of the diaphragm, lung, sternum, and vertebral column, drawn as a cross-section with the ribs removed.

the sternum forward. The resulting expansion of the chest in all three diameters can readily be observed.

Vertical expansion of the chest is mainly downward. Forming the floor of the chest and the roof of the abdomen is a large dome-shaped structure composed of muscle and tendon and known as the diaphragm. It is attached to the vertebral column, the rib arch, and the base of the sternum; the rear attachment is somewhat lower than the front. The dome of the diaphragm is supported by the upper abdominal organs: the liver on the right, the stomach on the left (*see Figure 3*).

When the muscles of the diaphragm contract, the dome flattens slightly. It presses down on the abdominal organs and, because of its lower attachment in the rear, forward as well, distending the abdominal wall at the waistline. If you will take one end of an ordinary rubber band in each hand, and then support the middle of the rubber band on the back of a chair, you will have a rough working model of the diaphragm, in cross section, during its phase of contraction. In the center, the rubber band presses down on the chair, as the diaphragm does on the abdominal organs. At the sides, the necessary opposite thrust of the rubber band can be felt pulling your hands upward. In much the same way, the diaphragm pulls upward at the sides, where it is attached to the rib arch; this upward pull is an important factor in the raising of the lower ribs.[1] The total action of the diaphragm in lowering the floor of the chest and helping to raise the ribs makes it an important muscle of inhalation.

As we have seen, the combined action of the diaphragm and the muscles between the ribs expands the chest in all three diameters. The resulting decrease in the internal pressure of the chest enables atmospheric pressure to force air in through the

---

[1] See George Dodds and J. D. Lickley, *The Control of the Breath* (Oxford: Oxford University Press, 1925), pp. 21–22.

breathing passages to the lungs. Inhalation is then complete. In quiet breathing, exhalation is largely automatic: the lungs and body wall, which have been distended by the muscular activity of inhalation, contract elastically when the forces of inhalation stop operating. The abdominal organs, which have been compressed by the contraction of the diaphragm during inspiration, spring back to their uncompressed position. Ribs and sternum fall back of their own weight. Thus in quiet breathing not much energy is needed for exhalation.

In speech and song, however, breath must be exhaled under varying degress of pressure, and under accurate control. Pressure and accuracy can best be regulated by the muscles of the abdominal wall, whose four layers work in opposition to the diaphragm, and are thus muscles of exhalation. When these muscles contract they flatten the abdominal bulge, push the abdominal organs up against the diaphragm, and indirectly bring pressure against the base of the lungs. By practice, these muscles can be controlled with a good deal of accuracy, and the pressure of the outgoing breath can be suited to the demands of the voice.

### The Vibrator

Voice itself is produced by forcing the outgoing breath between the vocal bands, two muscular and tendinous shelves which grow out of the side walls of the larynx and extend from front to back. The framework of the larynx consists of stiff cartilages so arranged as to form a valve at the top of the trachea, or windpipe.

The lowest of the laryngeal cartilages is the *cricoid*, so called because it completely encircles the air passage and has a signet-like elevation at the back. All these details suggested the term "ring-like" to the Greek anatomists who discovered and named the cartilage. The cricoid forms a base for the rest of the larynx.

Covering the front and sides of the larynx is a large angular cartilage, the two connected sides of which suggested, to the Greek anatomists, a pair of shields fastened together at an acute angle: hence the name *thyroid*, or "shield-like" cartilage. From the back of the thyroid two leg-like projections connect with the outer edge of the cricoid toward its rear, and form the crico-thyroid joints, on which pivoting is possible.

On the signet-like elevation at the rear of the cricoid are two smaller, "ladle-like" cartilages, the *arytenoids*, which can pivot in all directions, and also slide toward or away from each other in horizontal grooves. The vocal bands come together at the inner angle of the thyroid cartilage in front, and extend back

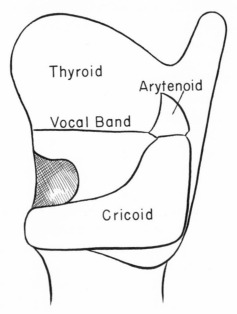

FIGURE 4

The mechanism of the larynx acts as a valve controlling the passage of air to and from the lungs through the movement of the two arytenoid cartilages, which are attached to the vocal bands and control their lateral movements.

along each side wall of the thyroid. In the rear, each vocal band is attached to the arytenoid on its own side of the larynx (*see Figure 4*).

When the larynx is used merely as a part of the breathing tract, the arytenoid cartilages pivot and slide toward the sides, thereby pulling the vocal bands close to the side walls. In this position the two bands form a V-shaped angle, with the apex of the V in front. The glottis, as the space between the vocal bands is called, is as wide as possible to permit free passage of air. At the other extreme, the arytenoids pivot and slide in so close together that the vocal bands come into contact with each other, and even slightly overlap, and thus prevent the passage of air. This valvular action takes place when for any reason it becomes necessary to compress the air in the lungs, as in bracing the chest before lifting a heavy weight, or in building up pressure for a cough. Between these two extremes lies the position for voice production: the vocal bands are stretched under tension from front to back, and are brought close enough together for the outgoing breath to set them into vibration as it forces its way out between them.

The movements of the vocal bands and of the laryngeal cartilages are controlled by a complicated musculature, part of which is located wholly within the larynx, and part of which connects the larynx with the sternum, the tongue, the base of the skull, and the soft palate in the roof of the mouth. Within the larynx the muscles adjust the position of the arytenoids and regulate the tension of the vocal bands by pivoting the cricoid and thyroid cartilages on the crico-thyroid joints. The musculature which connects the larynx with the other parts of the body adjusts the larynx as a whole to the vocal requirements of the moment. The details of muscular action need not, however, concern us, since both sets are largely involuntary. Control of laryngeal action for vocal purposes is almost entirely indirect, through the medium of hearing. For this reason those who become deaf before learning to speak never learn to speak well, and those who later become deaf often lose the finer shadings of sentence melody.

### The Physics of Sound Production

When the vocal bands are set into vibration by the pressure of the outgoing breath, they in turn impart a vibration to the column of air in the vocal tract, a vibration which we hear as sound. Since this vibration is the raw material out of which voice and speech are fashioned, it will be well for us to consider its nature in some detail.

As the vocal bands vibrate they alternately push the neighboring air molecules closer together and allow them to spring farther apart. That is, they impart alternate phases of condensation and rarefaction to the molecules which make up the column of air in the larynx. As soon as the molecules have been crowded together in the phase of condensation, they spring apart elastically, thereby compressing the molecules farther away from the source of vibration. Thus a sound wave is produced and transmitted in much the same way as a child may knock down a whole line of dominoes merely by knocking the first domino against the second.

But in contrast to the dominoes, which fall over only once, the air molecules spring back elastically, and are then ready to be compressed by the next impulse from the vibrating body. By means of the molecular vibration through a limited range, the energy of the sound wave is carried to a distance, and at the rate, in ordinary atmospheric temperatures, of somewhat more than a thousand feet a second. This speed, of course, far outstrips the speed at which the breath is being exhaled, and is entirely independent of the latter.

If the vocal bands vibrate at the rate of 250 complete cycles a second, the resulting pitch is roughly that of middle C in musical terminology. Since 250 separate condensations have been made while the sound has been traveling about 1000 feet, it is obvious that the points of maximum condensation must be located at intervals of about four feet along the path of the wave. If the vocal bands vibrate 500 times a second, 500 points of maximum condensation must be crowded into 1000 feet, about two feet apart. This distance between maximum points of condensation is known as the wave length of the sound. As the frequency of vibration increases, the wave length decreases; the relationship between them is reciprocal.

In changing the frequency of vibration, or musical pitch, of the vocal bands, or the strings of such musical instruments as the piano or violin, several physical factors play a part. If we look at the interior mechanism of the piano we see that the strings which produce the higher pitches are shorter, smaller in diameter and weight, and stretched under greater tension than the strings which produce the lower pitches. If we compare the violin with the bass viol, a larger instrument of the same family, we find the same relationship between the three physical factors: for its lower pitches, the bass viol has longer and heavier strings than those of the violin, and they are stretched more loosely. Furthermore, we notice that the violinist and the bass violist both regulate the pitch, in playing, by lengthening or shortening the vibrating section of the string by their fingering. In tuning their instruments, they regulate the pitch by adjusting the tension of the strings.

Thus, in order to produce a higher frequency, it becomes evident that we must either shorten the string, stretch it more tightly, use a lighter material, or combine all three factors. Specifically, the mathematical effect of these three factors is as follows: First, the frequency is inversely proportional to the length of the string; by reducing the string to half its former length, without altering the other factors, we double the original frequency, or, in musical terms, we produce the octave of the original pitch. Second, the frequency is directly proportional to the square root of the tension; to double the frequency without altering the other factors, we must increase the tension to four times its original value. Finally, the frequency is inversely proportional to the square root of the mass per unit of length; to double the frequency by this means, we must use a string which weighs only one fourth as much, per unit of length, as the original string. These three factors may all be combined in the following formula, in which F represents frequency, T tension, L length, and M mass:

$$F \text{ is proportional to } \frac{\sqrt{T}}{L\sqrt{M}}$$

Manufactured musical instruments utilize all three factors, as we have seen, though in actual playing the performer utilizes variations in length more than the other factors. In the vocal bands, which in most respects act like the vibrating strings of musical instruments, the change in tension is the greatest single factor in the control of the frequency. When the vocal bands are stretched for a higher note they are, to a degree, thinned out; that is, the mass per unit of length is slightly reduced, thereby helping to produce the higher frequency. The length of the bands is, however, slightly increased, thereby tending to produce a lower frequency. But the tension is increased so much that it becomes the dominant factor. This type of adjustment means that the control of vocal pitch is more closely analogous to the tuning of a violin than to the playing of it.

## Overtones

The frequencies that we have been examining depend upon the vibration of the string, or vocal band, as a unit. In addition, however, there are other vibrations, usually of weaker intensity, which occur at the same time as the fundamental vibrations. These additional tones result from the vibration of the string in halves, thirds, fourths, fifths, and successive unit fractions of its length; they are generally known as harmonics, partials, or overtones of the fundamental tone. Since the overtones vibrate at the same time as the fundamental, their occurrence involves no difference in the mass or tension of the vibrating string. Their frequencies depend solely on the differences in length of the vibrating segments: two, three, four, five times the frequency of the fundamental, and so forth. In musical terminology, the relationships between the frequencies of the fundamental and its overtones may be illustrated by the following table, in which middle C is used as the base:

|  | Approximate Frequency | Musical Notation |
|---|---|---|
| Fundamental............... | 256 | Middle C |
| First overtone.............. | 512 | C of first octave above |
| Second overtone........... | 768 | G of first octave above |
| Third overtone............. | 1024 | C of second octave |
| Fourth overtone............ | 1280 | E of second octave |
| Fifth overtone.............. | 1536 | G of second octave |
| Sixth overtone.............. | 1792 | B flat of second octave |
| Seventh overtone .......... | 2048 | C of third octave |

The B flat of the sixth overtone does not correspond exactly with the B flat of the tempered scale used for the piano; above the seventh overtone musical notation is inadequate. If some other note is used as the fundamental, the same arithmetical ratios hold, but the whole pattern must be fitted into the musical scale at a higher or lower point.

## Quality

Ordinarily the fundamental produces the greater part of the energy of the tone, and the overtones are not heard separately. Instead, their relatively weak intensities combine to produce what the listener identifies as the quality of the tone. Since some overtones may have more intensity than others, and hence be louder, the quality depends on the number and relative strength of those which combine with the fundamental in the complex pattern of the entire sound.

Different musical instruments have characteristic overtone patterns which enable us to distinguish a flute, for example, from a violin. Different speakers likewise have characteristic overtone patterns that enable us to distinguish one person's voice from another's. Furthermore, the overtone pattern of the individual's voice is less definitely fixed than that of a musical instrument. Changes in the overtone pattern indicate to the listener that the speaker is tired or that he has a cold, or otherwise reflect his momentary mental or bodily state. The quality of the vocal sound results partly from the number and relative strength of the overtones set up by the vocal bands, partly from the modifications of the overtone pattern that take place while the sound is coming out through the throat, mouth, and nose.

## Resonance

The air passages just mentioned have a selective action on the complex sound wave set up by the vocal bands. This action, known as resonance, is akin to the selective action of a radio receiving set on the electric waves it picks up. It is well known that a hollow cavity may have a definite musical pitch; blowing across the narrow mouth of a bottle sets up the characteristic cavity tone, or pitch. If the same pitch is sounded near the mouth of the bottle, the cavity will reinforce the tone or, as we say, resonate it.     Among musical instruments the most obvious illustration of this principle is provided by the marimbaphone, in which a hollow cylindrical resonator hangs immediately below each of the blocks of wood which are hammered to initiate the tone. Here there is a separate resonator for each pitch to be produced. In the trombone, on the other hand, a single resonator can be altered in length to produce the pitch required at any given moment.

The selective action of the resonator intensifies some frequencies at the expense of others, thus altering the overtone pattern and the quality. The cavity tone of the human mouth can be readily demonstrated: if you relax or slightly round your lips, then lightly tap your cheek with your finger or a pencil while you slowly move your jaw up and down, you will hear different musical pitches for each angle of the jaw. Rounding or unrounding the lips will produce a similar effect. The existence of the cavity tone is an indication of the ability of the cavity, in that particular adjustment, to resonate or intensify that particular pitch, if that pitch is being produced by the vocal bands either as the fundamental or as one of the overtones. The air passages of the throat, mouth, and nose act as selective, adjustable resonators of the vocal tone and are responsible, in large measure, for its quality.

In the mechanism of resonance, and particularly in the control of speech, the musculature is predominantly voluntary. Conscious control is possible by kinesthetic means, that is, by muscular sensation, as well as by hearing. The space within the larynx, above the vocal bands, though a part of the resonating mechanism, is of minor importance.  More important is the pharynx, or throat, into which the larynx opens.

The pharynx is a muscular tube which extends from the base of the skull down to the upper end of the esophagus, or food tube, behind the larynx.  In the front wall of the pharynx are openings into the larynx, mouth, and nose.  The whole structure is sometimes classified into three parts, according to the opening which lies nearest: the laryngopharynx, the oropharynx, and the nasopharynx.

The length of the pharynx can be varied slightly as the larynx is raised or lowered in speech.  The diameter may be narrowed by the large constrictor muscles which bind the pharynx to the vertebral column, and which are used chiefly in swallowing.  The nasopharynx can be cut off from the other two parts by raising and retracting the soft palate, the muscular back part of the roof of the mouth, until it comes into contact with the back wall of the pharynx, which moves slightly forward to meet it.  The pharyngeal wall consists in part of the musculature which connects the larynx with the upper parts of the speech mechanism.  It therefore acts as a link for integrating the adjustments of the larynx and the mouth.

The nasal passage consists of the external nares, or nostrils, and a tent-shaped passage extending back through the bones of the face to the nasopharynx.  The bony and cartilaginous septum, which divides the right and left external nares, extends back through the nasal passage about as far as the rear edge of the hard palate, the solid front part of the roof of the mouth, to which it is attached.

Leading off from the nasal passages are the paranasal sinuses, small passages leading to cavities in the forehead, the cheek bones, and the sphenoid bone at the base of the skull.  The vocal function, if any, of the sinuses remains debatable; it is possible that they resonate some of the sounds which emerge through the nose. The speaker has no control over their size or shape; they are not adjustable.

Control of the nose as a resonant passage is limited to slight dilation or contraction of the external nares, and to regulation of the size of the opening from the oropharynx into the nasopharynx by the action of the soft palate. The latter, as we have seen, may close the opening completely, or may open in varying degress. The rest of the nasal passage is fixed in size and shape, since its walls are the fixed bones of the face and skull.

Obstructions within the nasal passage—the swollen mucous membrane of a cold, the excessive growth of adenoid tissue, other nasal growths, or a deviated septum—may prevent normal nasal resonance. A short or inactive soft palate may, by failing to close the valve adequately, exaggerate nasal resonance. Altogether, however, the possible modifications of nasal resonance are strictly limited as compared with that of the mouth.

At the opening between the oropharynx and the mouth can be seen two muscular arches extending down from the velum, or soft palate, and known as the pillars of the fauces. With a mirror you should be able to locate them. The rear arches connect with the pharyngeal wall, the front with the under surface of the tongue. In combination with the tongue, the pillars of the fauces form a valve between the mouth and the pharynx. The separate resonant action of the pharynx, mouth, and nose depends upon the adjustment of these valves between the cavities.

The velum, pillars of the fauces, jaw, tongue, and lips are capable of so many adjustments that the resonance of the mouth is highly variable. Since the mouth plays so prominent a part in speech, it will be well to examine its structure in greater detail.

## The Mouth

The roof of the mouth begins with the alveolar ridge, or upper gums, which you can feel with your finger or the tip of your tongue, directly behind the upper front teeth. Behind the gum ridge is the hard palate, which stretches back in an ascending arc to the highest point of the mouth, and then curves slightly down and back. The final division is the velum, or soft palate, which forms a descending arc terminating in a hanging tip known as the uvula. Though the line between the hard palate and the velum is not visible, you can readily feel it with your finger or the tip of your tongue. All these anatomical divisions of the roof of the mouth are used in the production of distinctive differences in sound.

The tongue is a complex combination of muscles attached in front to the chin bone and in back to the hyoid bone in the upper part of the neck. The internal structure of the tongue is of little consequence to the phonetician, since its many movements are accomplished by the tongue as a unit, without voluntary control of its separate parts. The phonetician finds it convenient, however, to block out arbitrary regions on the upper surface of the tongue, according to their proximity to the anatomical divisions of the roof of the mouth. Thus the part lying nearest the front teeth is called the tip, or point. The part lying directly below the upper gum ridge is known as the blade; the part below the hard palate, as the front; and the part below the velum, as the back. The use to be made of this classification will become evident in the next chapter.

The size of the mouth cavity may be regulated by the angle of the jaw, which may be raised enough to permit a slight over-lapping of the upper and lower front teeth, or lowered enough to separate the lower teeth from the upper by about two inches.

The lips may be closed completely, spread in varying degress, or rounded in varying degrees.  Within the mouth the tongue is capable of a wide range of movements: it can move backward or forward, up or down, or in various unsymmetrical ways; the muscles which compose it can be tensed or relaxed.  All these adjustments involve resonant changes in the vocal quality, and all are utilized in speech.

# CHAPTER 3

# The Classification of Speech Sounds

In the first chapter we discovered that there are meaningful sounds and combinations of sounds, as well as meaningful letters and combinations of letters. We discovered that the relationship between sounds and letters is not always simple and straightforward, and that sounds, to be effectively understood, must be dissociated from the conventional spellings of present-day English and studied by themselves. Although listening to sounds may seem to be simple and obvious, you will almost certainly find, at least at first, that your listening is distorted by your recollection of the way letters look. In a sense you must learn to close your eyes to the appearance of letters on the printed page and spread your ears to catch the sounds of speech.

In the second chapter we examined the physical and physiological basis of speech sounds. You should get into the habit of referring to that chapter for verification of physical and physiological details. It now remains to examine the use we make of the physical mechanism of speech and to work out a systematic basis for the classification of English phonemes.

## The Place of Articulation

If we pronounce the words *tool* and *cool* alternately we notice that the difference in sound depends on a difference in the way we form the initial consonants. At the beginning of *tool* the tip of the tongue makes contact with the upper gum ridge. At the beginning of *cool* the back of the tongue arches up and makes contact with the velum. You should be able to feel this difference in articulation and to see some of it in a mirror. All other physical details are virtually the same in the two words. We can discover the same contrast between *dough*, in which the tip of the tongue touches the gum ridge, and *go*, in which the back of the tongue touches the velum. A less obvious contrast occurs between *sin*, in which the final consonant uses the tip of the tongue, and *sing*, in which the final consonant uses the back of the tongue. In short, the contrast between gum-ridge and velar contact is one means of distinguishing one word from another. Be sure to test these illustrative pairs for yourself.

If we compare *pool* with *tool* and *cool* we discover that the closed lips may provide another distinctive place of articulation. *Fin*, *thin*, *sin*, and *shin* provide still other places of distinctive articulation, which will be discussed in detail when we examine the formation of individual phonemes in later chapters.

Vowels may also be distinguished by their place of pronunciation. In comparing *hat* and *hot*, for instance, we notice that for the vowel of *hat* the tongue bunches in the front part of the mouth, and the front part of the tongue is active. For the vowel of *hot* the tongue bunches in the back part of the mouth, and the back part of the tongue is active. Similarly, we form the vowel of *tea* with the front part of the tongue; the vowel of *too*, with the back part. Thus the place of articulation is significant in the differentiation of both vowel and consonant phonemes.

## Voiced and Voiceless Sounds

*Fail* and *veil* illustrate another basis for classifying speech sounds and for differentiating meaning. Though we use virtually identical movements of the speech agents in the mouth for these two words, the initial consonants are clearly different. We find the same contrast between the final consonants of *leaf* and *leave*, and between the medial consonants of *wafer* and *waiver*. If you hold your fingers lightly on the tip of your larynx while you alternately pronounce *fail* and *veil*, you will feel laryngeal vibrations at the beginning of *veil*, but only after you've finished the initial consonant in *fail*. If you can artificially prolong the consonants, you'll sense the contrast more vividly. Similarly, you should be able to feel the laryngeal vibrations continuing into the last sound of *leave*, but feel them stop as you begin the last sound of *leaf*. Thus the vocal bands, whose vibrations you have been feeling, play their part in differentiating phonemes. For some phonemes, the [v][1] of *veil* and *leave*, for example, the vocal bands normally vibrate. For others, the [f] of *fail* and *leaf*, for example, the vocal bands must not vibrate. *Sink* and *zinc* are differentiated in the same way; so are *pill* and *bill*. Other pairs will be distinguished later on.

Vowels are normally voiced. So are such vowel-like consonants as [n], [l], and [r]. But they have voiceless allophones which we use occasionally in certain contexts which will be explained later, and of course in whispering. For the voiced-voiceless contrasts, such as the [v] and [f] of *veil* and *fail*, and the [b] and [p] of *bill* and *pill*, whispering reduces the sharpness of the contrast but does not altogether eliminate it, since the

[1] Symbols in square brackets represent sounds; they must be clearly differentiated, both in reading and writing, from symbols which are italicized or placed between quotation marks, and which represent spellings. For instance, the word *hour* has the spelling *h* (or "h"), but not the sound [h].

voiceless consonants are regularly pronounced more vigorously than their voiced counterparts, even in whispered speech.

## The Manner of Formation

In contrasting *dame* and *name* we discover that the initial [d] and [n], despite obvious acoustic differences, have the same tongue position. Both consonants, moreover, are voiced. The manner of formation is, however, different. For [d], we compress the breath, then suddenly release it; the velar valve remains closed, so that no air escapes through the nose. For [n], on the other hand, we open the velar valve by lowering the velum, so that the sound flows steadily out through the nose without either the compression or the percussive quality of [d]. Thus we may classify [d] as a voiced oral stop, or plosive, and [n] as a voiced nasal continuant. All sounds which are not stops are continuants; they provide continuous egress for the breath or voice.

We may illustrate stops by such sounds as the voiced [d] of *dame* and the voiceless [t] of *tame*. We may subdivide continuants into nasals, such as the [n] and [m] of *name*; fricatives, or consonants characterized by audible friction of the breath, such as the [s] and [v] of *save*; semivowels, such as the [w] and [l] of *will*; and vowels, such as the [e] of *veil* and the [o] of *go*. Distinctions between words depend on all such differences in the manner of producing and contrasting sounds.

In summary, consonants may be classified in three principal ways: (a) the place of articulation or principal narrowing of the passage for breath through the mouth; (b) the presence or absence of vocal vibrations in the larynx; and (c) the manner of formation. The details of this classification will be discussed as we examine the individual consonants in following chapters.

## Classification of Vowels

Vowels may be classified in four ways: (a) by the place at which the principal narrowing of the oral passage occurs; (b) by the height of the tongue; (c) by the tension of the tongue muscles; and (d) by the degree of lip rounding. You will notice that only the first of these classifications corresponds to a similar method of classifying consonants. The other three classifications apply only to vowels and to the complex vowels known as diphthongs.

## The Place of Articulation

The classification of the active regions of the tongue has already been mentioned. The front may be raised toward the hard palate, as in the vowels of *tea* and *take*. The back may be raised toward the velum, as in the vowels of *too* and *told*. Finally, the central part of the tongue may be raised toward the line between the hard palate and the velum, as in *turn* or the first syllable of *amount*. All languages make use of some such classification of vowels. All have front and back vowels, but not all have central phonemes. The English central vowels are therefore especially difficult for some foreigners.

## The Height of the Tongue

If you pronounce the sequence *sit, set, sat* you will observe that you lower your tongue and jaw from the high position of *sit* to the mid position of *set* and the low position of *sat*. Similarly the tongue is high in *look*, mid in *luck*, and low in *lock*. Most languages make use of differences in the height of the tongue, and most recognize at least three distinctive levels. But the exact levels in one language do not necessarily correspond very closely with the exact levels in another, and this variation regularly causes trouble for the foreigner learning a new language.

## The Degree of Muscular Tension

If you contrast *seat* with *sit*, or *pool* with *pull*, you will observe another important means of making meaningful distinctions. The primary difference is that for *seat* and *pool* the tongue muscles are tense; for *sit* and *pull* they are relaxed. You should be able to feel the difference of tension in your muscles. If you touch the skin leading back from your chin to your throat you should be able to feel the muscles bulge for the tense vowel but not for the lax. In addition, you should be able to see in a mirror how the muscles bulge and the point of the larynx rises for the tense vowels. The muscular bulge which you can feel under your chin has its counterpart in a muscular bulge on the upper surface of the tongue.

This variable muscular tension is a characteristic feature of English pronunciation. German has it to a lesser degree: the tense vowel of *bieten* contrasts with the lax vowel of *bitten*. Most other languages lack variable muscular tension as a phonemic distinction.

Differences in tension are likely to be accompanied by three kinds of incidental differentiation. The tense vowel is likely to be slightly longer than the lax. The tongue position is likely to be slightly higher for the tense vowel than for the lax. A slight rise in tongue position during the pronunciation of the tense vowel often produces a diphthongal allophone which contrasts with the monophthongal quality of the lax vowel. The first two of these incidental differences are likely to be more noticeable to the foreigner than the main difference in tension or the development of diphthongal quality. Concentration on the diphthongal quality is, however, the most efficient way for the foreigner to make the allophone sound normal. Only by making the difference in tension can the foreigner make such contrasts as that between *seat* and *sit* sound normal in English.

## Lip Rounding

Though lip rounding accompanies some back vowels, this feature is likely to be variable and slight in American English. Some degree of lip rounding is usual with the back vowels of *pool*, *pull*, *pole*, and *Paul*, and an energetic use of the lips in such words is likely to add to the distinctness of utterance. The vowels of words like *odd*, *on*, and *doll* are variable in American English. Some speakers in some areas of American English make use of lip rounding; most do not.

Lip rounding by itself does not ordinarily distinguish one word from another in American speech. Ordinarily it is incidental to one or more of the distinguishing factors already mentioned in this chapter. If in the pronunciation of some speakers lip rounding becomes the sole differentiating factor between *cot* and *caught*, *don* and *dawn*, the difference is likely to be wiped out altogether, leaving context as the sole factor enabling the listener to determine which word is intended.

## The Purposes of This Study

The first three chapters have given us a general notion of the material with which we are to work, and a general notion of the kinds of thinking we shall use in our subsequent investigation. Enough of the scope and methods is now apparent to enable us to examine the objectives of our investigation. What are the purposes of phonetic study?

The broadest answer is that phonetic study sharpens our understanding of the tool of speech that we use in the varied social situations of daily life. Viewed in this way, phonetic study parallels and complements the study of the written language which begins with the child's first fumbling efforts to read and write and which continues throughout his formal education and beyond. The study of written English is a heritage of the study of written Latin. Because systematic instruction in the mother tongue began at a time when Latin was studied largely as a means of written communication, it was but natural that the methods of teaching Latin should have been adapted to the teaching of English. The teaching of English grammar is still based largely on the Latin model, despite the structural differences between the two languages, and despite the great amount of fruitful research into the grammatical nature of the English language that we have seen in the last score of years. Thus far, such research has made little impact on English teaching.

It was natural, too, when English first made its appearance in the school curriculum, to overlook the difference in purpose between the English of everyday use and the Latin of learned writing. It was easy to forget that, whenever Latin had been the language of daily speech, instruction in spoken Latin had been considered at least as important as instruction in writing. Cicero and Quintilian were quite as interested in the training of speakers as of essay writers. But because of the historical accident that instruction in English began on the model of the contemporary instruction in Latin, all subsequent instruction in English has emphasized the written as against the spoken language. The realization of the place of the spoken language in education, and in the life of the educated man, though axiomatic to the scholars of antiquity, has been long overdue in present-day education. One objective of phonetic study should therefore be to help right the balance, to enable one to gain a sense of the language as a whole, not merely the written part.

On a more pedestrian level, the objective of phonetic study is the improvement of substandard speech, just as spelling, grammar, and theme writing are used to improve substandard writing. As the writing of many persons falls below what we have come to consider the educated use of the written language, so the speech of many individuals falls below the level of accuracy, ease, and good taste that we have come to consider the normal usage of educated speakers.

One who has been imperfectly grounded in grammar may say "He gave it to John and I" because he has been corrected for saying "John and me gave it to him" and has derived, to his own satisfaction, the rule that *I* normally comes after *and.* Similarly, one who has been imperfectly educated in speech may say *chicking* for *chicken*, because he has been forced to change *runnin'* to *running* without knowing why. The compensatory overcorrection of those who are not at ease in their command of the language is as much a problem for the teacher of speech as for the teacher of written English.

Another pedestrian advantage of an understanding of the spoken language is that it makes easier the acquisition of a foreign language. The emphasis now given to the spoken form of foreign languages is an indication that the teachers of foreign languages, unlike many of the teachers of written English, understand that the spoken form is quite as important as the written in any living language. The phonetically untrained student of a foreign language is at a disadvantage when he cannot make comparisons between the methods of producing distinctive sounds in his own language and those of the new language he is studying. Without the realization that some differences in sound are distinctive and others are not, his acquisition of the foreign language is likely to be little more than blind imitation.

On a more idealistic level, the production and appreciation of poetry suffers from neglect of the spoken language. The concepts of rhythm and rhyme are oral, not visual. One does not sit closeted with the score of a Mozart symphony or string quartet; the true lover of music responds to the playing of the music with his whole being. The mighty surge of Milton's *Paradise Lost* is more directly evident to the ear than to the eye. The loss of the oral sense is nowhere more evident than in Emerson, whose poetry looks well enough in print, but whose rhythms falter, and whose rhymes are all too often addressed to the eye, not the ear.

In short, the understanding and appreciation of language, from the lowliest to the loftiest plane, is hampered and incomplete if the spoken language is not included with the written. In the following chapters we shall begin our detailed examination of the spoken language.

# CHAPTER 4

# The Sounds of English
# [p, b, m, f, v, t, d, n, l]

We have already seen that the first requirement for the good visual representation of speech sounds is that each symbol shall represent one phoneme only and that each phoneme shall be represented by one symbol only. Despite the notorious lack of agreement between English spelling and sound, there are nevertheless a few letters each of which ordinarily calls to mind a single phoneme. These letters serve quite satisfactorily for phonetic symbols.

When we look at the letters *p*, *b*, *m*, *f*, *v*, *t*, *d*, *n*, *l*, *s*, *z*, and *k*, we ordinarily think of the phonemes which begin such words as *pay*, *bay*, *may*, *fine*, *vine*, *tie*, *die*, *no*, *low*, *so*, *zone*, and *key*. Sometimes, to be sure, these letters are "silent"; they correspond to no sound in the spoken word, for instance, *b* in *thumb*, *n* in *autumn*, *s* in *island*, *k* in *know*. Occasionally these letters represent, or help to represent, other sounds, for instance *f* in *of*, *p* in *graphic*, *t* in *thin*, *n* in *sing*, *s* in *ship*. In such words we shall need other symbols to represent other phonemes, and we shall study them later. On the whole, however, each of the letters at

the beginning of this paragraph calls to mind a single phoneme.
You are thus already familiar with a dozen phonetic symbols,
which we shall now examine individually. Remember that letters
enclosed in square brackets are phonetic symbols; italicized letters
refer to spellings.

## [p] as in *pipe*

We may define [p] as a voiceless bilabial stop. It is voiceless
because the vocal bands do not vibrate in its formation. It is
bilabial because both the upper and lower lips come together to
form the obstruction to the passage of the breath. It is a stop
because the obstruction to the passage of the breath is momen-
tarily complete; while the lips are closed the velum is also closed,
so that no breath can escape through the nose. In pronouncing
*pie* we compress the breath within the mouth, then explode it
as we move on to the rest of the word. In *up* we close the lips
as we finish the vowel, and have a choice between opening them
and leaving them closed at the end of the word. Thus [p] is
always a stop, not always a plosive. If we pronounce [p] in
isolation, or at the beginning of a stressed syllable, as in *pole*
or *appeal*, we notice a slight rush of breath, known as the aspirate,
which will be discussed later.

If we refer to the method of classifying consonants outlined
in Chapter 3, we find that our definition of [p] is adequate to
differentiate it from other phonemes, since we have pointed out
that it is made by breath without voice; have pointed out the
place of articulation, in this case the lips; and have indicated
the manner of formation, in this case by a complete stoppage
of the breath. The difference between the aspirated [p] in *pole*
and the unaspirated [p] in *up*, and the difference between keeping
the lips closed or opening them at the end of *up*, illustrate
allophonic variations of the phoneme; these variations cannot

be used, in English, to differentiate one meaning from another. [p] occurs at the beginning, middle, and end of words, and is usually spelled *p* or *pp*, as in *pipe* and *upper*. When *p* and *h* occur in successive syllables, as in *shepherd* and *uphill*, *p* is pronounced [p]. When, however, the letters *ph* occur within a single syllable, the combination represents other sounds: [f] in *photograph*, [v] in *Stephen*. The letter *p* is silent before other consonants in such words of Greek derivation as *psychology*, *ptarmigan*, and *pneumonia*.

Ordinarily the pronunciation of [p] causes little difficulty except that it may be too weakly articulated for distinctness. If it approaches the quality of [b] closely enough for *superb* to sound like the first two syllables of *suburban*, then it is probably too weak for good speech. On the other hand, the South regularly accepts *Babtist* and *babtize* for *Baptist* and *baptize*. In any of these instances, a more vigorous articulation is usually enough to restore the [p]. An overarticulated [p] which produces an aspirate in such words as *lamp* or *upper* is, however, equally faulty, and the speaker should be encouraged to relax.

### [b] as in *bob*

[b] is a voiced bilabial stop, formed with essentially the same adjustment of lips and velum as those for [p], but with the vocal bands vibrating and adding tone to the consonantal quality of the stop. [b] is normally articulated with less vigor than [p], a difference which enables us to distinguish it from [p] in whispered speech. [b] occurs at the beginning, middle, and end of words and is spelled *b* or *bb*, as in *bob* and *rubber*. After [m] in the same syllable, *b* is silent, as in *lamb* and *comb*, but may represent [b] at the beginning of a new syllable, as in *lumber*. The letter *b* is also silent in a few miscellaneous words like *debt* and *doubt*.

For native speakers of English, the pronunciation of [b] causes little difficulty. Speakers from Germanic countries, however, often have different allophonic and phonemic patterns in which aspirated and unaspirated [p] take the place of English [p] and [b]. To ears accustomed to English patterns, such Germanic patterns suggest a loss of the distinction between [p] and [b], and make the distinction between pairs of words like *rip* and *rib*, *tap* and *tab*, and even *pill* and *bill* difficult to hear.

## [m] as in *maim*

[m] is a bilabial nasal semivowel, formed with the lips closed and the vocal bands vibrating, as for [b], but with the velum lowered, so that a continuous stream of voiced breath passes out through the nose. [m] is thus similar to [b] in its voicing and bilabial articulation, but different in its manner of formation, because of the velar valve's remaining open. This difference is adequate to account for the phonemic contrast between [b] and [m], as in *bill* and *mill*, *hub* and *hum*.

We call [m] a nasal because the escape of the sound through the nose gives it the characteristic resonance of the nasal passage. We call it a semivowel because the free escape of the air through the nasal passage is similar to the free escape of the air through the mouth during the production of vowels. In contrast to [p], [b], and other stop consonants, [m] may also be termed a continuant, since there is no interruption of the continuously outgoing stream of breath, and the sound may be prolonged as long as the breath holds out. [m] occurs at the beginning, middle, and end of words and is spelled *m* or *mm*, as in *maim* and *summer*.

If the nasal passage is clogged by the swollen mucous membrane of a cold, or by enlarged adenoids or other growths, [m] will be muffled and, in extreme cases, will approach the quality of [b]. If, before another consonant, the lips are not completely closed, [m] may weaken and even become silent, and be replaced by a nasal quality added to the preceding vowel, as sometimes happens in the careless pronunciation of *campus* or *comfort*. Except as noted in this paragraph, the phoneme causes little difficulty.

## [f] as in *fife*

[f] is a voiceless labiodental fricative, formed by placing the lower lip lightly against the upper teeth, closing the velum, and forcing breath under moderate pressure out through the spaces between the teeth, or between the upper teeth and the lower lip. We call [f] labiodental because of the contact between the lip and the teeth; a fricative, because the most characteristic feature of the sound is the audible friction of the breath being forced past the teeth.  [f] occurs at the beginning, middle, and end of words, and is spelled *f*, *ff*, *ph*, or *gh*, as in *fife*, *offer*, *photograph*, and *cough*.

Occasionally in substandard speech [f] may be replaced by [θ], the first consonant in *thin*; most commonly this substitution occurs in *trough*, but sometimes it occurs in other words as well. Ordinarily [f] causes little difficulty to the native speaker of English.  In some languages, notably in Japanese, [f] is formed by the lips alone, without the aid of the upper teeth.  Such an [f] is weaker than its English counterpart, may sound odd to English ears, or may be completely inaudible.

## [v] as in *valve*

[v] is a voiced labiodental fricative, formed essentially like [f], except that the vocal bands vibrate.  It occurs at the beginning, middle, and end of words and is usually spelled *v*, as in *valve*

and *seven*, exceptionally *f* in *of*, *ph* in *Stephen*.  In *nephew*, [v] is normal in England; [f] in America.  Except for infrequent substitutions of [b] for medial [v] in such words as *rivet* and *culvert*, the phoneme causes no difficulty in native English pronunciation.

Since, however, [b] and [v] do not distinguish words in Spanish, but are positional allophones of a single phoneme, native speakers of Spanish often use the two sounds interchangeably in English and may also use sounds intermediate between English [b] and [v].  Such speakers regularly fail to differentiate such pairs as *bale* and *veil*, *marble* and *marvel*, *dub* and *dove*.  Once the Spanish-speaking student has learned to differentiate the bilabial stop [b] from the labiodental fricative [v], he will find English spelling a useful guide for this particular contrast.[1]

Native speakers of Germanic languages, including Pennsylvania German and Yiddish, often confuse [v] and [w] with each other, and sometimes use an intermediate sound for both phonemes.  Germans also frequently substitute [f] for English [v], partly because the letter *v* represents [f] in German, partly because voiced fricatives do not occur at the end of German words.  These two substitutions destroy the distinction between such pairs as *veil* and *wail*, *vine* and *wine*, and *vest* and *west*; and between *feel* and *veal*, *fat* and *vat*, and *safe* and *save*.  Once the distinctive formations of the three phonemes have been worked out, spelling is again a useful guide.

### [t] as in *taut*

[t] is a voiceless alveolar stop, formed by placing the tip of the tongue on the upper gums, or alveolar ridge, closing the

---

[1] Numerous exercises for this and other phonemic contrasts will be found in my *Handbook of Speech Improvement* (New York: The Ronald Press Co., 1956).

velum, compressing the breath, and then releasing the voiceless breath as the tongue moves to the position of the next phoneme. If [t] comes before a pause, as at the end of a sentence, it may be released weakly or not at all. At the beginning of a stressed syllable it is normally aspirated like the aspirated [p] previously mentioned. In fact [t] corresponds to [p] in all respects except the place of articulation on the alveolar ridge. [t] occurs at the beginning, middle, and end of words and is usually spelled *t*, *tt*, or *ed*, as in *taut*, *utter*, and *looked*. A less frequent spelling is *th*, as in *thyme* and *Thomas*.

In most languages [t] is dental rather than alveolar; that is, the tip of the tongue comes in contact with the upper teeth rather than with the gums. In English, the dental articulation is normal only when [t] occurs in a consonantal cluster with the dental *th* [θ], as in the ordinal *eighth*. In other contexts the dental [t] sounds foreign, especially in combination with similarly dentalized [d], [n], or [l]. Developing the habit of using alveolar articulation for these four phonemes will do much to reduce the foreign flavor in the foreigner's English.

[t] is a highly variable phoneme;[2] some allophones are normal; some suggest substandard speech. The principal shortcoming among native speakers is an excessive weakening of the sound, especially in the middle of a word. [t] may then change to a weakly articulated [d], to a variety of [r] produced by a short tap of the tip of the tongue against the gum ridge, or to a glottal stop [ʔ] formed by closing the vocal bands and allowing the compression of the breath to build up in the trachea instead of in the mouth. Or [t] may become completely silent. Though opinions differ as to what is standard and what is substandard in this type of variation, the weakened allophones of [t] frequently heard in

[2] See G. L. Trager, "The Phoneme 'T': a Study in Theory and Method," *American Speech*, XVII (1942), 144–48.

such words as *little*, *better*, *facts*, *mountain*, and *bottle* can usually be somewhat strengthened without laying the speaker open to the charge of artificiality.

## [d] as in *did*

[d] is a voiced alveolar stop, essentially like [t] in its formation except that the vocal bands vibrate, and the energy level is lower. [d] is analogous to [b] in all save the place of articulation. [d] occurs at the beginning, middle, and end of words, and is spelled *d* or *dd*, as in *did* and *sudden*. When -*d* or -*ed* represent the past tense or past participle of verbs without representing an added syllable, they are pronounced [d] after vowels and voiced consonants, as in *flowed* and *loved*, but [t] after voiceless consonants, as in *passed*, *hoped*, and *looked*. Details of this pattern will be discussed more fully in Chapter 6.

As already mentioned, foreign speakers often articulate [d] on the teeth instead of on the gum ridge. In English this dental articulation is normal only when [d] occurs in a cluster with the dental *th* [θ], as in *width*. Speakers of Germanic languages often substitute the voiceless [t] for the voiced [d] at the end of words, since final [d] does not occur in their native languages. This substitution destroys the distinction between such pairs as *ate* and *aid*, *heart* and *hard*, and *tent* and *tend*. Further confusion between English [t] and [d] may result from variations in the relative importance of aspiration and of voicing in some regional types of German. In native American speech, [d] is often weakened or eliminated, especially after [n] or [l], as in *land* or *old*, or in the neighborhood of a second [d], as in *candidate*. Here again opinions differ, but restoration of the [d] can be accomplished without exaggeration.

## [n] as in *nun*

[n] is an alveolar nasal semivowel, formed with the tip of the tongue on the upper gum ridge, and with the velum lowered to permit a continuous flow of sound through the nose. It is thus similar to [d] except that the velar valve is open; it is similar to [m] in all save the place of articulation on the gum ridge. This closing off of the mouth at the gum ridge produces the slight acoustic difference between [n] and [m], since for [n] there is a somewhat smaller resonant space.

[n] occurs at the beginning, middle, and end of words and is usually spelled *n* or *nn*, as in *nun* and *penny*. The letter *n* represents no sound after [m] in the same syllable, as in *autumn* and *condemn*, but may be pronounced [n] at the beginning of the next syllable, as in *autumnal* and *condemnation*. In such words as *think*, *longer*, and *anxiety*, the letter *n* represents a different sound, which will be discussed in Chapter 7.

Like [m], [n] may be muffled by adenoids or a cold. It then approaches the acoustic quality of [d]. Like [m], [n] may be weakened or lost before another consonant, or replaced by nasalization of the preceding vowel, as sometimes happens in *constant*. In many foreign languages [n], as we have seen, is dental rather than alveolar, an articulation which, in English, is normal only in combination with the dental *th* [θ], as in *tenth* and *ethnic*. Habitual dentalization of [n] is not likely to be noticeable unless it occurs in close proximity to other faultily dentalized consonants, as in *pint*, *kind*, *eaten*, *sudden*, and *sullen*.

## [l] as in *lull*

[l] is a lateral alveolar semivowel, formed by placing the tip of the tongue lightly against the upper gums, but with one side,

or both sides, of the tongue lowered to permit the escape of the voiced breath at the side. The velum remains closed. [l] occurs at the beginning, middle, and end of words and is spelled *l* or *ll*, as in *lull* and *follow*. Except for the first *l* in *colonel*, which represents either a vowel or a kind of [r], and for the silent *l* of such words as *calm*, *walk*, and *salmon*, *l* always represents [l] in American English.

[l] at the beginning of *lull* is, however, a noticeably different allophone from the final [l] represented by *ll*. In the final position, and before consonants, as in *field* and *milk*, [l] has an acoustic quality which is sometimes called "dark" in contrast to the "clear" quality of the initial allophone in *lull* and *please*. The dark quality results from a raising of the back of the tongue in addition to the contact between the tip of the tongue and the gum ridge. One noticeable regional pattern in the use of these two allophones is the predominance of the "clear" [l] between vowels, as in *village* and *follow*, in the South; and the predominance of the "dark" [l] in the same words in the rest of the United States and Canada.

In other languages the distribution of "clear" and "dark" [l] may be quite different. In French and German, for instance, [l] is normally "clear", even in positions corresponding to English *pool*, *gold*, and *fall*. In Polish, "clear" [l] and "dark" [l] are separate phonemes, used to differentiate words. For Polish, two phonetic symbols are essential. Since, however, in English, the two varieties are positional allophones of a single phoneme, we need only one, unless we wish to point out the difference between the northern and southern pronunciations of *village*, or to point out that some Scottish regional pronunciations include an initial "dark" [l] in such a word as *look*. In such cases we use [l] for the "clear" allophone, and [ł] for the "dark".

A third American allophone of [l] is a variety in which the

lateral emission is brought about by contact between the back of the tongue and the velum or uvula, in contrast to the usual contact between tongue tip and gum ridge. This is known as the velar [l]. If occurs most frequently before labial or velar consonants, as in *help*, *film*, *self*, and *milk*. Because the light contact between tongue and· velum necessary for the velar [l] is difficult to maintain, the speech agents often slip into a vowel position, as illustrated by the pronunciation *he'p yourse'f*. The velar [l], sometimes thought to be especially characteristic of the southern states, and specifically of Texas, is probably more widespread than many think, especially in *milk*. If the velar allophone spreads to other positions, particularly to the beginning of words, it sounds defective.

A final allophone is the dental articulation, used by many foreigners, often with a more marked dentalization than for [t], [d], or [n]. The dental [l] may be either "clear" or "dark". Dental [l] is normal in English only in combination with the dental *th* [θ], as in *health* and *deathly*; its use in other contexts denotes the foreign speaker.

### Summary

You should now review the consonants that have already been discussed, and familiarize yourself with their different manners and places of articulation. A small hand mirror is essential, since it will often enable you to discover facts about your speech which the sense of touch reveals inadequately, if at all. Placing your fingers lightly on the tip of the larynx will help you to determine the presence or absence of vocal vibrations. Holding a thin sheet of paper just below your nostrils, or placing your fingers lightly on the bridge of your nose, will often help to determine the presence or absence of nasal emission of sounds. Do not confuse the names of the letters of the alphabet with the sounds represented by the corresponding phonetic symbols. The letter "eff", for instance, corresponds to the phonetic symbol [f], but the name of the letter includes a vowel sound as well as the consonant [f]. Similarly, the letter "bee" corresponds to the phonetic symbol [b], but also includes a vowel. [f] can be pronounced in isolation, without any vowel. [b] cannot; you will produce something like "buh" if you try. The letter "ell" corresponds to the phonetic symbol [l], but if you produce [l] in isolation it will be the "dark" allophone. In short, you must begin to differentiate between letter names, visual phonetic symbols, and the sounds which the phonetic symbols represent.

## EXERCISES

In the following exercises, and in all others when you come to them, read the illustrative words aloud. Listen to the sound of the particular consonant you are studying at the moment, but don't distort it by prolonging it or exaggerating the amount of energy you would normally use for it. Watch the movements of the tongue, lips, jaw, and, if possible, the velum. Watch and listen for signs of voicing and of nasal quality. For Exercises 1–4 use the following word list:

big, took, lily, cease, fox, pension, twelve, building, roar, quarry, sphinx, many, improve, physics, murmuring.

1. Pick out those words in the list in which, at some point, the tip of the tongue touches the upper gum ridge.

2. Pick out the words which include voiceless consonants.

3. Pick out the words which, at some point, require complete closure of the lips.

4. Pick out the words which include labiodental consonants.

5. The following pairs of words are alike except for one distinguishing consonant sound. Indicate the phonetic symbols for the sounds which differentiate one word in each pair from the other word, and explain the means by which you produce the difference. For example, the difference between *dead* and *debt* is that the final [d] of *dead* involves vibration of the vocal bands, but that for the final [t] of *debt* the vocal bands are inactive. The difference between *dead* and *den* is that the velar valve remains closed for the final [d] of *dead*, but opens for the final [n] of *den*.

Do not indicate similarities. Do not comment on the action of the velar valve in comparing [d] and [t], since it takes no part in the contrast. Do not comment on the vocal vibrations in comparing [d] and [n], since both sounds are voiced. If you clutter up your analysis with similarities you will obscure your understanding of the contrasts. Though you will not be familiar with all the sounds in all the words, those sounds which distinguish one member of the pair from the other have all been explained in this chapter.

| | | | |
|---|---|---|---|
| bleed | plead | proof | prove |
| cap | cat | rub | rum |
| came | cane | fife | five |
| know | dough | toe | dough |
| fast | vast | debt | let |
| gnat | mat | best | vest |
| pride | fried | cheap | cheat |

# CHAPTER 5

# The Sounds of English
# [s, z, k, g, i, ɪ, ə]

## [s] as in *sister*

[s] is a voiceless alveolar fricative which requires a delicate adjustment of the speech mechanism.  First the sides of the tongue must be raised enough to force the air through a narrow groove along the mid-line of the tongue.  Then the air must be directed against the cutting edges of the lower teeth.  The velar valve must be closed, and the jaw must be high enough to bring the teeth together or almost together.  The tip of the tongue must not come in contact with either the upper teeth or the upper gums.  Since the lower teeth play an important, though passive, part in the formation of [s], differences in the pattern of the teeth make it necessary for different speakers to make slightly different adjustments of the tongue.  Most speakers with faulty [s] sounds are faulty only in the sense that they have not yet discovered the best adjustment of the tongue; the pattern of teeth and jaw can rarely be justifiably blamed for the difficulty.

The two most satisfactory adjustments for [s] are either to place the tip of the tongue against the lower gums below the lower teeth, or to place it about a quarter of an inch behind the upper teeth. In the upper position, the tip must be free from contact with the gum ridge. If actual contact takes place, the breath will either be stopped and an allophone of [t] substituted, or the breath will escape at the sides in a voiceless allophone of [l]. If in the lower position the tip creeps too high, there is danger of a whistle. If the tip comes high enough to touch both upper and lower teeth, there is a strong probability that [s] will be replaced by an allophone of [θ], the first sound of *thin*. Usually an unsatisfactory allophone of [s] can be improved by pulling the whole tongue slightly further back, but not so far back that the quality becomes confused with that of [ʃ], the first sound of *shin*.

[s] occurs at the beginning, middle, and end of words, with a variety of spellings: *s* in *see*, *ss* in *pass*, *sc* in *scent*, *sch* in *schism*, *c* in *race*, and *z* in *waltz*. The letter *x* represents [ks] in *box*. The letter *s*, on the other hand, represents a variety of other sounds, as in *sure*, *rose*, and *measure*; it is silent in a few words, such as *island*. Since the letter *s* represents a wide variety of sounds, and since a wide variety of spellings represents the phoneme [s], analysis will be difficult for foreign and native speakers alike. The foreigner will not know which sound any particular spelling represents, and the native speaker's attempts at analysis will be hampered by misleading cues from the spelling.

Most languages use some kind of [s] that is satisfactory in English, the main exceptions being Philippine languages which permit a wider range of [s] allophones than English, and which consequently encourage the confusion of English [s] with other English phonemes. The necessary delicacy of adjustment, however, causes difficulties for native and foreign speakers alike, and helps to account for the relative slowness with which children acquire a satisfactory [s]. It is all too easy to let the tip of the tongue get too close to the teeth or the upper gums.

## [z] as in *ooze*

[z] is a voiced alveolar fricative, formed with substantially the same tongue positions as [s], but with the vocal bands vibrating, and with slightly less breath force. [z] occurs at the beginning, middle, and end of words and is usually spelled *z*, *zz*, *s*, or *ss*, as in *zone*, *dizzy*, *rose*, and *dissolve*. In a few words of Greek derivation, initial *x* represents [z], as in *xylophone*. Medial *x* sometimes represents [gz], as in *exist*; sometimes [ks], as in *execute*. Because all these spellings represent other sounds in other words, the foreigner often confuses the sounds; false visual clues are common.

Though [z] is as difficult to pronounce as [s], the masking effect of the accompanying vocal tone makes a defective [z] less noticeable than a defective [s]. German and Spanish speakers regularly substitute [s] for final [z], thereby destroying the distinction between such pairs as *fuss* and *fuzz*, and *race* and *raise*. Germans also frequently substitute [z] for initial [s], making *sink* sound like *zinc*.

In America there is some variation in usage between medial [s] and [z] in such words as *absorb*, *absurd*, *desolate*, and *greasy*. Some of these variations represent regional variation. Others depend on personal preference. In the choice between [s] and [z], the student may have difficulty with unfamiliar words, a difficulty which can usually be overcome by nothing more time consuming than a trip to a good dictionary. Children have much the same difficulties in learning [z] as in learning [s].

## [k] as in *kick*

[k] is a voiceless velar stop, formed by bringing the back of the tongue into firm contact with the velum, closing the velar

valve, compressing the breath, and suddenly releasing the pressure by lowering the tongue. The vocal bands do not vibrate. [k] is thus analogous, except for the velar articulation, to [p] and [t]. [k] occurs at the beginning, middle, and end of words, and is spelled *k*, *c*, *ck*, *ch*, *q*, and, less commonly, *kh*, as in *kick*, *cat*, *chorus*, *quit*, and *khaki*. As previously noted, *x* represents [ks] in such words as *box* and *execute*. The letter *k* is silent before [n] in the same syllable, as in *known* and *unknown*, but [k] may be heard when [n] begins the next syllable, as in *acknowledge* and *acne*.

Like [p] and [t], [k] is aspirated at the beginning of stressed syllables, as in *kite*, *crime*, *climb*, and *account*, but not aspirated in other positions, such as those in *sky*, *thicken*, and *sick*. Variation in the patterning of aspirating or not aspirating in other languages often leads to the faulty patterning of the foreigner's English. Overeager native students of elocution and the theatre often add aspirates where no aspirate belongs, to the [t] in *water*, for instance. On the other hand, in careless native American speech, [k] sometimes weakens to a constricted velar fricative, similar to an exaggerated [h], as may occasionally be heard at the end of the first syllable of *technical*. Or it may occasionally weaken to a voiced stop [g], for example at the beginning of the last syllable of *significant*. If the speaker uses enough energy of articulation, [k] is likely to cause little difficulty.

### [g] as in *gag*

[g] is a voiced velar stop, formed substantially like [k], but with the vocal bands vibrating, and with slightly less breath force. [g] is analogous to [b] and [d] in all save the velar articulation. [g] occurs at the beginning, middle, and end of words and is spelled *g* or *gg*, as in *gag* and *beggar*, less commonly *gh*, as in

*ghost.* Note that in *gem* and *age* the letter *g* represents a different phoneme, a combination of sounds also represented by *j* in *jaw*, which will be discussed in Chapter 11. The letters *ng* represent four different sounds or combinations of sounds in *ungrateful, finger, singer,* and *danger.* In only the first two of these words does [g] occur; other sounds will be discussed in Chapter 7 and 11.

The letter *g* is silent before [m] or [n] in the same syllable, as in *gnaw, sign,* and *diaphragm,* but pronounced [g] when [m] or [n] begins the next syllable, as in *signal* and *pragmatic.* At the end of a syllable, *gh* may represent [f], as in *cough,* or be silent, as in *through.* There is little difficulty in the pronunciation of [g]; the problem is to known when to use it and when not to. The problem will be discussed in Chapter 7 in connection with the sounds represented by the letters *ng.*

### Summary of Stop Consonants

With the discussion of [g], we have completed our first survey of the six English stop consonants. Despite the obvious variability of English spelling, you will find that all English sounds which require a momentary stoppage of the breath are allophones of one or other of these six phonemes. We have briefly examined the aspiration of the three voiceless stops at the beginning of stressed syllables. Later we shall examine other details of their action, their interaction with one another, and with other sounds. The following diagram will help to make the physical relationships among them clear:

|           | *Bilabial* | *Alveolar* | *Velar* |
|-----------|------------|------------|---------|
| Voiceless | p          | t          | k       |
| Voiced    | b          | d          | g       |

### Vowels

Vowels are sounds whose audible quality results from the type of vibration set up by the vocal bands, and from the shape and size of the resonating chambers in the throat and mouth through which the sound leaves the body. Nasal vowels, by a lowering of the velum, add the resonance of the nasal chambers, but nasal resonance is never phonemic in the production of English vowels. For vowel production, the size of the resonant chambers is never reduced to the point of complete closure, nor even to the point at which audible friction sets in.

Since Anglo-Saxon times, English vowels have changed their quality more completely than have those of most European languages. Changes in spelling have not, however, kept pace with the changes in sound. As a result, spelling is an even less satisfactory guide to vowel phonemes than to consonants. In the International Phonetic Alphabet, as used in this book, the vowel symbols have been given what might be called their international value: each phonetic symbol represents the sound most likely to be associated with it in the greatest number of European languages. Since English, in comparison with most European languages, now has an eccentric system of spelling, the symbols for the vowel phonemes may seem to be more arbitrary to the native speakers of English than to others. The unfamiliarity should, however, decrease as you practice using the symbols.

### [i] as in *machine*

[i] is a high front tense vowel. The tongue is bunched in the front part of the mouth, and raised nearly to the level of the hard palate. The upper surface of the tongue becomes more and more convex from side to side as the sound continues. This is the

result of increasing muscular tension, which can be felt in the bulge of muscles under the chin. The lips are relaxed in a neutral position. Normally the upper and lower teeth are almost in contact with each other.

[i] occurs at the beginning, middle, and end of words and is commonly spelled *e* in *be*, *ee* in *see*, *ea* in *east*, *ei* in *conceit*, *ie* in *field*, and *i* in *machine*. Less common spellings occur in *people*, *subpoena*, and *Cæsar*.

## [ɪ] as in *bit*

[ɪ] is high front lax vowel, similar in formation to [i], but with the tongue muscles relaxed, the upper surface of the tongue less convex, and no muscular bulge under the chin. Though the tongue as a whole is slightly lower for [ɪ] than for [i], this difference is less important than the difference in tension. Increasing muscular tension, previously noted, produces a gliding [ɪi], which is one of the more important allophones of the phoneme [i]. The gliding allophone is most noticeable in the final position, as in *see* [sɪi]; least noticeable, before voiceless stops, as in *seat* [sit], where the duration is shortest. The gliding, or diphthongal, allophone [ɪi] of *see* is noticeably different from the French or Italian *si* [si] or [si:];[1] the foreigner may have the right phoneme, but not the typical allophone appropriate to the context. Variable muscular tension is much more characteristic of English than of most other languages.

[ɪ] occurs at the beginning and middle of words, and for some speakers also at the end. It is usually spelled *i* or *y*, as in *gift* and *myth*. Less frequent spellings occur in *women*, *build*, *business*, and *English*. In unstressed final positions, as in *city* and *coffee*, some speakers use [i], others [ɪ]. The use of final unstressed

[1] The symbol for length [:] is used to indicate a sound which is prolonged without audible variation in quality.

[ɪ] is most common to the south of a line drawn due west from Atlantic City to northern Missouri, thence southwest to New Mexico. There are also traces of unstressed final [ɪ] in eastern New England. Elsewhere the final unstressed vowel of *city* and *coffee* is [i], but not normally the gliding [ɪi] allophone of *see*. In this larger area most speakers make a distinctive difference between the unstressed [i] of such words as *Rosie's*, *taxis*, and *candied* and the unstressed [ɪ] which is frequently used in such words as *Rose's*, *taxes*, and *candid*. Since the use of unstressed [i] seems to be spreading southward, we can expect to find unstressed [ɪ] largely limited to older people outside the southern area, and an occasional unstressed [i] even in the South. Make a tentative test of your own habits in this variation. You may not get definite results immediately, because it will be difficult for you to pronounce any of these words without self-consciousness at first. But the ability to listen to your own pronunciation without distorting that pronunciation is one of the things you'll learn to do, and you can retest yourself later.

In medial syllables, the use of unstressed [i] is less frequent. Those who use [i] in the second syllable of *city* and *beauty* are likely to change it to [ɪ], or to the weaker vowel [ə] discussed later in this chapter, in the second syllables of *citified* and *beautiful*. Only in the neighborhood of Philadelphia does a clear and definite [i] seem to be characteristic of the medial syllables of such words as *beautiful*, *citified*, and *attitude*.

Before *r* in the same syllable, as in *hear*, *here*, *peer*, and *fierce*, earlier English [i] has changed to [ɪ]. Many people who actually pronounce [ɪ] in such words think they use [i], because of the spelling. If all such words were spelled with *i*, like *spirit* and *miracle*, the mistaken notion might not be so widespread. Only when [r] is immediately followed by another vowel, as in *hero* and *zero*, is there any choice between [ɪ] and [i]. If, like most

Northerners, we place the [r] at the end of the first syllable, we shall pronounce *zero* [zɪr-o]. If, like many Southerners, we place the [r] at the beginning of the second syllable, we shall pronounce *zero* [zi-ro]. In the country as a whole, the pronunciation with [ɪ] is by far the more frequent.

In stressed syllables, especially just before or after [r], [l], and the labial consonants, careless speakers often pull the tongue part way back toward the central position, and sometimes add lip rounding to [ɪ], thereby producing an obscured allophone in such words as *will, fill, building, river, spirit, miracle, superior,* and *beer.* Occasionally *such* and the adverb *just* (but not the adjective *just*) acquire the same pronunciation. A similar centralizing and blurring of [i] sometimes occurs in such words as *wheel, wield,* and *reel.* Well fronted allophones for the front vowel phonemes [i] and [ɪ] are a mark of good speech.

In a few words, such as *creek* and *breeches,* either [i] or [ɪ] may be used. In substandard speech there is an apparently growing tendency to substitute [i] for standard [ɪ] in the stressed syllables of such words as *initiate, tradition,* and *Patricia,* a tendency which possibly has its origin in the foreign-language neighborhoods of our larger cities. Both [i] and [ɪ] have numerous allophones; those for [ɪ] are probably the more numerous.

### [ə] as in *aroma* [əromə]

[ə] is a mid central lax vowel. The tongue is neither forward nor back, but central; neither high nor low, but mid. [ə] occurs at the beginning, middle, and end of words, but always in unstressed positions. This lack of stress is at once the most important characteristic of the phoneme and the reason for its historical development. [ə] may be spelled *a,* as in *about, geography,* and *aroma; e,* as in *taken* and *Nevada; i,* as in *April* and *anvil*; *o,* as in *commence* and *bacon*; *u,* as in *circus* and *column*; *y* as in *Pennsylvania.* Some unstressed syllables may have either [ə] or [ɪ], as in *heated, rugged, roses, bridges,* and *horrid*; others may have [ə], [ɪ], or [i], as in *began, defend, prevent, resign,* and *select.* Unstressed initial syllables afford the greatest opportunity for variation.

Many people remain completely unaware of the existence of [ə], partly because the variations in spelling conceal it, partly it is often interchangeable with unstressed [ɪ], and partly because of the natural tendency, when an unstressed syllable is examined, to add stress to it, thereby changing its quality. The vowel [ə] is, however, one of the most frequent in English, and its use is essential to good English pronunciation. Proper balance between emphatic and unemphatic material is as important in speech as is balance between singer and accompanist, or between foreground and background in a painting. It will probably take you a while to avoid stressing [ə] when you are analyzing words, but it is important for you to learn to recognize it without exaggeration.

## EXERCISES

For Exercises 1–4 use the following word list:

begins, case, possess, catches, logs, quartz, stages, not, longing, passion, zoo, chorus, taxation.

1. Pick out the words which include the phoneme [z].
2. Pick out the words which include the phoneme [s]
3. Pick out the words which include the phoneme [g].
4. Pick out the words which include the phoneme [k].
5. Indicate the distinctive phonemes which differentiate each of the following pairs of words, and explain the physical means by which the difference is produced. For example, in *seat* the

phoneme [i] is produced with tense tongue muscles; in *sit* the phoneme [ɪ] is produced with lax tongue muscles. Do not indicate similarities:

| | | | |
|---|---|---|---|
| rat | rack | loose | lose |
| rum | run | greet | grit |
| back | bag | bag | gag |
| breast | pressed | steel | still |
| close (verb) | close (noun) | lacy | lazy |
| candid | candied | flax | flags |
| anchor | anger | vile | file |

6. Make a phonetic transcription of your own pronunciation of the words in the following list. Repeat each word aloud till you are certain of the phonemes it contains. Then set down the correct symbol for each phoneme, not necessarily one for each letter in the spelling, since there may be more or fewer phonemes than letters. Record your own pronunciation; do not change to pronunciations recommended to you by other people or by books. This exercise is not designed as a test of your familiarity with opinions about pronunciation, but for practice in auditory analysis. Arrange your transcription in vertical columns, one word to a line, leaving the rest of each line for the instructor's comments. The required symbols have all been discussed in this and the preceding chapter. They are [p, b, m, f, v, t, d, n, l, s, z, k, g, i, ɪ, ə]; use no others. Examples: *need* [nid], *stiff* [stɪf], *amid* [əmɪd].

leaf, mill, veal, keep, zeal, kill, pin, fizzes, sieve, kneel, niece, limb, scene, knit, bliss, schemes, sleepy, gives, teases, leaves, seizes, seated, pities, licks, needed, misses, needs, begin, insignia, mixed, civility, indivisibility.

# CHAPTER 6

# The Sounds of English
# Inflectional Endings in -*ed* and -*s*

# [w, j, e, ɛ]

### Inflectional -*ed*

If we contrast *begged* with *baked* we note that the final -*ed* is pronounced [d] in *begged*, [t] in *baked*. The pronunciation of this inflectional ending is one of the few variations in English which can be reduced to rule. When -*ed* represents the past tense or past participle of a verb, without forming an extra syllable, it is pronounced [d] when the immediately preceding phoneme is voiced, as in *begged*, *rubbed*, *lived*, *bathed*, *charged*, *screamed*, *oozed*, *gained*, *cared*, *pulled*, or *flowed*. Pronounce these words aloud and convince yourself of the vocal-band activity in the phoneme preceding the final [d].

The inflectional -*ed* is pronounced [t] when the immediately preceding sound is voiceless, as in *baked*, *wrapped*, *reached*, *passed*, *laughed*, and *rushed*. Pronounce these words aloud and convince yourself of the voiceless quality of the phoneme preceding the final [t]. If the vocal bands vibrate for the immediately preceding sound, they vibrate for the sound represented by -*ed*; if they do not vibrate for the immediately preceding sound, they do not vibrate for the sound represented by -*ed*.

But in such words as *heated* and *heeded*, the pronunciation of -*ed* as either [t] or [d] after an immediately preceding [t] or [d] would be awkward and not in keeping with English speech habits. The [t] or [d] of the ending would merge with the [t] or [d] of the root word, and the distinction between present and past tenses would be lost. This merging has actually taken place in a few words, such as *bet, cast, cost, hit, hurt, let, put, rid, set, shed, shut, spread, cut*, and *thrust*, in which we distinguish the past tense from the present by the context of the sentence, not by any difference in sound.

In still other words, such as *heated* and *heeded*, modern English retains the older pronunciation of -*ed* as [ɪd] or [əd], and as a separate syllable. Since the vocal bands, which vibrate for [ɪ] and [ə], normally continue to vibrate for the final consonant, the final phoneme is usually [d] rather than [t]. Occasionally, however, in a belt extending from southern New Jersey to the neighborhood of Norfolk, Virginia, and westward through Pennsylvania and Maryland, one may hear [ɪt] or [ət] at the end of such words, but only occasionally.

Adjectives ending in -*ed*, such as *ragged* and *crooked*, also retain the older ending in [ɪd] or [əd]. *Crooked* has one syllable as a verb, two as an adjective. So does *blessed*, but in liturgical use there is often confusion in the linguistic tradition, with the two-syllable pronunciation often used for both verb and adjective. In all words discussed thus far in this chapter, the vocal bands continue to do what they have been doing just before the last sound in the word: vibrating bands continue to vibrate; bands at rest remain at rest. This tendency of sounds to agree with neighboring sounds in one or more particulars is known as assimilation; it will be discussed more fully in Chapter 19.

## Inflectional -s, -es, and -'s

A similar patterning occurs when -s, -es, and -'s indicate the plural or possessive forms of nouns or the third person singular form of verbs. In such words as *goes*, *rubs*, *comes*, *dogs*, *gives*, *birds*, *sins*, *sings*, *cars*, *halls*, and *Fred's*, the final sound is [z], because the preceding sound is, in every instance, voiced, and the vocal bands continue to vibrate. In such words as *caps*, *hats*, *docks*, *fifes*, and *Frederick's*, on the other hand, the final sound is [s], because the vocal bands are at rest during the preceding sound, and remain at rest.

In such words as *races*, *raises*, *fish's*, *reaches*, and *bridges*, however, it would be awkward to pronounce either [s] or [z] immediately after the final consonant in the root form of the word. Such a pronunciation would necessitate a cluster of consonants within a single syllable that English does not use. Consequently these words retain the older ending in [ɪz] or [əz], and the inflectional form adds a syllable to the word.

But not all singular nouns ending in voiceless consonants form their plurals with [s], [ɪz], or [əz]. During the earlier period when English plurals regularly included an extra syllable, final voiceless consonants of the singular noun were frequently changed to their voiced counterparts in anticipation of the vowel of the plural form. Modern spelling sometimes indicates the change, as in *thief* and *thieves*, *life* and *lives*, in which the final [f] of the singular was changed to the voiced [v] by the vowel of the plural ending before that vowel dropped out of the pronunciation.

The same kind of variation, but without any change of spelling, occurs in *bath* and *baths*, in which the *th* of the singular represents a voiceless [θ] and the *th* of the plural a voiced [ð]. For *th*, however, the lack of any distinguishing spelling has resulted in the formation of a new plural for *bath* on the analogy of the plural of *bat*. Thus in present-day speech, on all social levels, such words as *baths*, *paths*, *booths*, *truths*, *youths*, and *oaths* sometimes have the traditional voiced ending [ðz], sometimes the new voiceless ending [θs]. Other *ths* plurals, like *deaths*, *myths*, *widths*, and *fourths*, always end in [θs]. For full discussion of the sounds [θ] and [ð], see Chapter 7.

Until you thoroughly understand the principles just set forth, you will need to listen very carefully to the *-ed*, *-s*, *-es*, and *-'s* endings, because the spellings often fail to differentiate the voiced from the voiceless forms, and because usage varies. If you complacently follow the conventional spellings you will simply be evading any serious analysis of the sounds.

### [w] as in *wet*

[w] is a bilabial velar semivowel, formed by rounding the lips, closing the velum, raising the back of the tongue part way toward the velum, and expelling the voiced breath as the speech agents move away from the position just described toward whatever vowel follows. It is better to think of [w] as characterized by movement rather than by position, that is, to think of it as a glide.

[w] occurs at the beginning and middle of words, before vowels, but not at the end, and not before consonants. It is spelled *w* or *u*, as in *wet*, *aware*, *swell*, *guava*, and *quite*. Less frequently, in proper names with French spellings, it has the spelling *ou*, as in *Ouida* and *Ouachita*.[1] The spelling of [w] in *choir* is unique.

---

[1] A Parish (county) in Louisiana. Washita County, Oklahoma, presumably derives from the same American Indian source.

The similarity of [w] to the vowels of *pool* and *pull* may be illustrated by the word *woo*, in which the change from consonant to vowel, both in sound and formation, is very slight. So close are they, in fact, that foreigners often fail to hear the change from consonant to vowel in such words as *woo*, *wood*, and *wolf*. Some of them, especially native speakers of Chinese, Russian, or Spanish, frequently omit [w] from such words.

Speakers of Germanic languages, as noted in Chapter 4, often confuse [w] and [v]; Iranians and Afghans often do the same. For most foreigners, the vowel-like quality of [w] needs to be emphasized. The foreigner should think of [w] as a kind of shortened, intensified, and gliding relative of the vowel of *pool*.

Difficulties with [w] are rare in native English. Some speakers occasionally intrude [w] between *o* and *u* and a following vowel, as in the overemphatic pronunciation of *going* or *go on*.[2] In old-fashioned rural speech, [w] sometimes drops out of unstressed syllables, in such words as *awkward* and *backward*. Sometimes, especially in childish speech, [w] and [r] may be confused with each other. Usually the easier [w], or something like it, replaces the more difficult [r]. Less frequently, when the word includes both [r] and [w], a second [r] may replace [w], as sometimes happens in *prerequisite*. These difficulties are, however, all minor.

### [j] as in *yeast* [jist]

[j] is the phonetic symbol for the sound represented by *y* in *yeast* and *i* in *onion*. The English letter *j* represents a double sound which will be discussed later, and which should not be confused with the phonetic symbol [j]. The phoneme [j] is a palatal semi-vowel, formed by raising the front of the tongue toward the hard

---

[2] It is worth noting, in passing, that those investigators who record *go* as [gow] have no means of indicating this intrusive [w].

palate, closing the velum, and expelling the voiced breath as the speech agents move away from the position just described toward the position of whatever vowel follows. Remember that the front of the tongue is the part which lies directly under the hard palate; do not confuse it with the tip. For [j], the tip remains at rest behind the lower front teeth. Like [w], which it parallels in all save the point of onset, [j] is characterized by motion of the speech agents rather than by position.

Like [w], [j] occurs at the beginning and middle of words, before vowels, but not at the end, and not before consonants. In addition to its usual spelling in *yeast* and *onion*, it occurs in a few words of French or Spanish origin, such as French *chignon* and Spanish *piñon*, in which the spellings *gn* and *ñ* represent [nj] in the fully Anglicized pronunciations of these words. [j] also occurs as the first element of the sequence [ju] popularly known as "long *u*", which is represented by various spellings in such words as *unit, feud, few, view*, and *beauty*. The pronunciation of "long *u*" varies greatly, and detailed examination will be postponed to Chapter 14.

Most foreign languages make use of some kind of [j], but some, notably the Scandinavian and American Spanish, use a tenser and more audibly fricative variety which, to American ears, is acoustically intermediate between the initial consonants of *yoke* and *joke*. The use of this intermediate sound leads to an apparent, and sometimes an actual, interchange of these two phonemes.

The acoustic similarity of [j] and [i] sometimes makes it difficult for the foreigner to hear the change from consonant to vowel in such words as *yeast* and *year*, with the result that they sometimes pronounce them like *east* and *ear*. In native American speech there is an occasional instrusion of [j] after [i] or [e] before a following vowel, as in the pronunciation [hi jɪz] for the phrase *he is*. In standard American speech, either [j] or [ɪ] may occur before [ə] in such words as *alien, champion, California*, and *Pennsylvania. Virginia*, however, always has [j], never [ɪ].

## A Note on [h]

A brief note on the phoneme [h] will be useful at this point, though the main discussion of [h] will be postponed to Chapter 15. We have already seen that the letter *h* is silent in a few words like *hour* and *honest*. We have seen that *ph* represents [f] in *photograph*; and that *gh* may represent [f] in *cough*, but be silent in *through*. We have seen that *th* represents two different phonemes, one in *thin*, the other in *this*.

Most occurrences of the letter *h* represent the phoneme [h], which may be described as a puff of air whose mouth position is determined by the mouth position of the following sound. English [h] occurs only before vowels, and, in the speech of most Americans, before [w] and [j]. It is normal before vowels, as in *heal* [hil] and *hill* [hɪl]. For most Americans it is normal before [j], as in *huge*, though some omit [h]. For some Americans, probably for most, it is normal before [w], as in *wheel* [hwil] and *whisk* [hwɪsk], though more Americans omit [h] before [w] than before [j]. In making phonetic transcriptions, use [h] when you need it.

## [e] as in *gate*

[e] is a mid front tense vowel. The tongue is bunched in the front part of the mouth, and is raised mid high. The tongue muscles are tense, the upper surface of the tongue is slightly convex, and the tension of the muscles can be felt in the bulge under the chin, as for [i]. In contrast to the relatively short vowel in *gate* [get], a longer allophone, as in *gay*, develops a diphthongal

offglide similar to the [ɪ] of *sit*, so that an allophonic transcription of *gay* might be [geɪ]. The diphthongal allophone is most likely to occur when the vowel is lengthened in the final position, as in *gay*, or before voiced consonants, as in *game* and *grade*. A monophthongal allophone is more likely to occur before voiceless consonants, as in *gate*, or in weak syllables, such as the first syllables of *vacation* and *chaotic*.

Other diphthongal allophones of [e] occur in addition to [eɪ], and will be discussed later. Notice, however, that the difference between [e] and [eɪ] represents no phonemic difference; a change from one to the other will never produce a change in the meaning of any English word. A diphthongal allophone also develops when the [i] of *seat* is prolonged in a word like *see* or *seem*. This allophone occurs as [ɪi] or something similar, but there is no phonemic difference between [i] and [ɪi]. Though [eɪ] and [ɪi] are not distinctive, they do have a stylistic value in most parts of the United States except for Michigan, Wisconsin, and Minnesota, where monophthongal [e:] and [i:] are frequent. Elsewhere the long monophthongal forms sound foreign in English, and are, in fact, part of the pattern by which we recognize foreign speech. Since, however, we are at present primarily concerned with phonemic differences, you should use the basic forms [i] and [e] in preference to [ɪi] and [eɪ] in your transcriptions.

Beside the *a* and *ay* spellings already noted, [e] is commonly represented by *ai* in *stain*, *ea* in *steak*, *ey* in *they*, and *ei* in *veil*. Native speakers are likely to have little difficulty with the sound. A raised allophone, in which the tongue position more nearly approaches the high level of [i] is frequent in South Carolina, especially in the Charleston area, and in a broad band across the northern part of the country from Michigan to eastern Washington. The raised allophone makes *grain* sound somewhat more like *green*, and *lake* somewhat more like *leak*. It is probably too early to determine whether this shift represents a general trend, though it is in accord with previous English vowel shifts.

Foreigners, who are usually accustomed to more nearly pure vowels in their native languages, are likely to slight the allophonic diphthongization, as well as the changes in sentence melody which ordinarily accompany and emphasize the diphthongal quality. Such foreigners should use the diphthongal transcriptions [ɪi] and [eɪ] as a reminder of their stylistic importance in English speech.

## [ɛ] as in *get*

[ɛ] is a mid front lax vowel. The position of the speech agents is similar to that for [e], but the muscles are relaxed, the upper surface of the tongue is less convex, and no bulge can be felt in the muscles under the chin. The whole tongue is slightly lower than for [e], but the difference in tension is the characteristic feature. The lower tongue position, however, distinguishes [ɛ] from [ɪ], as may be noted by comparing *sit* [sɪt] and *set* [sɛt].

In most forms of American speech, [ɛ] occurs at the beginning and in the middle of words, but not at the end, and only when the syllable carries more than minimal stress. In such words as *where* and *there*, [ɛ] is normally followed by either [r] or [ə], the latter serving as a vocalic offglide for those speakers who do not pronounce final *r*. In New York City, and to a less noticeable degree in the South, [r] may be lost without the substitution of [ə], leaving [ɛː] at the end of the word. Such a loss of [ə] is often frowned upon in the South; in New York City it seems to attract less notice.

[ɛ] is usually spelled *e*, as in *best* and *berry*; its spelling in *any*, *says*, *said*, and *bury* is exceptional. Before final *r*, as in *fare*, *fair*, and *pear*, [ɛ] is usual, but other vowels, to be discussed later, also occur. In *Mary* and *dairy*, [ɛ] is usual in the North, [e] in the South. Before *r*, [ɛ] is likely to be somewhat longer than before other sounds; the added length depends on the phonetic context, and is thus allophonic. But the distinction between *fed* [fɛd] and *fade* [fed] is phonemic, since the other sounds in the two words are alike.

In the South, [ɛ] sometimes replaces [e] in such words as *great*, *snake*, and *naked*. Southern opinion is divided on the social status of such pronunciations; from a Northerner they will sound quaint. In other parts of the country, notably from upstate New York westward, [ɛ] is often produced with the tongue further back in the mouth when [r], [l], or labial consonants are nearby, as in *well*, *very*, and *American*. Such a pronunciation of *very*, popularly indicated by the spelling *vurry*, is almost a rhyme for *furry*. Retraction of [ɛ], usually considered substandard, parallels the similar retraction of [ɪ] mentioned in Chapter 5. All in all, it becomes evident that [ɛ] is the least stable of the vowel phonemes we have thus far examined.

## EXERCISES

Use the following word list for Exercises 1–4:

myth, wake, friend, squeak, year, fringe, senior, quest, persuade, chairs, getting, greeting, parents, guessed, been, wield, sieve, cute, million, steak, fierce, yes, liquor, quarantine, penguin, annual, cheer, miracle.

1. Pick out the words which include either the tense [i] or the tense [e].
2. Pick out the words which include either the lax [ɪ] or the lax [ɛ].
3. Pick out the words which include [w].

4. Pick out the words which include [j].

5. Indicate the distinctive phonemes which differentiate each of the following pairs of words, and explain the physical means by which the difference is produced.  Do not indicate similarities:

| | | | |
|---|---|---|---|
| peg | pig | well | yell |
| fail | fell | bleed | blade |
| peer | pair | wetter | waiter |
| sense | since | thieves | thief's |
| build | belled | slept | slipped |
| lever | liver | west | waste |
| beer | bear | vest | west |

6. Make a phonetic transcription of your own pronunciation of the following words; arrange them in columns, as before.  In addition to the symbols used in the last chapter, you will need [w, j, h, e, ɛ].  Refer to Exercise 6 in Chapter 5 for detailed directions.

bend, came, wheels, flexes, queen, begs, amazed, deaf, vague, says, silly, sweat, pavement, welcome, whiff, leaves, quickness, steaks, yell, whale, phases, sleepy, yet, daisies, been, quest, baby veiled, pecked, pays, penny, quaked, days, wasted, fixed, knave, laced, knell, Yale, festive, festival, festivity, wheeze, Mexican, Canadian.

# CHAPTER 7

# The Sounds of English
# [θ, ð, ŋ]

### [θ] as in *thin*; [ð] as in *this*

In compound words like *courthouse* and *anthill*, the letters *th* represent [t] in the first syllable and [h] in the second. But in such words as *thin* and *this*, *bath* and *bathe*, *th* represents one or other of a pair of sounds for which English spelling is thoroughly misleading. If we prolong the first phoneme of either *thin* or *this*, or the last phoneme of either *bath* or *bathe*, we discover that each *th* represents a single fricative consonant which may be prolonged to the limit of the breath capacity.

Closer examination reveals that *th* represents a voiceless fricative in *thin* and *bath*, but a voiced fricative in *this* and *bathe*. If you don't hear the voiced-voiceless contrast clearly, press your fingers lightly on the larynx as you produce the sounds; for the voiced sounds you should readily feel the vocal vibrations through the skin. In short, we have two new phonemes: a voiceless [θ] in *thin* [θɪn], and a voiced [ð] in *this* [ðɪs].

Both [θ] and [ð] are formed by placing the tip of the tongue against either the cutting edges or the back of the upper teeth

77

and forcing the breath out through the remaining space. Either sound may occur at the beginning, middle, or end of words. Aside from minor exceptions, as in *thyme*, *Thomas*, and *Esther*, in which *th* represents [t], and compounds like *courthouse* and *anthill*, in which *th* represents [th], the letters *th* regularly represent one or the other of these fricative phonemes. Though there is no simple rule for determining in advance which of the two phonemes is normal in any English word, the following hints may be helpful.

Before [w] or [r] in the same syllable, *th* always represents the voiceless [θ], as in *thwart* and *throw*. At the beginning of nouns, verbs, and adjectives, and of adverbs derived from adjectives, *th* normally represents [θ], as in *thumb*, *thank*, *thick*, and *thickly*. These are idea-carrying words, usually found in emphatic positions in the sentence, and as such have acquired the more energetic pronunciation of the voiceless sound.

On the other hand, initial *th* usually represents [ð] in pronouns, conjunctions, and adverbs not derived from adjectives, as in *them*, *than*, and *then*. Pronouns, conjunctions, and many of these adverbs are more likely than nouns, verbs, and adjectives to have a grammatical than a graphic function. Hence they are less likely to be pronounced emphatically. Hence they have acquired the less energetic voiced pronunciation. Since early English [θ] and [ð] were not separate phonemes, were not used to distinguish words, as we distinguish *teeth* [tiθ] from *teethe* [tið], phonetic factors alone determined the early distribution of these two phonemes.

Unfamiliar words beginning with *th*, like *thence* and *thither*, often lead the student astray. Consider any such new words in terms of the principles explained in the two preceding paragraphs, and then confirm your guess by reference to your dictionary.

Before final silent *e*, *th* represents [ð], as in *bathe* and *soothe*.

In other contexts of sounds and spellings no rule is satisfactory. In the middle of words, *th* represents [θ] in *ether* and *author*, but [ð] in *either* and *father*. At the end of words, *th* represents [θ] in *truth*, but [ð] in *smooth*. Usage varies between [θ] and [ð] in a few words, of which *with* is the best known. Some nouns have [θ] in the singular, as in *bath* and *mouth*, but [ðz] in the plural, as in *baths* and *mouths*. As previously noted, however, there is a growing tendency to lose this distinction, and to form the plural "regularly" with [θs]. Unfamiliar words like *blithe* and *lathe* are likely to provide pitfalls for the unwary student who does not consult a good dictionary.

Foreigners usually have difficulty with [θ] and [ð], not because of any intrinsic difficulty in the formation of the sounds, but simply because they are unfamiliar. Even Spaniards, who have both [θ] and a more constricted variety of [ð] in their own language, have difficulty with the corresponding English sounds because the English spelling is different.

The dental articulation of [t] and [d] characteristic of most European languages makes it difficult to differentiate [θ] from [t] or [ð] from [d]. Sometimes the foreigner makes too firm a contact between tongue and teeth. More often he substitutes [s] or a dental [t] for [θ], as in [sɪn] or [tɪn] for [θɪn]; and [z] or a dental [d] for [ð], as in [zɪs] or [dɪs] for [ðɪs].

In native English, [θ] and [ð], or approximations to them, often occur as lisping substitutions for [s] and [z], as in [ðɪθ] for *this* and [ðɪð] for *these*. In childish speech, [f] and [v] sometimes replace [θ] and [ð], as in [bof] for *both* and [vɪs] for *this*. Less common is the reverse substitution, [θ] and [ð] for [f] and [v]. Native substitution of [t] and [d] for [θ] and [ð] is probably less common than it used to be, and is now largely confined to the poorer speakers in the larger cities, and to foreign-language communities.

Since *th* is an ambiguous symbol, be on your guard when you encounter the letters in an unfamiliar word. You should at least get dictionary opinion, even though the dictionary may represent conservative usage. And you will need to listen carefully when you attempt to identify and analyze [θ] and [ð].

## [ŋ] as in *thing*

If you pronounce *thin* and *thing* slowly and alternately, you will notice that the final sounds in the two words are similar but not identical. You should also notice that *ng* in *thing* represents a single sound which you can prolong as long as your breath holds out, not a succession of [n] and [g] of the sort you hear in *ungrateful*. The final sound in *thing* may be symbolized by [ŋ], and may be described as a velar nasal semivowel. It is formed by lowering the velum, raising the back of the tongue until it establishes firm contact with the velum, and expelling the voiced breath through the nose. [ŋ] is thus similar to [m] and [n] in all save the place of articulation, which it shares with [k] and [g]. The three nasal consonants of English can now be added to the chart of Chapter 5, to show their structural relationships to the stop consonants:

| *Stops and Nasals* | *Bilabial* | *Alveolar* | *Velar* |
|---|---|---|---|
| Voiceless stops; velum raised | p | t | k |
| Voiced stops; velum raised | b | d | g |
| Nasals; voiced; velum lowered | m | n | ŋ |

It should be noted that nasals are normally voiced, but that whispering produces no difference in their meaning. If you whisper such a word as *meaning* [minɪŋ], the nasals, along with the vowels, become voiceless, but the meaning of *meaning* remains unchanged. The nasals do not share with the stops and the fricatives the phonemic contrast between voiced and voiceless sounds. Nothing in the nasals corresponds to such phonemic contrasts as those between the voiced [d] of *din* [dɪn] and the voiceless [t] of *tin* [tɪn], or between the voiced [z] of *zinc* and the voiceless [s] of *sink*. Voiceless nasals are allophones of the corresponding voiced nasals.

If you compare the native English pronunciations of *singer* and *finger*, you will observe that *ng* represents [ŋ] alone in *singer*, but [ŋg] in *finger*. Historically, [ŋg] is the older pronunciation; the existence of [ŋ] as an independent phoneme results from the historical loss of [g] in certain contexts. Rules for the use of these sounds in English follow:

1. At the end of a word, only [ŋ] occurs, as in *sing, hang, long, tongue*, and *eating*.

2. Except as noted in rule 3, inflectional forms and compounds use [ŋ] alone if the root word ends in [ŋ], as in *sing, sings, singer, singing, longing, tongues, banged, Springfield, Bingham, Binghamton, Birmingham*, and *Washington*. The endings *-ham* and *-ton* of English place and personal names are compounds, the unstressed forms of the older pronunciations of *home* and *town*. *Length* and *strength*, which are derivatives of *long* and *strong*, sometimes have [ŋ] alone, sometimes [ŋk]. *Gingham*, though neither a compound nor an inflectional form, but the English approximation of the French *guingan*, has [ŋ] alone on the analogy of *Bingham*.

3. The exceptions, which have [ŋg], are comparatives and superlatives of adjectives: *longer, longest, stronger, strongest, younger*, and *youngest*, and a few miscellaneous words like *elongate* and *prolongation*. A few uncommon words, like *monophthongal* and *diphthongize*, which historically have [ŋg], are sometimes heard with [ŋ] alone. The French *hangar*, a shelter for

airplanes, usually had [ŋg] when first used in English, but has now been thoroughly Anglicized as *hanger*, with [ŋ] alone.

4. In the middle of the root form, as in *finger, hunger, angle, England, English, anguish,* and *distinguish,* [ŋg] occurs in standard speech, [ŋ] alone in the speech of some Americans of German descent whose speech habits have been influenced by the German pattern of pronouncing *ng* as [ŋ] alone. German family names like *Engelman* are pronounced with [ŋg] in English, but with [ŋ] alone by those who are still under the influence of the German pattern.

5. Compounds formed by prefixing *in-, on-,* or *un-* to words beginning with [g], such as *ingratitude, ongoing,* and *ungrateful,* have [ng] in standard speech, sometimes [ŋg] when the speech is rapid or unemphatic.

6. Final *-nge,* as in *change* and its derivatives, has [n] plus "soft *g*", a sound which will be discussed in Chapter 11.

The velar nasal [ŋ] is also represented by *n* before [k], in such words as *chunk, distinct, anchor,* and *lynx.* [ŋ] also occurs in *anxious,* from which the historical [k] is sometimes lost, and in *anxiety,* from which the [k] has been completely lost. English [ŋ] occurs at the middle and ends of words, but never at the beginning. Since the spelling is so confusingly unphonetic you will need to give special attention to the identification and analysis of the sound.

The history of [ŋ] and [ŋg] varies in different languages to such an extend that the foreign student of English is likely to have great difficulty in differentiating them. In German, at one extreme, [ŋg] has simplified to [ŋ] in all words and all positions, including such words as *Finger* and *Hunger.* Accordingly, the German's first impulse will be to omit [g] from the English cognates of such words as these. Later, as he learns of the existence of [ŋg], he may confuse [ŋ] with [ŋg], or [ŋg] with [ŋ], as the association of the moment prompts him. Speakers of Thai, Tagalog, and other languages of southeast Asia have [ŋ] initially, medially, and finally, but not always [ŋg]. Their problem in English is likely to parallel the Germans'.

At the other extreme, in Spanish, Italian, Hungarian, Turkish, Yiddish, and the Slavic languages, [ŋ] has no existence except as the allophone of [n] used before [k] or [g]; as such, it has no phonemic contrast with [n]. Yiddish split off from High German before the latter had lost [g] from the [ŋg] cluster.[1] Consequently the association of [ŋ] with [g] and [k] is so strong that any attempt to establish [ŋ] as an independent phoneme is extremely difficult. The tendency to pronounce English *sing* as [sɪŋg] or [sɪŋk] will persist strongly. The difficulty is often complicated by muscular tension, which often closes the velum before the release of the tongue. Proper timing of the muscular movements for [ŋ] and [ŋg] is therefore important, and these must be more relaxed when [ŋ] is not to be followed by [g] or [k].

In native English there is little variation between [ŋ] and [ŋg] except in *England*, *English*, and a few unfamiliar words like *diphthongal*. In the north of England the old [ŋg] survives, especially before vowels, as in *singer* and *long enough*, and there are traces of this usage in native American speech, especially in the Southern Mountains. But most instances of the substitution of [ŋg] for [ŋ], as in *Long Island*, can be traced to foreign-language neighborhoods.

The commonest variation in native American speech is the substitution of [n] for [ŋ] in the unstressed ending *-ing* of such

[1] See Edward Sapir, "Notes on Judeo-German Phonology," *Jewish Quarterly Review*, n.s., VI (1915), 231–66.

words as *running* and *nothing*. Popularly known as "dropping the *g*," this substitution illustrates the confusion between spelling and pronunciation. When the speaker realizes that he should form the sound with the back of the tongue, rather than with the tip, and that there are the same number of sounds in each pronunciation, he is more likely to restore the conventional pronunciation than if he starts chasing after a "dropped *g*" that was never there in the first place.

In childish speech, [ŋ] and [n] may be confused in any position, and the child may use [ŋ] for [n], even in such a word as *nice*. In *length* and *strength*, anticipation of the final [θ] sometimes pulls the tongue forward to the position of a dental [n], producing the pronunciations [lɛnθ] and [strɛnθ], which rhyme with *tenth* [tɛnθ]. Insertion of [k] between [ŋ] and [θ] is usually enough to normalize the pronunciation, since [lɛŋkθ] and [strɛŋkθ] are usually accepted, along with [lɛŋθ] and [strɛŋθ], as normal.

## EXERCISES

Use the following word list for Exercises 1–4:

think, angry, withering, eight, changed, northern, engine, gathering, Thompson, withstood, pothook, sanguinary, thus, eighth, nothing, bothering, athletic, congress, belonging, either, anchor, anesthesia.

1. Pick out the words which include [θ].
2. Pick out the words which include [ð].
3. Pick out the words which include [ŋ].
4. Pick out the words which include [g].
5. Find the distinctive contrasting sounds in the following pairs; label them with phonetic symbols; explain the difference in their physical formation:

| thin | thing | | teeth | teethe |
|------|-------|---|-------|--------|
| wreathe | wreath | | singer | sinner |
| thin | fin | | ham | hang |
| his | hiss | | mean | main |
| worth | worse | | linger | limber |
| beliefs | believes | | hand | hanged |
| rug | rung | | lesson | listen |

6. Make a phonetic transcription of your own pronunciation of the following words. Use only [θ, ð, ŋ], and the symbols discussed in previous chapters:

Christmas, bathing, deathly, theme, thinks, winking, lengths, quibbling, within, indistinct, stealthy, England's, flinging, myth, mingling, hymns, teething, escaped, lynxes, strengthen, tingles, themselves, withheld, Binghamton, women, singled, seethes, sphinxes, building, tinkling.

# CHAPTER 8

# The Sounds of English
# [r, æ, ɑ]

## [r] as in *red*

The sounds of *r* in *red*, *very*, and *far* have a long, complicated, and controversial history. The earliest type of [r], so far as we know, was a strong trill formed by allowing the tip of the tongue to vibrate or flutter against the upper gums while voiced breath was forced out under moderately strong pressure. Such a tip trill survives in some Scottish varieties of present-day English, is cultivated by some singers, and is taught to telephone girls for use in the word *three*. The excessive energy required for the trill has, however, led to a weakening of the sound in most parts of the English-speaking world.

One weaker form is the reduction of the trill to a single tap, which is hardly distinguishable from a weak [d]. This variety survives, between vowels, as in *very* and *merry*, in the south of England, and in the speech of a few Americans who ape the British style. Weakening of American [t] between vowels sometimes produces a similar sound, so that British *berry* may sound

86

like *Betty* to American ears, and vice versa.  In either dialect, considered without reference to the other, the two words are recognizably distinct.

As the historical process of weakening the [r] continued, there developed first a frictional type formed with the tongue close to the roof of the mouth, and later a semivowel without audible friction, and with the tongue somewhat lower.  In America a slight amount of friction is sometimes audible after tongue-tip consonants, as in *three*, *tree*, and *dream*.  The more usual American type lacks audible friction.  It is formed by closing the velum, vibrating the vocal bands, and either by pointing the tip of the tongue toward the roof of the mouth, or lowering the tip and raising the central section of the tongue toward the line between the hard palate and the velum.  It is virtually impossible to detect, by hearing alone, which variety a speaker is using at any given moment, provided he uses the variety more familiar to him.  Of course, if one attempts to demonstrate both varieties, one will usually sound better than the other.

At a somewhat earlier period, speakers in the north of England replaced the tip-trilled [r] with a trill of the uvula, which was allowed to vibrate in a narrow groove along the mid-line of the back of the tongue.  This uvular trill came to be known as the Northumbrian burr.  It developed independently in some parts of France, and later spread to neighboring parts of Germany.  As heard today, it rarely survives as a trill, but has weakened to a uvular fricative or semivowel.

In some parts of the English-speaking world, the weakening of [r] led to its complete elimination from certain positions. First, [r] dropped out of a limited number of words, chiefly before voiceless consonants.  Because this happened before the development of some of our present-day vowels, the loss of [r] gave the earlier vowels a chance to survive.  Thus informal *bust* and *cuss* survive along with standard *burst* and *curse*, and informal *passel* along with standard *parcel*.

Later, in the early decades of the nineteenth century, a more extensive loss of [r] took place in some regional varieties of English. In the south of England, and in the speech of many Americans in eastern New England, New York City, and the lowland South, *r* is not now pronounced as [r] at the end of a word or before a consonant. In these dialects [r] dropped completely out of such words as *far* and *farm*, and was replaced by compensatory lengthening of the vowel. In some areas, notably New York City and the South, the added length of the vowel may be the sole factor that distinguishes *hard* from *hod*, *dark* from *dock*, and *harp* from *hop*.

Dialects which limit the use of [r] regularly replace it with a weak allophone of [ə] in such words as *fear*, *feared*, *fare*, *fares*, *poor*, *fire*, and *flour*. In words like *for*, and sometimes in those like *four*, [r] may be replaced by [ə] or by vowel lengthening. In the south of England, and to a limited extent in the lowland South, and to a greater extent in eastern New England, [r] may survive at the end of a word if the next word begins with a vowel and there is no pause between the words. Thus *r* may be silent in *far*, but pronounced [r] in *far away*.

The variety just described is sometimes called the linking or liaison [r], because it breaks the hiatus between consecutive vowels. It leads to the intrusion of [r] where no historical [r] has existed, as in *vanilla* [r] *ice cream*, and *law* [r] *of the land*. An intrusive [r] may also result from mixture of dialects. If one sometimes hears *dear* with [r] and sometimes without, it is but a step to the pronunciation of *idea* sometimes with and sometimes without a final [r].

The intrusive [r] of *law* and *idea* is common in the south of

England, in eastern New England, and in the New York City
area. It is less common in the South, for two reasons: first, the
Southerner often omits *r* between vowels, not oɪ.ly in *far away*,
but also within single words, like *very* and *Carolina*. Second,
there is less mixture of the major varieties of English in the
lowland South than in New York City, eastern New England,
or the south of England.

The rest of the country regularly uses [r] or an [r]-colored
vowel wherever *r* or *rr* occur in the spelling, except for a few
cases of dissimilation which will be discussed in Chapter 20.
Some speakers in eastern New England and the border areas of
the South, and a good many speakers in the New York City
area, also retain final and preconsonantal [r], at least part of
the time. A generation ago Kenyon estimated[1] that about two-
thirds of the American population normally pronounce *r* in all
positions. At present I would estimate the proportion as nearer
to three-fourths of the total population.

Though consonantal [r] is a single phoneme in English, the
vocalic [r] that differentiates *stirring* from *string* is a separate
phoneme that will be discussed in Chapter 9. For the present,
use the single symbol [r] wherever the sound occurs in your
speech. If you hear an [r] in *fear*, record it as [fɪr]; if you hear
a weak [ə] instead of [r], record it as [fɪə]. If you hear no [r]
in *card*, record it as [kɑ:d], using the length mark [:] to avoid
possible confusion with *cod*, which may be [kɑd] in your speech.
At this stage of your transcribing, it is much more important to
discover your own usage, even your own inconsistencies, with
respect to [r], than to transcribe according to some rule which
will give you no help in developing your hearing.

[1] John S. Kenyon, "Some Notes on American R," *American Speech*, I
(1926), 333.

### [æ] as in *cat*; [ɑ] as in *cart*

We shall compare two new vowels at this time. [æ] is low and front, and usually lax, though a tense allophone occurs in some phonetic contexts, and in the speech of some individuals. [æ] occurs at the beginning and middle of words but not ordinarily at the end. It is spelled *a*, as in *cat* and *ash*. In most American areas, but not in all, it is spelled *au* in *aunt* and *laugh*. Before [r] plus a vowel, as in *carry*, *barren*, and *parrot*, [æ] occurs regularly along the Atlantic and Gulf coasts, in Pennsylvania and the South, but [ɛ] occurs more frequently in other areas.

[ɑ] is low, back, and lax. It occurs at the beginning and middle of words, and is spelled *a*, as in *arm*, *calm*, and *farm*. In a few foreign words, such as *Shah* and *spa*, and in the speech of those who omit [r] from *far* and similar words, it occurs finally. The exact quality of [ɑ] varies greatly; there are many regional allophones, and, in some words, an actual choice of other phonemes. These variations will be discussed in Chapter 12.

[æ] and [ɑ] are distinguished by the active region of the tongue: you should be able to feel the whole tongue moving forward for [æ] and back for [ɑ], and should be able to see that movement in a mirror. Since both phonemes are produced with the tongue low in the mouth, there is plenty of room for slight allophonic variations, which will be discussed later on. For the present, at least, treat [æ] as the symbol for your vowel, or vowels, in *cat* and *man*; and [ɑ] as the symbol for your vowel, or vowels, in *cart* and *cot*.

Few foreign languages have a contrast similar to that between [æ] and [ɑ]. Most languages lack a vowel phoneme which is very close, acoustically, to English [æ]. A good many foreign languages use a variety of [ɑ] which is either very similar to English [ɑ] or made with a slightly more forward tongue position. The more forward [ɑ] usually sounds passable if used for English [ɑ] but noticeably strange if used for English [æ].

In native American English, the chief difficulty in the use of these sounds is the frequent occurrence of an overtense, overlong, overnasalized [æ] in such words as *bad*, *man*, and *land*. What is needed in such cases to produce a more pleasant quality is to use a more relaxed, shorter vowel, with less nasality, not always an easy quality to produce. The common elocutionary solution of shifting the vowel quality toward that of [ɑ] is no solution at all; it invariably makes the vowel seem either foreign or artificial.

## EXERCISES

Use the following word list for Exercises 1–4:

strap, vary, far, Carolina, surprise, farmer, through, carry, third, governor, horrible, Marion, southerner, Martha, prisoner, thermometer, borrow, particularly, actor, flatterer, quarry, recreation, secretary, strangle, stenographer, area, crash, library, parachute, Palmer, dairy, forest, warrant.

1. Pronounce the words at normal speed; do not slow them down. Then indicate which *r*'s represent either [r] or some kind of [r]-colored vowel in your speech.

2. Pick out the words which include [ɑ].

3. Pick out the words which include [æ].

4. Pick out the words which include [ɛ].

5. Indicate the phonetic and physical contrasts in your own pronunciation of the following pairs of words:

| | | | |
|---|---|---|---|
| reed | weed | red | led |
| fresh | flesh | red | dead |
| wedding | wearing | cue | crew |
| flax | flecks | man | men |
| hamper | hanker | merry | marry |

6. Make a phonetic transcription of your own pronunciation of the following words:

palm, marred, drank, damn, sang, farce, thanks, valley, wax, wreath, heart, lathe, lambs, wring, anvil, garments, bargains, April, vanity, capitol, actress, rang, barque, creek, wrapped, scars, scarce, tardy, wrinkle, wreathes, angry, vanguard, parson, carrying, fierce, Antarctic, pairs, spirit, various, clearly, appearance, fearful, Maryland, parents, æsthetic, marital.

7. Make a phonetic transcription of your own pronunciation of the following sentences. Read each sentence at normal speed. If you slow down you will risk changing the pronunciation of the weaker syllables. Leave every other line on your paper blank for the instructor's comments:

Terry married Grace in April.
The actress drank some tea in the garden.
The appearance of spring was delayed till May.
The bargain basement was filled with angry women.
They laid a red carpet at the building's entrance.

# CHAPTER 9

# The Sounds of English
# [r] and the Central Vowels

# [r, ɝ, ɜ, ɚ, ə]

In the last chapter we noted that all normal speakers of English pronounce [r] in *red*. Except for some Southerners, all pronounce some kind of [r] in *very*. In *far*, more than two-thirds of the American population pronounce [r]; less than one-third omit it. In these three positions—before, between, and after vowels—[r] is consonantal and nonsyllabic; it involves the characteristic hindering of the free flow of breath that we associate with consonants. The [r] of *red* serves as a kind of springboard for the [ɛ] which follows it. The [r] of *very* interrupts the flow of sound just enough to mark the boundary between syllables. The [r] of *far* closes the syllable somewhat more definitely than the prolonged vowel of the pronunciation [fɑ:]. In these words [r] is nonsyllabic; the characteristic sonority of the syllable depends on the vowel [ɛ] in *red* and *very*, and on [ɑ], or something similar, in *far*.

Now compare *string* and *stirring*. In *string*, [str-] provides the initial springboard, the vowel [ɪ] is the syllabic element, and the nonsyllabic [ŋ] closes the syllable; [r] is still nonsyllabic. But in *stirring*, only the initial [st-] is the springboard; a kind of vowel-like *r* completes the syllable, and the rhythm of the whole word is very close to that of *staying* [steɪŋ]. For this vowel-like *r* which distinguishes *stirring* from *string*, we use the symbol [ɝ] and transcribe the whole word [stɝɪŋ], in contrast with *string* [strɪŋ]. Shortening the word to *stir* gives us the transcription [stɝ]. We may define [ɝ] as a mid central tense vowel with [r]-coloring, the [r]-coloring being indicated by the hook on the upper right side of the symbol. Physically, the [r]-coloring is produced either by raising the central portion of the tongue fairly high, like the central [r], or simultaneously raising the tip of the tongue, like the tongue-tip [r].

But just as not all Americans pronounce [r] at the end of *far* and *star*, not all use [r]-coloring at the end of *stir*. To record a mid central tense vowel without [r]-coloring, we simply omit the hook and transcribe *stir* as [stɜ]. Obviously [stɝ] and [stɜ] do not indicate separate words; the vowels represent corresponding phonemes in different regional types of speech. A typical speaker from the coast of Maine or the coast of Georgia will make no use of [ɝ]; he will pronounce *stir* [stɜ]. A typical speaker from Pennsylvania or Oregon will make no use of [ɜ]; he will pronounce *stir* [stɝ]. Only in border areas, such as some parts of Maryland, some parts of Arkansas, and in the mixed speech sometimes heard in the New York City area, will you find people who sometimes say [stɝ] and sometimes [stɜ]. Other typical spellings for [ɝ] and [ɜ] may be illustrated by such words as *stern, heard, work, turn,* and *journal.*

Both [ɝ] and [ɜ] have allophonic variations of their own. They may vary in length without affecting meaning: [ɝ] and [ɝː], [ɜ] and [ɜː]. When a vowel follows, as in *stirring*, the vowel and the [r]-coloring may be pronounced separately, as in [stɜrɪŋ], a variation more frequent among those who use [ɜ] in *stir* than for those who use [ɝ]. [ɜr] represents the historical sequence of vowel plus [r] from which [ɝ] developed. The sequence may occasionally be heard before consonants, as in [bɜrd] for *bird*, especially in upstate New York,[1] but [ɝ] is unquestionably more frequent.

Before consonants, [ɜ] has an important diphthongal allophone [ɜɪ], as in [wɜɪk] for *work* and [bɜɪd] for *bird* a regional variation frequent in the New York City area and the Deep South. Dialect writers sometimes try to suggest the diphthong by spelling *bird* "boid," less frequently "buyd." Neither spelling indicates the diphthong very accurately, and the "oi" spelling frequently misleads the reader into thinking that a pronunciation identical with that of the name *Boyd* is intended. Note that [ɜɪ] does not ͵normally occur in the final position, as in *stir*, nor before vowels, as in *hurry*, nor when following sounds constitute inflectional endings, as in *stirs*, *stirred*, and *stirring*.[2]

The social status of [ɜɪ] varies greatly. Southerners usually take it for granted, and some Southerners prefer [bɜɪd] to [bɜːd]. Though speakers of all social levels in the New York City area use [ɜɪ],[3] New Yorkers generally condemn the use of the diphthong, and the number of younger New Yorkers who use [ɜɪ] seems to be decreasing.

Attempts to explain [ɜɪ] as the result of foreign influence may be dismissed on two counts. In most foreign speech [r] is strongly

---

[1] See my "Pronunciation in Upstate New York," *American Speech*, X (1935), 110–12.

[2] See my "Pronunciation in Downstate New York," *American Speech*, XVII (1942), 150–51.

[3] See A. F. Hubbell, *The Pronunciation of English in New York City* (New York: King's Crown Press, 1950). Hubbell uses a smaller sampling of speakers than those referred to in the previous note, but collects a larger sampling from each individual speaker.

pronounced, and the foreigner is quite likely to pronounce English [ɜr] with a definitely consonantal [r]. So long as [r] or [r]-coloring remain, no [ɜɪ] develops. Furthermore, the percentage of foreigners, though high in New York City, is well below the national average in the South, where [ɜɪ] spreads over a wider area than in New York. [ɜɪ] occurs in southern villages in which no foreigners live.

A better explanation will be found in the characteristic diphthongizing of all long, tense English vowels, a diphthongization we have already observed in the [eɪ] of *say* and the [ɪi] of *see*. The diphthong [ɜɪ] seems to have been more common in the nineteenth century than today. Small groups, especially older people, continue to use it in eastern North Carolina, in New London, Connecticut, and in northeastern Maine.

In unstressed positions the mid central lax vowels [ɚ] and [ə] replace [ɝ] and [ɜ]. [ɚ] has [r]-coloring, produced in much the same way as the [r]-coloring of [ɝ]; [ə] has no [r]-coloring. Some people pronounce *murmur* [mɝmɚ], some [mɝmə]. In addition to its already familiar use in *aroma*, *amid*, and *soda*, [ə] replaces both the nonsyllabic [r] of *fierce* and the syllabic [ɚ] of *bitter* when the [r]-coloring is lost, as in the pronunciations [fɪəs] and [bɪtə]. Spellings for both [ɚ] and [ə] are represented by the endings of such words as *attar*, *paper*, *tapir*, *actor*, *murmur*, *glamour*, and *martyr*. As we have seen in Chapter 5, we all use [ə]. Not all of us use [ɚ].

The unstressed [ɚ] and [ə] almost never diphthongize, but [ər] may occur as a bridge between syllables. The speaker who pronounces *batter* [bætɚ] normally pronounces *battery* [bætɚi]; but one who pronounces *batter* [bætə] is quite likely to pronounce *battery* [bætəri].[4] Either type of speaker may also pronounce

---

[4] Compare J. S. Kenyon, *American Pronunciation* (8th ed.; Ann Arbor: George Wahr, 1940), pp. 158–59.

*battery* [bætri] in rapid speech. The sequence [ər] is not, of course, a diphthong, since the two elements occupy separate syllables.

Note especially the limitations on the use of these central vowels. [ɝ] and [ɜ] occur only as the main syllabic elements of stressed syllables, though [ɜ] may be diphthongized as [ɜɪ]. [ɚ] and [ə] are always unstressed. [ɚ] occurs only in unstressed syllables. [ə] occurs in unstressed syllables, as in *bitter* [bɪtə] and *amid* [əmɪd], and also as an unstressed offglide in stressed syllables after the main vowel, as in *fierce* [fɪəs] and *there* [ðɛə].

In the analyses and transcriptions of this chapter and of those that follow, you will need to take special care to pronounce words and sentences with normal rhythm and stress. The addition of stress to normally unstressed syllables is almost certain to distort vowel quality and to produce unnatural pronunciations. You will need to be particularly cautious with little words like *that* and *and*, which have a grammatical rather than a graphic function in the sentence.

## EXERCISES

For Exercises 1–4, use the following word list:

author, occurrence, myrtle, personnel, thorough, nadir, lurk, hurry, colonel, persist, personal, victory, worship, encouragement, history, Virginia, idea, currant, arrange, miraculuous, mere, garage, absurd, where, little, syrup, poor, tourist, flourish.

1. Pick out the words which include [ɝ] in your own natural pronunciation.

2. Pick out the words which include [ɜ] in your own natural pronunciation.

3. Pick out the words which include [ɚ] in your own natural pronunciation.

4. Pick out the words which include [ə] in your own natural pronunciation.

5. Make a phonetic transcription of your own pronunciation of the following words:

purse, frequent, birth, England, worth, wagon, first, sermon, swerve, hearth, worthy, bargain, turn, farther, colonel, dearth, never, dirty, ferry, learn, murder, verse, dairy, sir, lather, third, carry, yearn, curl, furtive, absurd, connect, carrots, American, occur, prefer, disturbed, matters, gravity, merciless, characteristics, martyrs.

6. Make a phonetic transcription of your own pronunciation of the following sentences:

The ring was buried in the sand.
The man gazed at the fierce animal.
Several nurses attended the meeting.
They failed to make the battery work.
The bag was taken in the railway train.
The girl had a dress made of purple silk.
He was busily reading a history of Greece.

# CHAPTER 10

# The Sounds of English
# Unstressed Syllables

Since the unstressed vowels discussed in Chapters 5 and 9 are more difficult to comprehend than stressed vowels, it will be well to review them, and to enlarge our understanding of them before going on to other sounds.

We have already seen that inflectional endings of such words as *freezes* and *needed* may have either [ɪ] or [ə]: [frizɪz] or [frizəz], [nidɪd] or [nidəd]. In such unstressed prefixes as those of *beneath*, *develop*, *prevent*, and *select*, on the other hand, we may have not only [ɪ] or [ə], but also unstressed [i]. Since [i] and [ɪ] may also occur in stressed syllables, it will be useful, in order to avoid ambiguity, to place the stress mark [ˈ] before the stressed syllable. Thus we may record *beneath* as [bəˈniθ], [bɪˈniθ], or [biˈniθ]; *select*, as [səˈlɛkt], [sɪˈlɛkt], or [siˈlɛkt]. When the stress pattern varies as well as the quality of the unstressed vowel, we may hear *details* as [dəˈtelz], [dɪˈtelz], [diˈtelz], or [ˈditelz].

Unstressed [i] has only a limited use in inflectional endings, in a few words of Greek or Latin derivation, such as *theses*

[ˈθisiz], the plural of *thesis* [ˈθisɪs].  In *bases*, [ˈbesiz] the plural
of *basis*, we have a contrast with *bases*, the plural of *base*, which
is normally [ˈbesɪz] or [ˈbesəz].  The extension of the Greco-Latin
plural [-iz] to words to which it does not historically belong,
such as *processes*, is a feature of recent substandard speech,
especially that of the radio and television commercial.

At the end of the root form of the word, as in *city*, or before
a vowel, as in *create*, the unstressed [i] is normal: [ˈsɪti] and
[kriˈet].  Apparently this use of [i] is a development of the last
half century or so.  Older people who learned to speak before
the current fashion developed may say [ˈsɪtɪ] and [krɪˈet], pronunciations which are also frequent in the South, where the speech
is more conservative than in other areas.

In unstressed medial syllables, such as those of *animal* and
*cemetery*, the choice is usually restricted to [ə] or [ɪ]: [ˈænəməl]
or [ˈænɪməl], [ˈsɛməˌtɛri][1] or [ˈsɛmɪˌtɛri].  Words pronounced with
unstressed [i] at the end of the root form, like *city* and *pity*,
normally retain unstressed [i] in nonsyllabic inflectional endings,
like *cities* [ˈsɪtiz] and *pitied* [ˈpɪtid], or before an extra syllable
beginning with a vowel, as in *pitying* [ˈpɪtiɪŋ].  Before a suffixed
syllable beginning with a consonant, however, most Americans
change the unstressed [i] to [ɪ] or [ə], as in *citizen* [ˈsɪtɪzən] or
[ˈsɪtəzən] and *pitiful* [ˈpɪtɪfəl] or [ˈpɪtəfəl].  Only in the Philadelphia
area are such pronunciations as [ˈsɪtizən] and [ˈpɪtifəl] at all
frequent.

In unstressed syllables, especially those spelled with *a*, *e*, or *i*,
you must beware of preconceived notions about the quality of
the unstressed sounds.  Do not assume that unstressed syllables
with *a* have the sounds [e] or [æ], nor that those with *e* have the

---

[1] Where it seems desirable to indicate a stress weaker than the main stress,
but stronger than minimal stress, the stress mark may be placed below instead
of above the line.

sound [ɛ].  The sounds [e], [ɛ], and [æ] rarely, if ever, occur in syllables with minimal stress.  If you listen carefully, you will discover that variations in your own use of unstressed [i], [ɪ], and [ə] do not follow any simple pattern.  Your own pronunciation may show differences in the corresponding unstressed syllables of such pairs as *terrible* and *terribly*, *package* and *packages*, and *carpet* and *carpeted*.  You will need to be especially cautious in analyzing such a word as *indivisibility*, in which the spelling suggests a series of [ɪ] sounds, but for which you will probably find the spelling deceptive.  In your own speaking, recognize that unstressed [i], [ɪ], and [ə] have a valid, useful, and unavoidable function in English.  Do not make the mistake of thinking that in substituting [e], [ɛ], or [æ] you are improving the distinctness of your speaking.  You aren't.  You're only making it sound artificial.

### Syllabic Consonants

We have already seen that in such words as *better* and *ladder* what was once a consonantal [r] has become syllabic [ɚ] or [ə].  Two other consonants regularly become syllabic; they become more vowel-like, though without completely losing their consonantal quality.  They are vowel-like in sound, and vowel-like in function, in that no other vowel is needed to complete the syllables in which they occur.

If you repeat *sadden* and *saddle* at an ordinary rate of speed, you will notice that the tip of the tongue makes contact with the gum ridge at the beginning of [d] and remains there till the completion of [n] or [l].  While the tongue remains on the gum ridge no vowel sound develops; [n] and [l] constitute the second syllables.  Ordinarily the syllabic consonants may be recorded in the same way as the nonsyllabic, thus *sadden* [ˈsædn] and *saddle* ['sædl]. The only way in which [n] or [l] can be pronounced in this context is syllabically; you cannot, in English, pronounce either set of four sounds as one syllable. Hence there is no ambiguity. Similarly, in *sadness* ['sædnəs] and *sadly* ['sædli], the vowels [ə] and [i] constitute the syllabic element of the second syllables, and again there is no ambiguity in the transcription.

Occasionally, however, we need a special symbol to avoid ambiguity between the syllabic and nonsyllabic uses of the consonants. The transcription ['sædnɪŋ] for *saddening*, for instance, looks as if two syllables were intended. If we wish to indicate the usual three-syllable pronunciation we place the syllabic marker [ˌ] under the [n], thus ['sædn̩ɪŋ]. The need for the special syllabic-consonant marker does not often arise, but occasionally we need to distinguish such a word as *lightening* with [n̩] from *lightning* with [n]. For *sadden* and *saddle*, and most other occurrences of syllabic [n] or [l], the syllabic marker may be used or omitted as you prefer, since no ambiguity results.

When they are preceded by stressed vowels, we normally use the syllabic combinations [dn], [dl], [tn], and [tl], as in *sadden*, *saddle*, *beaten* ['bitn], and *beetle* ['bitl]. In all these four combinations the tip of the tongue remains on the gum ridge from the beginning of the stop to the end of the continuant. For [dn] and [tn], the velum drops, allowing the breath to escape through the nose for [n]. For [dl] and [tl], the sides of the tongue drop, allowing the breath to escape laterally for [l]. If you try to insert a weak [ə] in the middle of any of these combinations, as in ['sædən] for *sadden*, ['sædəl] for *saddle*, ['bitən] for *beaten*, or ['bitəl] for *beetle*, the pronunciation will sound forced and artificial.

When, however, a consonant precedes [t] or [d], we normally insert [ə] before [n] or [l], and its omission regularly reduces the clarity of utterance. Normally we pronounce *abandon* [ə'bændən], *candle* ['kændəl], *piston* ['pɪstən], and *pistol* ['pɪstəl].   When an unstressed vowel precedes [n] or [l], usage varies.  *Accident* may be ['æksədənt] or ['æksədnt]; *capital*, ['kæpətəl] or ['kæpətl].  You should repeat words of this type till you can both feel and hear the difference.

The use of syllabic consonants depends on two factors.  First, the places of articulation of the successive consonants must be close enough together for them to be quickly and easily linked.  When the places of articulation are identical for two or more consonants we say that they are *homorganic*.  Thus [t], [d], [n], and [l] are all homorganic with one another, since we articulate each with the tip of the tongue on the gum ridge.  Similarly, [p], [b], and [m] are homorganic with one another, since each is formed by the articulation of the upper and lower lips.  [s] and [z] are homorganic with each other since, whichever choice of articulation we make for [s], we also make for [z].  We are most likely to use syllabic consonants when the successive consonants are homorganic.

Syllabic consonants may be used, however, when the successive consonants, though not homorganic, can readily be formed without the insertion of a vowel between them.  Thus for *apple* and *ribbon* the pronunciations ['æpl] and ['rɪbn] are possible because the tongue tip can be placed in position for [n] or [l] while the lips are forming [p] or [b].  For *reason* and *trestle* the pronunciations ['rizn] and ['trɛsl] are possible because the tongue can slide from the position of [s] or [z] to the position of [n] or [l] without dropping down to the position of the vowel [ə].  Begin to rid yourself, therefore, of your first impulse to record [ə] without actually hearing it or without feeling the break between consonants.

On the other hand, in *eagle* ['igəl], *wagon* ['wægən], *tickle* ['tɪkəl], and *bacon* ['bekən], the tongue must move from the velar position of [k] or [g] to the alveolar position of [n] or [l], a movement which is almost certain to carry the tongue through the position for the vowel [ə]. In such sequences the use of syllabic [n] or [l] sounds muffled. The muffling is even greater if another consonant precedes [k] or [g]. Thus we normally pronounce *tingle* ['tɪŋgəl] and *Lincoln* ['lɪŋkən], not ['tɪŋgl] and ['lɪŋkn].

Secondly, the consonant which precedes the syllabic consonant must be strongly enough articulated to mark the syllabic boundary and avoid blurring in the linking. If we pronounce *women* as ['wɪmn], the [m] is acoustically too weak to mark the end of the first syllable clearly and too much like [n] to avoid indistinctness. Normally we retain distinctness by pronouncing *women* ['wɪmən]. Similarly, *Helen* is normally ['hɛlən], *cannon* is ['kænən], *barren* is either ['bærən] or ['bɛrən]; in no such words is syllabic [n] normal. On the other hand, [n] is definite enough to provide the syllabic boundary in *flannel* ['flænl], and we use syllabic [l] in words of this type.

If the consonant preceding the syllabic consonant is a stop, the explosive release of the stop is reduced. Thus in *cattle* ['kætl], the release of the [t] is restricted to a lowering of the sides of the tongue; in *fatten* ['fætn] the release of the [t] is restricted to a lowering of the velum. If we place another consonant before the stop, the beginning of the stop is restricted, as in *apt* [æpt] or *list* [lɪst]. Restrictions both before and after the [t], if we pronounce *captain* ['kæptn] with a syllabic [n], result in a lowering of the articulative and acoustic quality of the stop to the point at which it frequently drops out. Thus ['kæptn] usually changes to ['kæpn], and may go on to ['kæpm]. To avoid the loss of [t] we cannot, in English, separate [t] from the preceding [p], but we can substitute [ən] for the syllabic [n]. Ordinarily, in good speech, we pronounce *captain* ['kæptən]. Where [t] has been bolstered by [ə] it has been retained, as in *captain*, *pistol* ['pɪstəl], and *piston* ['pɪstən]. Where [ə] has not been retained, [t] has been lost, as in *listen* ['lɪsn] and *thistle* ['θɪsl].

Syllabic [m] may occur in a few words like *chasm* ['kæzm] or ['kæzəm] and *prism* ['prɪzm] or ['prɪzəm], but it is not common. Syllabic [ŋ] occurs only in rapid or substandard speech, as in ['bekŋ], which may represent either *bacon* or *baking*. Stops and fricatives are never syllabic in any English words, though the syllabic noises [s:] and [ʃ:] may be used to indicate disapproval or a demand for quiet, respectively.

Since the variations between [ən] and [n], and between [əl] and [l], are subtle and complicated, you will need to give them close attention. If you can hear [ə], or can feel the tongue tip leave the gum ridge and return to it, write [ə] in your transcription. If you can't hear [ə], and if the tongue tip remains on the gum ridge, write a syllabic consonant. But don't jump to conclusions too quickly. The duration of [ə], if it occurs at all, is likely to be very brief; be sure you don't miss it. On the other hand, be sure you don't imagine it.

## EXERCISES

Use the following words for Exercises 1–3:

little, numskull, pointed, capstan, poison, button, jungle, bulletin, policy, hated, raisins, person, uncle, bugle, Bingham, venom, castle, poultry, nation, husband, awful, cradle, ample, butler, felony, criminal, possible, possibly, quarantine.

1. Pick out the words which include [ə].
2. Pick out the words which include syllabic [n].
3. Pick out the words which include syllabic [l].
4. Make a phonetic transcription of your own pronunciation of the following words:

nerves, burden, dresses, nurses, ended, dressers, lantern, scandal, whistle, treason, cannibal, elected, fixes, dazzled, risked, rested, raisins, parcel, glistens, breathless, flattery, sadness, candidates, myrtle, spirit, limited, physical, single, Christmas, guesses, battering, kitten, captaincy, whiskers.

5. Make a phonetic transcription of your own pronunciation of the following sentences.

The man was seated beneath a maple tree.
The girl's appearance fascinated the man.
Next Saturday will be the twelfth of April.
Mrs. Miller was making pickles in the pantry.
The dentist filled the cavities in eleven teeth.
Melons and blackberries can be seen in the market.
The carpenter fixed many things with little bits of string.

# CHAPTER 11

# The Sounds of English
# [ʃ, ʒ, tʃ, dʒ, ɔ, o]

**[ʃ] as in *mission* [ˈmɪʃən]**
**[ʒ] as in *vision* [ˈvɪʒən]**

We now come to a group of consonants that, though not ordinarily difficult for native speakers of English to pronounce, offer some obstacles to easy comprehension and analysis. If you pronounce *see* and *she* alternately, disregard spelling, and merely listen, you will notice that what you can actually hear is a difference in the musical pitch. Both sounds, of course, have pitches well above what you can reach with your voice, but the ratio of [s] in *see* [si] to [ʃ] in *she* [ʃi] is about that of C on the piano to the next lower F. If you whisper the words you can hear the contrast more easily. Better still, contrast an isolated and prolonged [s:], a hiss that you might use to express disapproval, with an isolated and prolonged [ʃ:], that you might use to demand quiet.

If you look in a mirror while doing this, you should be able to see that the whole tongue is drawn slightly further back for [ʃ] than for [s], and that the tongue is somewhat more widely spread from side to side. Consequently the breath stream comes out in a broad sheet for [ʃ], in contrast to the narrower channeling that characterizes [s].

We may therefore redefine [s] as a voiceless narrow fricative articulated with the blade of the tongue and the fore part of the gum ridge. This is the place at which the passage will be narrowed, regardless of whether the tip of the tongue is up or down. We may define [ʃ] as a voiceless wide fricative articulated with the blade of the tongue and the back part of the gum ridge. The exact place and degree of narrowing will, of course, vary with different speakers. So will the amount of lip rounding with which some speakers reinforce the lower-pitched quality of [ʃ].

[ʃ] occurs at the beginning, middle, and end of words, and with a variety of spellings: *sh* in *she* and *fish*, *s* in *sure*, *ssi* in *mission*, *ti* in *nation*, *sch* in *schist*, *ci* in *vicious*, and *ch* in *machine*. [ʃ] also occurs in *pressure* [ˈprɛʃɚ], *conscience* [ˈkɑnʃəns], and *anxious* [ˈæŋkʃəs] or [ˈæŋʃəs]. The variety of the spellings obviously means that you must use your ears, not your eyes, in analysis.

The voiced counterpart of [ʃ] is [ʒ], as in *vision* [ˈvɪʒən] and *azure* [ˈæʒɚ]. It is formed with the same adjustments of the speech mechanism as [ʃ], but with the addition of voice. In English, [ʒ] occurs with spellings *s* and *z* in the middle of words of French derivation. In a few words taken over from French more recently, it occurs in the middle and at the end of words, with spellings *j* and *ge*, as in *bijoux* and *rouge*. [ʒ] is never used at the beginning of any English word.

### [tʃ] as in *church* [tʃɝtʃ]
### [dʒ] as in *judge* [dʒʌdʒ]

In *church* English uses a closely blended combination of the stop [t] with the fricative [ʃ]; such a combination is known as an *affricate*. To the casual listener, [tʃ] sometimes seems to be a single sound, but if you try to prolong it you discover that you prolong only the fricative [ʃ]. Phonemically, however, it functions as a single unit which contrasts with both [t] and [ʃ], as in *tin* [tɪn], *shin* [ʃɪn], and *chin* [tʃɪn]. [tʃ] occurs at the beginning, middle, and end of words, usually with the spellings *ch* or *t*, as in *church* and *nature* [ˈnetʃɚ].

The voiced counterpart of [tʃ] is the affricate [dʒ], phonetically a compound, phonemically a unit. [dʒ] occurs at the beginning, middle, and end of words, and is spelled *j*, *g*, *d*, or *dg*, as in *judge*, *age* [edʒ], and *grandeur* [ˈgrændʒɚ]. Words like *change* [tʃendʒ] and *fringe* [frɪndʒ] illustrate still another sound represented by the letters *ng*; see Chapter 7 for previous discussion. As with [tʃ], the compound phonetic structure of [dʒ] can be demonstrated by trying to prolong it.

The four phonemes [ʃ], [tʃ], [ʒ], and [dʒ] present difficulties to foreigners, since most languages lack one or more of them. French lacks [tʃ] and [dʒ]; consequently French speakers are likely to substitute [ʃ] and [ʒ]. German lacks [ʒ] and [dʒ]; German speakers are likely to substitute [ʃ] and [tʃ], especially at the ends of words. Italian lacks [ʒ]; Spanish lacks all but [tʃ]. Scandinavians, Siamese, and a good many speakers of American Spanish confuse [tʃ], [dʒ], and [j] with one another. Chinese sometimes confuse [s], [ʃ], and [tʃ], and [z], [ʒ], and [dʒ]. Speakers of Tagalog and other Philippine languages generally substitute [s] for any of these four phonemes. All foreigners have difficulty resulting from the bewildering English spelling which represents these phonemes.

In native English speech, [ʃ] and [ʒ] occasionally occur as lisping substitutes for [s] and [z]. Other native difficulties, which involve the substitution of one of these four phonemes for one of the others in substandard speech, will be discussed in Chapter 19.

**[ɔ] as in *caught***
**[o] as in *coat***

The vowel [ɔ] is formed with the tongue low, though usually not quite so low as for [ɑ]. The tongue is bunched in the back part of the mouth, the lips are usually slightly rounded, and the muscles of both tongue and lips are slightly tense. The use of so many qualifying adverbs in the previous sentences suggests that the allophones of [ɔ] vary a great deal. As a matter of fact, illustrative words may suggest varying allophones, and even other phonemes, to some readers. These variations will be discussed later. For the present, regard [ɔ] as the vowel phoneme of the illustrative words which follow, even though your own allophones may vary considerably. [ɔ] occurs at the beginning, middle, and end of words and is spelled *a* in *all* [ɔl], *au* in *caught* [kɔt], *aw* in *lawn* [lɔn], *o* in *horse* [hɔrs], and *ou* in *bought* [bɔt].

The vowel [o] is mid back tense and accompanied by lip rounding. It occurs at the beginning, middle, and end of words and is spelled *o* in *go*, *oa* in *oak*, *ou* in *soul*, *oe* in *toe*, and *ow* in *crow*. Irregular spellings represent [o] in *sew* [so] and *beau* [bo]. Just as prolonged [e] and [i] develop the diphthongal allophones [eɪ] and [ɪi], so a prolonged [o] develops the diphthongal allophone [oʊ]. The meaning remains unchanged, however, whether we pronounce *coat* [kot] or [koʊt]. Foreigners, who usually have a monophthongal [o] in their native languages, will usually sound more like native English speakers if they learn to use the diphthongal [oʊ].

For native speakers of English, the difference between the monophthongal and diphthongal allophones is usually automatic, depending on the duration of the allophone. If the vowel is lengthened, as in *go*, it is more likely to be diphthongal than if it is short, as in *coat*. The degree of diphthongization varies with different individuals and different localities. There is probably less diphthongization in the north central states, Wisconsin and Minnesota in particular, than elsewhere in the country. The exact shadings of the allophones of [o] also differs in various parts of the country: the sound begins with the tongue slightly further forward in the Middle Atlantic area, and slightly higher in the South, than in other areas.

Before *r*, there is a historical distinction between [ɔ] and [o] which has been maintained in some parts of the English-speaking world, but lost in others. Those who maintain the distinction pronounce *horse* as [hɔrs], [hɔəs], or [hɔːs]; and *hoarse* as [hors], [hoəs], or [hoːs]. Similar distinctions may be made between *for* with [ɔ] and *four* with [o]; between *morning* with [ɔ] and *mourning* with [o].[1]

In the south of England, in the New York City area, and generally across the northern part of the United States west of New England, the distinction has been almost completely wiped out, and all these words customarily have [ɔ]. The South regularly maintains the distinction between [ɔ] and [o] before *r*. So does the upper New England coast, though the distinction seems to be losing ground in the Boston area. The distinction remains in the Middle Atlantic area southward from central New Jersey, and westward through the midland areas, but not as sharply as in the South. There is a broad transitional area extending from north to south, with the distinction gradually weakening toward the north. For those who have difficulty in distinguishing the historical [or] words from those historically [ɔr], all good Ameri-

[1] For some of the American regional variations, see Hans Kurath, "Mourning and Morning," in *Studies for William A. Read*, ed. N. M. Caffee and T. A. Kirby (Baton Rouge: Louisiana State University Press, 1940), pp. 166–73.

can dictionaries distinguish the two classes of words with one set of symbols or another.

When [o] occurs before *r*, it usually has a slightly lower tongue position than [o] in other contexts. Normally it does not diphthongize to [oʊ] unless the following [r] can be placed at the beginning of the next syllable, as in *glory* [ˈglorɪ] or [ˈgloʊrɪ]. At the end of words, as in *four*, or before consonants, as in *hoarse*, it is normally [o], not [oʊ]. The similarities of the spellings for [or] and [ɔr] have probably contributed to the loss of the distinction in some localities, and to inconsistencies in its retention in others.

The distinction between [or] and [ɔr] is not, of course, vital for the foreigner, who usually adopts the indigenous regional pattern without much difficulty. Except for inconsistency in the transitional geographical areas, there is likely to be little native difficulty either.

### EXERCISES

For Exercises 1–6, use the following word list:

passing, passion, measure, mishap, fortune, oriole, gorge, glory, feature, possession, Virginia, presume, audition, village, corrosion, insurance, camouflage, education, confusion, natural, auction, commotion, Beauregard, quarter, portion, shore, machinery, orator, oration, social, coronation, enclosure, crutches, associate, furniture, gymnasium, joke, gashouse, orchid, growing.

1. Pick out the words which include the phoneme [ʃ].
2. Pick out the words which include the phoneme [tʃ].
3. Pick out the words which include the phoneme [ʒ].
4. Pick out the words which include the phoneme [ʤ].
5. Pick out the words which include the phoneme [ɔ].

6. Pick out the words which include the phoneme [o].

7. Indicate the phonetic and physical differences between the following pairs:

| | | | |
|---|---|---|---|
| coat | caught | chin | gin |
| chip | ship | flaw | flow |
| porch | ports | toast | tossed |
| chalk | choke | ridge | rich |
| paltry | poultry | person | Persian |
| correspondent | co-respondent | confusion | Confucian |

8. Make a phonetic transcription of your own pronunciation of the following words:

flashes, cheap, shore, shin, glorious, largest, chin, shawl, reached, omission, chink, forty-fourth, avaricious, ginger, sketches, sergeant, pleasure, ditches, decision, short, changing, adjourn, leash, menagerie, regiment, course, commission, porch, shall, jail, natural, soldier.

9. Make a phonetic transcription of your own pronunciation of the following sentences:

The sergeant ate three large tomatoes.
The champion ran in the 50-yard dash.
Mr. Jones was ill with German measles.
They served maple syrup with the pancakes.
The porch was screened against mosquitoes.
They saw fourteen graves in the churchyard.
St. Jerome lived early in the Christian era.

# CHAPTER 12

# The Sounds of English
# Low-Vowel Variants
# [a] and [ɒ]

For most Americans the vowels [æ], [ɑ], and [ɔ] form an auditory series in which each vowel represents a distinctive phoneme. Thus most Americans pronounce *cat* [kæt], *cart* [kɑrt], *cot* [kɑt], and *caught* [kɔt]. Most Americans distinguish *cart* and *cot* by the presence or absence of [r], not by vowel quality or length. Because of the loose position of the tongue in the lower part of the mouth, however, numerous intermediate sounds may develop in the [æ-ɑ-ɔ] series. Though in most American regional types of speech these intermediate sounds are allophones of [æ], [ɑ], or [ɔ], in some areas they may have phonemic status, and at least two of them are widely enough used and important enough stylistically to warrant special attention.

### The intermediate [a]

Many people pronounce *rather* [ˈræðɚ], to rhyme with *gather*. Some say [ˈrɑðɚ], to rhyme with *father*. Still others strike an auditory compromise between [æ] and [ɑ], and say [ˈraðɚ]. This [a] may be defined as a low lax vowel formed with the tongue bunched in either the central or the frontcentral area, and sounding intermediate in quality between [æ] and [ɑ]. It is the vowel most frequently heard in French and Spanish *la*, and the vowel corresponding to [æ] in some varities of Scottish and Irish English. No single word can be used to illustrate [a] in American English, since many Americans do not use it at all, and others use it as an allophone of either the phoneme [æ] or the phoneme [ɑ]. [a] is also used in some of the allophones of the phonemic diphthongs, which will be discussed in Chapter 15.

The use of [a] is a comparatively recent development. During the second half of the eighteenth century a number of words which had previously had [æ] began to change to [ɑ]. In the south of England such words as *far* and *farm* began to change from [fær] and [færm] to [fɑr] and [fɑrm];[1] and *ask, dance,* and *path* began to change from [æsk], [dæns], and [pæθ] to [ɑsk], [dɑns], and [pɑθ]. The fashion spread across the Atlantic, but met with varying receptions. Most parts of the United States accepted the new [ɑ] in *far* and *farm*, but in eastern New England the shift was incomplete. Some New Englanders accepted [ɑ], but most shifted only as far as [a], which remains to this day the characteristic eastern New England vowel of *far, farm,* and similar words.

In *ask, dance,* and *path,* the new fashion took hold even less completely. Only in eastern New England and eastern Virginia did the change affect any large segments of the population. In most forms of present-day American speech, such words as *ask, dance, path, half, aunt,* and *command* normally have [æ].

---

[1] The regional loss of [r] occurred later. For an account of the vowel shift, see "Fashion and the Broad A," in Charles H. Grandgent's *Old and New* (Cambridge: Harvard University Press, 1920).

In the south of England they have [ɑ]; in eastern New England and eastern Virginia they sometimes have [a], sometimes [ɑ], sometimes [æ]. There are indications, however, that both in eastern New England[2] and eastern Virginia the use of [a] and [ɑ] is declining in favor of [æ] in this class of words.

Partly as a result of the New England elocutionary tradition, now chiefly maintained in the small dramatic schools in New York City and Hollywood, scattered individuals in other parts of the country have adopted [a], often self-consciously and unsystematically. Such speakers usually retain [æ] in some of the words in which eastern New England traditionally uses [a]. On the other hand, they often use [a] in words like *bad, grand, fancy*, and *thanks*, in which the south of England and all standard American varieties use [æ]. For such people, [a] represents an allophone of [æ], an allophone which, in their own opinion, represents prestige. For the New Englander who uses [a] for both the *farm* and *ask* classes, [a] represents an independent phoneme.

When used consistently, [a] occurs chiefly before voiceless fricatives, as in *ask, half*, and *path*, but not before [ʃ], as in *crash* [kræʃ] and *passion* [ˈpæʃən]. [a] occurs also in a few words before [n] and a second consonant, as in *dance* and *command*, and in a few words of foreign origin like *lava, pajamas*, and *canasta*. There are, moreover, numerous exceptions to the categories listed above. One who sets out to acquire a consistent use of [a] must, in practice, memorize the complete list of slightly more than a hundred words in which [a] is traditional in New England, and [ɑ] in southern England. All dictionaries identify such words in one way or another, not for the purpose of prescribing [a], but merely in order to keep the categories straight. If a speaker acquires [a] early in life, like many New Englanders,

---

[2] See Virginia Rogers Miller, "Present-Day Use of the Broad A in Eastern Massachusetts," *Speech Monographs*, XX (November, 1953), 235–46.

he is likely to be reasonably consistent, but if he acquires [æ] first and later tries to shift to [a] or [ɑ], his inconsistency may very well attract unfavorable attention.

Sometimes [a] and [ɑ] replace the usual [æ] before [l] or [r] and a following vowel, as in [ˈvali] for *valley*, [haloˈin] for *Halloween*, [ˈkarɪdʒ] for *carriage*, and [ˈbarəl] for *barrel*. Here again [a] represents an allophone of [æ]. These variations occur with some frequency in Pennsylvania. [a] before [l] is common in upstate New York. [a] before [r] is common in the South. Both variations occur sporadically elsewhere.

As an allophone of [ɑ], [a] also occurs in such words as *hot* [hat], *stop* [stap], *lock* [lak], *odd* [ad], *on* [an], and *barn* [barn] in upstate New York and westward through the Great Lakes basin. There are traces of it in northern Ohio, Indiana, and Illinois, and frequent use of it in southern Ontario, Michigan, Wisconsin, Minnesota, and the eastern half of the Dakotas. There is also a trace in northern Iowa. Critics from outside this area often regard such a use of [a] as substandard, but within its home territory the allophone is accepted without any particular notice.

### The intermediate [ɒ]

Many people pronounce *forest* [ˈfɔrəst] and make the first syllable identical with *for* [fɔr]. Others say [ˈfɑrəst], and make the first syllable identical with *far* [fɑr]. Still others strike a compromise between [ɑ] and [ɔ], and say [ˈfɒrəst]. This [ɒ] may be defined as a low back lax vowel, usually with enough lip rounding to differentiate it from [ɑ]. To the ear, it lies between [ɑ] and [ɔ]. For most of those Americans who use it at all, it represents an allophone of either [ɑ] or [ɔ]; when it comes to represent both, it may become a separate phoneme. Like [a], [ɒ] is not used by all Americans; hence, there may be some difficulty in hearing and understanding it. [ɒ] is, however, more widely used than [a]; it occurs as a widespread allophonic variant in three major categories.

The first category includes words in which all three vowels [ɑ], [ɒ], and [ɔ] normally occur in one or another major type of American speech. This category includes words spelled with *o* plus *r* or *rr* plus a vowel, such as *forest, orange, horrible,* and *correspond.* It also includes words in which *o* is followed by a velar consonant, such as *log, frog, mock, honk,* and *gong.* Finally it includes miscellaneous words like *God, warrant, laurel, laundry, doll, golf,* and *on.*

For words like *forest,* in which [r] follows the vowel, the variation is predominantly geographical.[3] Thus in western Vermont, upper New York and westward, Illinois and south-westward, [ɔ] predominates. Along the New England coast, in New York City, southward along the Atlantic Coast, and for some distance inland in the South, [ɑ] predominates. Everywhere there are, of course, some good speakers who do not use the predominant form, including some who use the intermediate [ɒ]. Some vary their pronunciation from word to word and from time to time, especially near the boundary line between the two predominant types. Many good speakers, for instance, use different vowels in *forest* and *borrow;* they may use [ɔ] in one and [ɑ] in the other, or [ɒ] in either.

When stressed, *on* is usually [ɑn] in the Northeast, [ɑn] or [an] from upper New York to the central Dakotas, and [ɑn] in much of the farm country west of the Mississippi and from the latitude of Omaha north. Southward from southern New Jersey,

---

[3] See my article, "The Dialectal Significance of the Low-Back Vowel Variants before *R*," in *Studies in Speech and Drama in Honor of Alexander M. Drummond* (Ithaca: Cornell University Press, 1944). Data subsequently collected indicate the need for no more than minor modifications of the boundary line drawn on the map on p. 249.

southern Pennsylvania, and the Ohio Valley, and in the western cattle country, [ɔn] and [ɒn] predominate.

*Doll* and *solve* are usually [dɑl] and [sɑlv] in the North as far west as the Dakotas, and in the South. In western Pennsylvania, and in the Pennsylvania-derived speech of the southern mountains and the cattle country, they are frequently [dɒl] and [sɒlv] or [dɔl] and [sɔlv]. *Mock* is [mɑk] in most parts of the country, but often [mɒk] or [mɔk] in upstate New York and Ohio. *Mockingbird* regularly has [ɔ] in the South.

*Water* usually has [ɔ] along the Atlantic Coast and in the South. Further inland, [ɒ] becomes more frequent, and eventually, as we move west, [ɑ] becomes predominant. In California and along the Oregon coast, [ɔ] again predominates. Before velar consonants, as in *log*, *frog*, and *honk*, the pattern is extremely complicated, but with [ɔ] usually predominant outside of New England and the New York City area, and with [ɒ] fairly frequent. This first category includes words which regularly run the gamut from [ɑ] through [ɒ] to [ɔ].

The second major category includes a large group of words in which *o* precedes a voiceless fricative or a nasal, as in *off*, *toss*, *soft*, *broth*, *long*, and *gone*. Here the usual American vowel is [ɔ]. In western Pennsylvania, however, and occasionally in eastern New England, western New York, the Mormon country, western Canada, and sporadically in other areas, one may frequently hear [ɒ]. In western Pennsylvania, the shift may go as far as [ɑ] in such words as *off* [ɑf], *lost* [lɑst], *long* [lɑŋ], *law* [lɑ], *office* [ˈɑfɪs], and *coffee* [ˈkɑfi], though [ɒ] is usually more frequent. In general, the words of this second class stay fairly close to [ɔ], and [ɒ] is clearly an allophone of [ɔ].

The third category consists of a large group of words in which *o* precedes any of the stop consonants not hitherto mentioned in this chapter. In such words as *hop*, *rob*, *hot*, *nod*, and *lock*, the usual American vowel is [ɑ], which is identical in quality with the [ɑ] of *farm* and *father*, but normally of shorter duration. So widespread is this use of [ɑ] that Krapp, early in the century, gave *not* as the key word for the symbol.⁴ More recently, Kenyon gave *fodder* as the key word for General American [ɑ] and British [ɒ].⁵ In the south of England, in eastern New England, in western Pennsylvania and the Ohio valley, [ɒ] is the traditional vowel of these "short *o*" words, but [ɑ] is frequently heard in eastern New England, occasionally in the western Pennsylvania area, and increasingly in the south of England. In the United States as a whole, [ɑ] is most frequent, [ɒ] is occasional except for widespread use in limited areas, and [ɔ] is rare except in western Pennsylvania.

In the New York City area, in the various midland types, and in the South, [ɒ] may occur in words like *far*, *farm*, and *calm*. New York City may have [fɒr] and [fɒrm] or [fɒ:] and [fɒ: m]. Philadelphia and Baltimore often have [fɒr] and [fɒrm], and these pronunciations extend westward through Pennsylvania and the Ohio valley to Missouri and Oklahoma. In southern Iowa there are spots where [fɒr], [fɑr], and even [far] overlap. *Calm* may be [kɒm] throughout this entire area and in the South.

The South may have [fɒ:] and [fɒ: m], in extreme cases [fɔ:] and [fɔ: m]. New Orleans sometimes has [fɔr] and [fɔ:] for *far*, but [ɒ] is the more usual vowel. This usage contrasts sharply with that of eastern New England, where [fa:] and [ka: m] are usual; and with the north central area, Wisconsin, for example, where [far] and [ka: m] are frequent. Opinions regarding the social status of these varying forms differ widely in different areas.

Since [a] and [ɒ] are highly variable allophones, the physical

⁴ G. P. Krapp, *Pronunciation of Standard English in America* (New York: Oxford University Press, 1919), p. XIV.

⁵ J. S. Kenyon, *American Pronunciation* (10th ed.; Ann Arbor, George Wahr, 1950), p. 24.

characteristics of the sound waves which transmit them are likely to be highly variable too. Photographs of sound-spectograph records of [a] in *ask* and [ɒ] in *not* show [a] nearer to [æ] in *at* than to [ɑ] in *father*, and [ɒ] midway between [ɑ] in *father* and [ɔ] in *all*,[6] but the same speaker or other speakers might record quite different spectographs at different times. *Ask* may range all the way from [æsk] to [ɑsk], and *not* is quite as likely to have [a] as [ɒ], and even more likely to have [ɑ]. A laboratory analysis of such a variable allophone as either [a] or [ɒ] is not likely to tell us much unless accompanied by something we can listen to.

We can now see that the simple phonemic pattern for *cat*, *cart*, *cot*, and *caught*, with which this chapter began, needs to be revised and expanded, because the regional patterns differ. Without showing all possible variations, the table on page 122 will at least throw light on the different means by which the different areas distinguish different meanings. Since *cat* is normally [kæt], except for an occasional [kat] in New York City, it is not included in the table.

The table does not, moreover, show minor differences. The [ɑ:] of southern British *cart* is not identical with the [ɑ:] of New York City, but is slightly nearer to the eastern New England [a:]. The [ɔ] of southern British *caught* is nearer to the [o] of *coat* than are the other varieties of [ɔ] shown in the table. The [ɑ] of New York City *cot* is sometimes lengthened to [ɑ:], in which case the distinction between *cot* and *cart* must be determined by the context of the sentence. In eastern New England and western Pennsylvania, [kɒt] sometimes serves for both *cot* and *caught*; again the meaning must be determined from the context.

---

[6] As shown in Potter, Kopp, and Green, *Visible Speech* (New York: D. Van Nostrand Co., Inc., 1947), p. 55.

| Area | Cart | Cot | Caught |
|------|------|-----|--------|
| Eastern New England | [kaːt] | [kɒt] | [kɔt] |
| New York City | [kɑːt] | [kɑt] | [kɔt] |
| North Central | [kart] | [kat] | [kɔt] |
| Middle Atlantic | [kɒrt] | [kɑt] | [kɔt] |
| Western Pennsylvania | [kart] | [kɒt] | [kɒt] |
| Central Midland | [kɒrt] | [kɒt] | [kɔt] |
| Southern Mountain | [kɒrt] | [kɑt] | [kɔt] |
| South | [kɒːt] | [kɑt] | [kɔt] |
| Northwest | [kart] | [kɒt] | [kɔt] |
| Southwest Coast | [kart] | [kɑt] | [kɔt] |
| Southern England | [kɑːt] | [kɒt] | [kɔt] |

In summary, the vowels [a] and [ɒ], though not universal, are widely used, and may add to the characteristic flavor of a regional type, even on the standard level. You should therefore be prepared to hear them in the speech of others, if not in your own, and should not assume that only your own phonemic pattern is possible or respectable.    Sometimes you may be surprised to discover instances of [a] or [ɒ] which you hadn't known to be in your speech. The whole auditory series from [æ] through [a], [ɑ], and [ɒ] to [ɔ] needs careful analysis. Above all, you should not assume that a shift from [æ] to [a], or from [ɑ] or [ɔ] to [ɒ], will necessarily improve your own speech. Such a shift is usually but one aspect of a shift from one phonemic pattern, or dialect, to another. It is usually irrelevant to speech improvement, and may have no greater result than that of creating inconsistencies in your normal phonemic pattern.

## EXERCISES

Use the following words in Exercises 1 and 2:

cart, cot, caught, Boston, Toronto, north, cost, costume, patio, coral, canasta, corrugated, sorry, haunt, borrow, jaunt, foggy, laundry, clogged, honk, bother, ball, lava, fault, possible, water, alcohol, alcoholic, golf, mockery, wash, volley, watch, Halloween, coroner, volume, doll, awkward, involve.

1. Pick out the words which include [ɑ] in your pronunciation.

2. Pick out the words which include [ɔ] in your pronunciation.

3. Make a phonetic transcription of your own pronunciation of the following words:

caught, class, knot, paths, fancy, strong, horrid, jaunt, catalogue, corresponding, branches, moth, aunt, quarries, honk, mocking, resolve, crosses, calves, Gothic, mass, boxes, brought, often, audience, passionate, corridors, grasped, coarse, coerce, accident, foreigner, northern, grandfather, wharf, sparkling, quarantine.

4. Make a phonetic transcription of your own pronunciation of the following sentences:

A fox ran between the rows of tall corn.
A black launch went ashore on the sand bar.
The actor bought a bizarre mask at the bazaar.
After classes the girls walked along the corridor.
She purchased three pairs of ornamented silk pajamas.
The sportsman caught a large salmon near the waterfall.

5. In which section of the country would you be most likely to hear each of the following sentences? Why?

A. [ʃi pɑ꞉kt ðə ɑrɪnʤ kɑ꞉on ðə græs əkrɔs frəm ðə bɑ꞉n]
B. [ʃi pa꞉kt ði ɑrɪnʤ kar ɑn ðə gras əkrɒs frəm ðə ba꞉n]
C. [ʃi parkt ði ɔrɪnʤ kar an ðə græs əkrɔs frəm ðə barn]
D. [ʃi pɒrkt ði ɑrɪnʤ kɒr ɔn ðə græs əkrɔs frəm ðə bɒrn]
E. [ʃi pɒrkt ði ɔrɪnʤ kɒr ɒn ðə græs əkrɒs frəm ðə bɒrn]
F. [ʃi parkt ði ɔrɪnʤ kar an ðə græs əkrɔs frəm ðə barn]

# CHAPTER 13

# The Sounds of English
# [u, ʊ, ʌ]

**[u] as in *pool*; [ʊ] as in *pull*; [ʌ] as in *pump***

Various pronunciations of *soot* illustrate three vowels which bear a close historical relationship to one another. When pronounced [sut], *soot* rhymes with *boot*, and has the same vowel phoneme as *pool* [pul], *soup* [sup], *rude* [rud], and *do* [du]. When pronounced [sʊt], it rhymes with *put* [pʊt] and has the same vowel phoneme as *could* [kʊd], *look* [lʊk], and *wolf* [wʊlf]. When pronounced [sʌt], it rhymes with *cut* [kʌt], and has the same vowel phoneme as *flood* [flʌd], *come* [kʌm], and *rough* [rʌf]. Historically, [ʊ] developed as a relaxed variety of [u], and [ʌ] as a still more relaxed variety of [ʊ], during the seventeenth and early eighteenth centuries. The same spellings, *u*, *ou*, *oo*, and *o*, represent all three phonemes.

## [u]

[u] is a high back tense vowel with strong lip rounding. It occurs at the beginning, middle, and end of words, as in *ooze* [uz], *soup* [sup], and *do* [du]. When lengthened, [u] may develop

into a diphthongal [ʊu], which parallels the development of [i] into [ɪi], [e] into [eɪ], and [o] into [oʊ]. These diphthongs are nondistinctive allophones of [i], [e], [o], and [u] phonemes; shifts between diphthong and monophthong have no effect on the meanings of the words in which they are used.[1]

In some parts of the country, notably in the South, in much of the Midland area, and along the Atlantic Coast as far north as New York City, [u] is formed with the tongue further forward in the mouth than is normal in, for instance, upper New York, Michigan, Minnesota, or Oregon. The more fronted articulation carries with it a suggestion of [i] quality, or of the high front tense rounded [y] of French *rue* [ry] or German *Brüder* [ˈbrydər]; fronted allophones may be monophthongal or diphthongal.

## [ʊ]

[ʊ] is a high back lax vowel with less lip rounding than [u]. It occurs only in the middle of words, as in *pull* [pʊl], *wolf* [wʊlf], *look* [lʊk], and *should* [ʃʊd]. Because of the identical spellings, and the differences in muscular tension of the tongue and lips, which characterize [u] and [ʊ], foreigners usually have great difficulty in differentiating the two phonemes. In most languages there is no phonemic distinction between [u] and [ʊ]. For most foreigners, [u] is likely to be the principal allophone of the phoneme, and [ʊ] merely an accidental and occasional allophone without phonemic value, and without enough conspicuousness to call attention to its phonetic difference from [u]. The foreigner is likely, therefore, to use [u], or a vowel of inter-

[1] Sound spectrographs of these four sounds are recorded on pages 55–56 of Potter, Kopp, and Green, *Visible Speech* (New York: D. Van Nostrand Co., Inc., 1947), where [e] and [o] occur in both monophthongal and diphthongal forms, but [i] and [u] only in monophthongal forms. Only in word-end position is the diphthongal quality visible, and it is notably less visible than in the phonemic diphthongs [aɪ], [aʊ], and [ɔɪ].

mediate tension, for both *fool* and *full*, and must therefore depend on the context to make his meaning clear. To help master the difference, the foreigner should aim at the diphthongal allophone [ʊu] for the phoneme [u], and at a short relaxed [ʊ] for contrast.

In some words, for instance *hoof*, *roof*, *root*, and *soot*, native standard English offers a choice between [u] and [ʊ]. In other words, only one pronunciation is standard: [u] in *food*, [ʊ] in *butcher*. Such pronunciations as [fʊd] for *food* and ['butʃɚ] are substandard. Before [r] or [ə] in the same syllable, the historical [u] has relaxed to [ʊ], as in *poor* [pʊr] or [puə], *tour* [tʊr] or [tuə], and *sure* [ʃʊr] or [ʃuə]. Before [r] and a following vowel, either [ʊ] or [u] may be heard, but [ʊ] is much more frequent, as in *injurious* [ɪn'dʒʊriəs] and *tourist* ['tʊrɪst]. This development parallels the similar relaxation of [i] to [ɪ] before [r] or [ə], as we have already seen in *clear* [klɪr] or [klɪə] and *zero* ['zɪro] or ['ziro]. In some areas the vowel drops down to a lower level, so that *sure* changes from [ʃʊr] to [ʃor] or [ʃɔr]. In this country, such a lowering of the vowel usually suggests the cowboy; to Englishmen, it suggests the curate.

In unstressed syllables before a following vowel, [u] regularly relaxes to [ʊ], as in *casual* ['kæʒʊəl], *graduate* ['grædʒuet], and in the phrase *to Ithaca* [tʊ 'ɪθəkə]. Unstressed [o] may also shift to [ʊ] or a weak [u], as in *window* ['wɪndʊ] or ['wɪndu], rhyming with *Hindu* ['hɪndʊ] or ['hɪndu]. The weakened [u] or [ʊ] parallels, to some extent, the weakened [i] or [ɪ] of *any* ['ɛni] or ['ɛnɪ].

## [ʌ] as in *cup*

[ʌ] is a lax unrounded vowel phoneme whose allophones are different in different parts of the English-speaking world. In the south of England the tongue drops almost to the level of [ɑ] or [a]. In America the tongue position is usually mid, on about the level of [o], and is usually back, although an allophone fronted almost to the central area of [ɜ] is common in the Southern Mountains. [ʌ] occurs at the beginning and middle of words, but not at the end. It is found only in syllables which carry more than minimal stress. In the weakest syllables it changes to [ə], as do many other unstressed vowels. Compare *unable* [ˌʌnˈebəl] with *enable* [ənˈebəl], or *seagull* [ˈsiˌgʌl] with the name *Siegel* [ˈsigəl]; these contrasts depend quite as much on the difference in vowel quality as on the stress.

[ʌ] is spelled *u* in *under* [ˈʌndɚ], *o* in *come* [kʌm], *oo* in *flood* [flʌd], and *ou* in *rough* [rʌf]. When [ʌ] has the *o* spelling, there is an apparently growing tendency to shift the pronunciation to other vowels. *Donkey* may be heard as [ˈdʌŋki], [ˈdaŋki], [ˈdɒŋki], or [ˈdɔŋki]. *Constable* has almost completely shifted from [ʌ] to [ɑ]. *Hover* may have [ʌ] or [ɑ]. *Covert* is still [ˈkʌvɚt], but *covert* cloth is [ˈkovɚt] in most clothing stores. *Compass* is sometimes [ˈkɑmpəs], but this may be merely a passing foreignism, and all these variations may reflect uncertainty based on spelling.

In such words as *hurry*, *worry*, and *courage*, a variation between [ʌr] on the one hand and [ɝ] and [ɜr] on the other has survived from the eighteenth century. Thus [ˈhʌri], [ˈhɝi], and [ˈhɜri] represent present-day *hurry*, with the variations largely geographical.[2] Thus [ˈhʌri] predominates along the Atlantic seaboard, throughout most of Pennsylvania, and for a good distance inland in the South. *Worry*, *courage*, *nourish*, and similar words in the same class follow similar but less clearly marked regional patterns.

Since English [ʌ] has few foreign counterparts, foreigners are likely to substitute [u], [ɔ], or [ɑ], under the influence of either the spelling or inaccurate hearing. The chief native difficulties

[2] See my "Notes on the Pronunciation of *Hurry*," *American Speech*, XXI (1946), 112–15. Data subsequently gathered do not substantially effect the conclusions reached in this article.

AMERICAN ENGLISH VOWELS

| | Front | Half Front | Central with [r]-Coloring | Central no [r]-Coloring | Back Unrounded | Back Rounded |
|---|---|---|---|---|---|---|
| High tense .......... | i | | | | | u |
| High lax .......... | ɪ | | | | | ʊ |
| Mid tense .......... | e | | ɝ | ɜ | | o |
| Mid lax .......... | ɛ | | ə | ə | ʌ | |
| Low tense .......... | | a | | | | ɔ |
| Low lax .......... | æ | | | | ɑ | ɒ |

are the use, generally considered substandard, of [ɪ] or a centralized [ɪ] in such words as *such* and *just*, and of [ɛ] or a centralized
[ɛ] in such words as *such, just, judge,* and *brush.* In old-fashioned
speech, *won't* [wont] occurs as [wʌnt]; in the substandard speech
of the New York City area, as [wʊnt]. For *gums,* the old-fashioned
rural pronunciations [gumz] and [gʊmz] survive, along with
standard [gʌmz].

We have now analyzed all the vowel phonemes of American
English. The chart on page 128 will remind you of their relationships.

### EXERCISES

Use the following word list for Exercises 1–3:

through, though, thought, pool, poor, courage, workroom,
foolish, pudding, pulpit, Brewster, bouquet, burnish, ugly, purpose, public, looking, lurid, loon, knuckle, lose, rooted, aloof,
rough, trough, glue, goodness, cuckoo, insurance, Moore, crude,
statue.

1. Pick out the words in which you yourself use [u].
2. Pick out the words in which you yourself use [ʊ].
3. Pick out the words in which you yourself use [ʌ].
4. Indicate the phonetic and physical differences between the
words in the following pairs:

| wooed | wood | should | shoed |
|-------|------|--------|-------|
| book  | buck | luck   | look  |
| rough | roof | ten    | ton   |
| look  | lick | fooled | fold  |
| buck  | balk | stood  | stud  |
| mode  | mood | poor   | purr  |

5. Make a phonetic transcription of your own pronunciation of the following words:

moving, motion, nurses, nourish, occurrences, pulpit, comfort, crumbs, doing, doesn't, woolen, pushes, grooved, pudding, Cumberland, hurricane, druggist, flourished, florist, quarantine, turrets, axiomatic, aloof, crushes, spoons, umbrella, grievous, wonders, upon, unworthy, ruby, woman.

6. Make a phonetic transcription of your own pronunciation of the following sentences:

He pushed a plunger into the clogged drain.
The cat scurried across the room after a rat.
They discovered a purple comb in the ancient tomb.
The jury acquitted the defendant of the charge of perjury.
The woman bought a comfortable chair at the furniture store.
Woodrow Wilson was president of this country in the First World War.

# CHAPTER 14

# The Sounds of English [ju] as in *cube* [kjub] and its variants

In Chapter 6 we first analyzed [j] in *yes* [jɛs] and *onion* [ˈʌnjən], and defined it as a palatal semivowel formed by raising the front, but not the tip, of the tongue to a position close to the hard palate, and allowing the tongue to glide away from this position. If we compare *you* [ju] with *unit* [ˈjunɪt], or *ooze* [uz] with the verb *use* [juz], we discover another important function of the semivowel [j]. Though all the phonemes to be discussed in this chapter have been discussed in previous chapters, the spelling with the single letter "u" often traps the unwary into thinking that only a single sound is involved, instead of the sequence [ju]. Other less frequent spellings occur in such words as *feud* [fjud], *beauty* [ˈbjuti], *few* [fju], and *view* [vju].

The sequence [ju] occurs at the beginning, middle, and end of words, as the preceding paragraph illustrates. Except at the beginning, it may have [ɪu] as a nondistinctive variant, as in [fɪud] and [vɪu] for *feud* and *view*, though of course [j] and [ɪ] are separate phonemes. The essential physical difference between [ju] and [ɪu]

131

is in the stress patterning. In [ju] the energy level rises during
the first element, reaching its peak in the latter part of the
sequence, thus [jˈu]. For [ɪu], on the other hand, the energy level
decreases, the peak coming at the beginning of the sequence,
thus [ˈɪu]. [ju] is generally more frequent than [ɪu].

All standard forms of English agree in retaining initial [ju],
as in *unit* [ˈjunɪt] and *eulogy* [ˈjulədʒi]. After [p], [b], [m], [f],
[v], [k], and [g], that is, after labials and velars, either [ju] or,
occasionally, [ɪu] may occur, as in *pew* [pju], *beauty* [ˈbjuti], *muse*
[mjuz], *few* [fju], *view* [vju], *cube* [kjub], the family name *Gulick*
[ˈgjulɪk], and the heraldic term *gules* [gjulz]. After [h], [j] is either
retained, as in *hue* [hju], or blended with [h] to form a single
voiceless palatal fricative [ç], as in *hue* [çu], the voiceless counterpart of [j]. The fricative [ç] is familiar to students of German
as the consonant of the pronoun *ich* [ɪç]; in English it is merely
a nondistinctive variant of the sequence [hj].

In other phonetic contexts [j] is frequently lost. After [tʃ]
and [dʒ], [j] is usually absorbed and eliminated by the preceding
consonants, as in *chew* [tʃu] and *June* [dʒun]. Occasionally we
may hear [tʃɪu] and [dʒɪun], but not [tʃju] or [dʒjun]. After [r]
and [l], we usually omit [j], as in *rude* [rud] and *lucid* [ˈlusɪd],
though occasionally we may hear [rɪul] and [ˈlɪusɪd]. A few
people make the effort to pronounce the rare word *lute* as [ljut],
a shibboleth to the old-time elocutionist, instead of the more
usual [lut].

In the south of England, and to a lesser degree in New
England, [j] survives after [θ], [t], [d], [n], [s], and [z], as in
*enthusiasm* [ɪnˈθjuziæzəm], *tune* [tjun], *due* and *dew* [dju], *new*
[nju], *assume* [əˈsjum], and *resume* [rɪˈzjum]. In the American
South, normal usage retains [j] after [t], [d], and [n], as in New
England, but not after [θ], [s], or [z]. Radio announcers some-

times affect the [sj] sequence in words like *suit* and *superior*, often with embarrassing results.   Outside of New England and the South, [j] normally drops out after all the consonants in this group.   Individual speakers, of course, occasionally depart from the pattern of distribution of [ju] and [u] just described.   In all the instances described thus far in this chapter, either the monophthongal [u] or the diphthongal [ʊu] may occur.   *Ooze* may be [uz] or [ʊuz]; the verb *use* may be [juz] or [jʊuz].

You will notice that the greatest variation in the use of the palatal [j] occurs immediately after consonants articulated close to the palatal region.   In [tjun], [dju], and [nju], the quick change of tongue position from the gum ridge to a nearby section of the hard palate requires a delicacy of adjustment which the speaker does not always have at his command.   With less than complete control, [tjun] shifts readily to [tʃun], [dju] to [dʒu]. After consonants articulated at a greater distance from the hard palate, [j] requires less delicacy of articulation, as in [pju], ['bjuti], [mjuz], [fju], [vju], [kjub], and [gjulz].   Hence we normally retain [j] in this latter group, but most Americans pronounce *tune* [tun], *due* [du], and *new* [nu].

Before *r* in the same syllable, [ju] relaxes to [jʊ], as in *pure* [pjʊr] or [pjʊə]; this is of course the same type of relaxation already noted in *poor* [pʊr] or [pʊə].   In some types of British pronunciation the tongue drops low enough to result in [pɔ:] for *poor* and [pjɔ:] for *pure*.   In this country the Midland and Southern types sometimes use a low enough tongue position for [por], [poə], or [po:] for *poor*; and [pjor], [pjoə], or [pjo:] for *pure*.   The traditional pronunciation "shore" for *sure* in cowboy dialect stories usually represents [ʃor].   Before [r] and a following vowel, [jʊ] is the more frequent, as in ['bjʊro] for *bureau*; [ju] is less frequent, as in ['bjuro].

Under weakened stress, [ju] relaxes to [jə], as in *accusation* [ˌækjəˈzeʃən], in contrast to the fully stressed [ju] of *accuse* [əˈkjuz]. An intermediate [ju], as in [ˌækjuˈzeʃən], is likely to sound artificial except on the most formal occasions. Under weakened stress, [j] is more likely to be retained after [n] or [l] than in stressed syllables, because the preceding consonant is almost invariably a part of the preceding syllable, and the new syllable begins with [j]. *Volume* normally ranges between [ˈvɑljəm] and [ˈvɔljəm], but *voluminous* is normally [vəˈlumɪnəs]. *Annual* is normally [ˈænjʊəl], but *annuity* is often [əˈnuəti]. For *manufacture*, both [ˌmænəˈfæktʃɚ] and [ˌmænjəˈfæktʃɚ] occur, though some critics consider the former substandard.

After [t] and [d] in unstressed syllables, [j] normally assimilates to [ʃ] and [ʒ], as in *nature* [ˈnetʃɚ] and *education* [ˌɛdʒəˈkeʃən]. Toward the end of the eighteenth century, usage varied between retaining [j], as in [ˈnetjʊr] and [ˌɛdjuˈkeʃən], dropping [j], as in [ˈnetɚ] and [ˌɛdəˈkeʃən], and using the assimilated forms. Since then the retention of the unassimilated [j] has become obsolete, and the complete dropping of [j] has been relegated to rustic speech.

Teachers who have insisted on [tjun] for *tune* and [dju] for *due* in regions where the normal pronunciations were [tun] and [du] have unconsciously encouraged the use on an intrusive [j] in words in which it has no historical place. Thus we often hear [ˈkɑljəm] for *column*, perhaps on the analogy of *volume*; [ˈpɚˈkjə-letɚ] for *percolator*, on the analogy of *circulate*; and similar intrusions of [j] in *coupon, escalator, Marguerite, similar, stabilize, tremendous, sterilize,* and *metabolism.* The judicious speaker will avoid the intrusive [j], and will pronounce *column* [ˈkɑləm], *coupon* [ˈkupɑn], *percolator* [ˈpɚkəletɚ], *escalator* [ˈɛskəletɚ], *stabilize* [ˈstebəlaɪz], *metabolism* [məˈtæbəlɪzəm], and *Marguerite* [mɑrgəˈrit].

## EXERCISES

Use the following words for Exercises 1–2:

pewter, booty, brooch, tube, picture, prunes, revenue, particular, Pennsylvania, avenue, aqueduct, alien, mature, induce, sure, flute, pasture, California, Quebec, presume, fortune, soldier, shoes, jury, window, jaguar, juvenile, young.

1. Pick out the words in which you yourself use [j].
2. Pick out the words in which you yourself use [u].
3. Make a phonetic transcription of your own pronunciation of the following words:

abuse, plunger, puny, rubbish, cures, gloves, musical, knew, accumulation, customer, purity, argument, obscure, jungle, governor, manufactures, sure, absolute, monkey, funeral, cousin, enthusiasm, sugar, Susan, bushel, student, community, alluring, cruelty, municipality, incongruous.

4. Make a phonetic transcription of your own pronunciation of the following sentences:

Gasoline is manufactured from crude petroleum.
The cuckoo clock showed that it was one o'clock.
The tourist drove through New Jersey in a Buick.
The popular musician played a tune on the trombone.
The shrewd business man jumped aboard the Duluth express.
Admiral George Dewey defeated the Spanish fleet in Manila
    Bay.

# CHAPTER 15

# The Sounds of English
# [h, hw, hj, aɪ, ɔɪ, ɑʊ]

### [h] as in *hat*

As we have already seen in Chapter 6, *h* is sometimes a purely orthographic sign used with some other letter to indicate either a single consonant sound, as in *thin* [θɪn], *this* [ðɪs], *phase* [fez], *rough* [rʌf], and *fish* [fɪʃ]; or a consonant cluster, as in *cheese* [tʃiz]. The letter *h* distinguishes the spelling of *thin* from that of *tin*, but gives no clue to the phonemic contrast between the [θ] of [θɪn] and the [t] of [tɪn]. In a few words, *h* has no phonetic value whatever, in *ghost* [gost], *rhapsody* [ˈræpsədi], *honor* [ˈɑnɚ], *khaki* [ˈkæki] or [ˈkɑki], and *dough* [do]. In some of these words [h] was at one time pronounced; in others it has never been pronounced.

When *h* has independent phonetic value, as in *hat* [hæt], *heal* [hil], and *haul* [hɔl], its use distinguishes these words from *at* [æt], *eel* [il], and *all* [ɔl]. The sound [h] is a glottal fricative, or aspirate, formed by exhaling the breath in a slight puff, with the vocal bands close enough together to produce audible friction. [h] has no characteristic position of the speech agents in the mouth, but takes the mouth position of whatever sound follows it. Hence its auditory quality differs slightly in each of the illustrative words of this paragraph. [h] occurs only as the first sound of a syllable which has more than minimal stress, as in *hook* [hʊk] and *apprehend* [ˌæprɪˈhɛnd].

In unstressed medial and final syllables of compound words [h] normally drops out: compare *shepherd* [ˈʃɛpɚd] with *sheep herder* [ˈʃip ˌhɝdɚ], *prohibition* [proɪˈbɪʃən] with *prohibit* [proˈhɪbɪt]. At the beginning of the stressed syllable, [h] survives, otherwise not.

Except when stressed or located at the beginning of a phrase, the pronouns and auxiliary verbs *he*, *his*, *him*, *her*, *have*, *has*, and *had* normally lose [h] in much the same way, as in the sentence: *He would have hurt him if he had had his gun with him* [hi wəd əv ˈhɝt ɪm ɪf i əd ˈhæd ɪz ˈgʌn wɪð ɪm]. At normal speeds this sentence would sound forced if the omitted [h] sounds were restored.

Such losses of [h] should be regarded neither as carelessness nor as indications of Cockney dialect, but as one aspect of the normal English pattern of reducing unstressed syllables to the background, in order that stressed syllables and stressed ideas may occupy the foreground of attention. Failure to differentiate the functions of foreground and background leads to stilted artificial speech, a fault to which singers and radio announcers are especially likely to succumb.[1] Radio announcers frequently attempt [ˌfɪlhɑrˈmɑnɪk] instead of the normal [ˌfɪlɚˈmɑnɪk] when announcing the New York Philharmonic Symphony. The needless [h] and the unavoidable stress on the second syllable some-

---

[1] In the old English hunting song "John Peel", a favorite of men's choruses, occurs the phrase, "With his horse and his hounds in the morning." I have heard musical directors repeatedly insist on the pronunciation of [h] in both occurrences of *his*.

times sound like an incipient cough in the middle of the word.

## [hw] and [ʍ] in *when*
## [hj] and [ç] in *huge*

The words *when* and *huge* illustrate special uses of [h]. In *huge*, the sequence of [h] and [j] produces a closely linked cluster. Some speakers maintain it as a cluster, as in *huge* [hjudʒ] and *human* [ˈhjumən]. Others blend [h] and [j] so closely that they lose their separate identities and merge in a single sound [ç], a voiceless palatal fricative, the voiceless counterpart of [j]. If the blending takes place, *huge* becomes [çudʒ] and *human* [ˈçumən]. Since, however, no change in meaning is effected by the shift from [hj] to [ç], most students will prefer not to bother with the extra symbol [ç].

Words like *when* and *what* began with the letters *hw* in Old English, a spelling which suggested the order of sounds more accurately than our present-day reversed order. Today some people pronounce *when* as [hwɛn], with a closely blended cluster [hw] in which, as in the cluster [hj], the two elements retain their separate identities. Sometimes, however, [h] and [w] blend so closely that they lose their separate identities and merge in a single sound [ʍ], a voiceless fricative formed by rounding the lips and raising the back of the tongue nearly to the velum. [ʍ] is the voiceless counterpart of [w]. Since no change in meaning accompanies the shift from [hw] to [ʍ], most students will prefer not to bother with the extra symbol [ʍ].

Loss of the aspirate [h] from the sequence [hj], as in [judʒ] and [ˈjumən] for *huge* and *human*, is usually considered substandard in all English regional types, though common in most large cities. Similarly, the substitution of [w] for [hw], as in [wɛn] for *when* and [ˈsʌmwɑt] for *somewhat*, is often considered substandard in America, though also common in most large cities. In the south of England, on the other hand, the substitution of [w] for [hw] is normal.

Since we have now examined all the consonants of standard English, the chart on page 140 may be used to compare their formations.

### Diphthongs

In the diphthongs [ɪi], [eɪ], [oʊ], and [ʊu], which have previously been mentioned, the diphthongization is accomplished by gradually moving the jaw and tongue upward, and by changing the tension of the tongue muscles. For [oʊ] and [ʊu] there is also a gradual increase in lip rounding. We may therefore define a diphthong as a vocalic glide within the limits of a single syllable.

Such vocalic sequences as those in *react* [riˈækt] and *coerce* [koˈɜˈs] are not diphthongal, since the syllabic division separates the two elements and prevents a true glide from one to the other.

The vocalic elements in *peel* [pɪil], *pail* [peɪl], *pole* [poʊl], and [pʊul] are, however, true diphthongal glides: the vocalic elements are continuous gliding sounds, for which the phonetic symbols represent the approximate points of beginning and ending. Since all four of the glides are slight, and since the contrast between diphthongal and monophthongal pronunciations does not change the meaning of any of the words, we often fail to notice the diphthongs. Some phoneticians have noticed the [eɪ] and [oʊ] glides, but have failed to notice the more subtle [ɪi] and [ʊu]. Others have noticed all four, but have failed to comprehend the difference in function between these four and the phonemic diphthongs we are about to examine.

Because of the allophonic nature of these four diphthongs, there is no compelling necessity for our transcriptions to show

AMERICAN ENGLISH CONSONANTS

| | Lips | Lip-Teeth | Point-Teeth | Point-Gums | Point-Retroflex | Blade: Narrow Channel | Blade: Wide Channel | Palatal | Central | Velar | Glottal |
|---|---|---|---|---|---|---|---|---|---|---|---|
| Voiceless stops......... | p | | | t | | | | | | k | |
| Voiced stops........... | b | | | d | | | | | | g | |
| Nasals................ | m | | | n | | | | | | ŋ | |
| Voiceless fricatives..... | ʍ | f | θ | | | s | ʃ | ç | | ʍ | h |
| Voiced fricatives ....... | | v | ð | | | z | ʒ | | | | |
| Semivowels ........... | w | | | l | r | | | j | r | w | |

Note: [w] and [ʍ] each appear in two places on the chart because each has a double articulation; the lips and the back of the tongue are activated simultaneously. [r] appears in two places to indicate two alternative articulations.

them.  There is no ambiguity in transcribing [pil] for *peel*, [pel] for *pail*, [pol] for *pole*, or [pul] for *pool*.  Any diphthongal transcription of these four vowel phonemes is chiefly useful in calling the attention of the foreigner to their stylistic value, and in dialect studies.

When, however, we compare *pound* [paʊnd] with *pond* [pɑnd], *oil* [ɔɪl] with *all* [ɔl], and *life* [laɪf] with the eastern New England pronunciation of *laugh* [laf], we see that the difference between a diphthong and a monophthong may have meaningful significance.  The diphthongs [aʊ], [ɔɪ], and [aɪ] are phonemic; they are meaningfully distinct from the monophthongs [ɑ], [ɔ], and [a]. The diphthongs [ii], [eɪ], [oʊ], and [ʊu] are not phonemic; they are not meaningfully distinct from the monophthongs [i], [e], [o], and [u].  The phonemic diphthongs must always be transcribed as diphthongs; the nonphonemic diphthongs may be transcribed as simple monophthongs without ambiguity.

## [aɪ]

The diphthong [aɪ] occurs at the beginning, middle, and end of words, and is usually spelled *i* or *y*, as in *ice* [aɪs], *mine* [maɪn], and *fly* [flaɪ].  The beginning of the diphthong varies allophonically.  It may shift toward [ɑɪ], in extreme cases even to [ɒɪ]; extreme allophones are likely to be considered substandard.  In eastern Virginia, northern New York, northern New England, and Canada, an older variant [ɜɪ] occasionally survives.  When used before voiceless consonants, as in [ɜɪs] for *ice*, it is usually accepted as standard.  When used before [r] or [l], as it may occasionally be in northern New York and northern Michigan in [fɜɪr] for *fire* and [fɜɪl] for *file*, its social status is somewhat more debatable.

In the Midland and South, the diphthong is often reduced to

a monophthong before *r*. *Fire* becomes [far], less commonly [fɑr], in the Midland; [faə] and [fɑ:], less commonly [faə] and [fɑ:], in the South. In other phonetic contexts, [aɪ] also simplifies to [a:], less commonly [ɑ:], in the South. [mɑ:lz] for *miles* seems to be more frequent in South Carolina and Alabama than elsewhere; [ma:lz] is frequent all over the South. Southerners are more likely to accept this simplification as standard before voiced consonants, as in [ma:lz], than before voiceless, as in [ma:t] for *might*.

## [ɔɪ]

The diphthong [ɔɪ] occurs at the beginning, middle, and end of words and is usually spelled *oi* or *oy*, as in *oil* [ɔɪl], *boil* [bɔɪl], and *boy* [bɔɪ]. There are several allophonic variations. In Pennsylvania, Maryland, Delaware, southern New Jersey, and to a lesser extent westward through the Midland areas, [ɔɪ] sometimes approximates [oɪ]. In the South, [ɔɪ] frequently simplifies to [ɔ:], as in [ɔ:l] for *oil*. To northern ears the resulting confusion between *all* and *oil*, *fall* and *foil*, and the like may be baffling, but the confusion can usually be resolved by the context, and the Southerners themselves seem to be committed to the simplification.

In the New York City area the first element [ɔ] of the diphthong [ɔɪ] may be overlong and overtense but is not to be confused with the midland [oɪ], which has a higher tongue position, normal tension, and normal length. The traditional New York pronunciation is [ɜɪ], used for both [ɔɪ] and [ɝ], as in [vɜɪs], which may represent either *voice* or *verse*. Although [ɜɪ] continues to be used in New York City as a substitute for [ɝ], its use as a substitute for [ɔɪ] is now comparatively rare. The substitution of [vɝs] for *voice* and [vɔɪs] for *verse* is more likely to be heard in self-conscious imitations of the New York City dialect than

in the dialect itself.[2]   Note in passing that [vɜɪs] in Michigan
and northern New York means neither *verse* nor *voice*, but *vice*.

In a few words, the eighteenth-century confusion of [ɔɪ] with
[aɪ] survives in rural speech and in the speech of older people,
as in [baɪl] for *boil* and [dʒaɪn] for *join*.   Probably the most
persistent survival is [haɪst] for *hoist*.

### [aʊ]

The diphthong [aʊ] occurs at the beginning, middle, and end
of words, and is usually spelled *ou* or *ow*, as in *out* [aʊt], *round*
[raʊnd], and *now* [naʊ].  The spelling is likely to confuse foreigners,
since *ou* may represent [ɔ] in *bought* as well as [aʊ] in *bout*, and
*ow* may represent [o] in *crow* as well as [aʊ] in *cow*.

The principal allophones are [ɑʊ] and [aʊ], which shade into
each other.  [ɑʊ] predominates across the north from New England
through the Great Lakes country, and on into Minnesota and the
farm country of the eastern Dakotas.   It predominates in the
northern two thirds of Iowa and the northeastern quarter of
Nebraska, and again on the Pacific Coast.

Though [ɑʊ] predominates in New England, [aʊ] is frequent
in the eastern part.  In the New York City and Middle Atlantic
areas, [aʊ] predominates, but there is a frequent third allophone,
the strongly fronted, overtense [æʊ].  In the South, both [aʊ] and
[æʊ] are frequent, [ɑʊ] relatively scarce.  In the South, too, the
second element of the diphthong sometimes drops out, leaving
[na:] or [næ:] for *now*, especially before a vowel in the following
word.  Westward through the Midland areas, [aʊ] usually predominates, but with [æʊ] frequent.  In the North, [æʊ] is usually
considered substandard; in the Midland and Southern areas, it
is less likely to attract unfavorable attention.

[2] Compare Henry Alexander, "Soiving the Ersters," *American Speech*, I
(1926), 294–95; see also the discussion of this point in Chapter 9.

In Virginia, Canada, and to a lesser extent in northern New England, northern New York, upper Michigan, Wisconsin, and Minnesota, a regular allophone for [ɑʊ] before voiceless consonants is [ɜʊ], as in [hɜʊs] for *house*. This allophone, the survival of a form generally used in the eighteenth century, sometimes sounds odd to speakers from other localities, but is socially respectable across the northern belt of territory and in the Virginia Tidewater area.

## Diphthongs resulting from the loss of [r]

In eastern New England, New York City, and the South, the loss of final and preconsonantal [r] gives rise to a set of glides which have some features in common with the true diphthongs already described. When *fear* becomes [fɪə], *feared* [fɪəd], *pair* [pɛə], and *insured* [ɪnˈʃʊəd], the combinations [ɪə], [ɛə], and [ʊə] involve a certain amount of blending, though the blending is not as close as in [aɪ], [ɔɪ], and [ɑʊ].

For most users, the diphthongs [ɪə], [ɛə], and [ʊə] are distinctively different from the monophthongs [ɪ], [ɛ], and [ʊ]; compare *beard* [bɪəd] with *bid* [bɪd], *shared* [ʃɛəd] with *shed* [ʃɛd], and one pronunciation of *gourd* [gʊəd] with *good* [gʊd]. The glides [ɪə], [ɛə], and [ʊə] are not, however, distinctively different from [ɪr], [ɛr], and [ʊr], since they represent alternative ways of pronouncing the same words.

In the New York City area, and to a lesser extend in other areas which omit final and preconsonantal [r], the diphthongs [ɪə], [ɛə], and [ʊə] sometimes lose the second element [ə], as in [bɪ: d] for *beard*, [ʃɛ: d] for *shared*, and [gʊ: d] for *gourd*. Here length distinguishes the vowels from those of *bid*, *shed*, and *good*.

In such words as *pour* and *poured*, loss of [r] may result in the glides [oə] or [ɔə], but again the blending is not close. In eastern New England, *pour* and *poured* may have virtually two syllables: [po-ə] and [po-əd]. In the New York City area, [pɔə] and [pɔəd] predominate; [pɔ:] and [pɔ: d] are slightly less frequent. In the South, [poə] and [poəd] predominate; [po:] and [po: d] are frequent, but some Southerners consider the forms without [ə] substandard. With either pronunciation, Southern *court* [koət] or [ko: t] is distinct from *coat*, which is usually [koʊt], occasionally [kot]. Loss of [r] after [ɑ], as in *far* [fɑ:] and *farm* [fɑ: m], usually produces no diphthong; [ɑə] in this context is rare.

Loss of [r] after [aɪ] or [ɑʊ] sometimes produces an unstable double glide, or triphthong, as in *fire* [faɪə] and *flour* [flɑʊə]. In eastern New England the triphthongs almost break up into separate syllables, as in [faɪ-ə] for *fire* and [flɑʊ-ə] for *flour*. In the South, they often simplify by losing the middle element, as in [faə] for *fire* and [flɑə] for flour. After [ɔɪ], the [r]-colored element is normally syllabic, as in *foyer* [ˈfɔɪɚ]. If the [r]-coloring is lost, the resulting [ə] is also syllabic, as in [ˈfɔɪə].

## EXERCISES

1. Indicate the phonetic differences in your own pronunciation of the following pairs, and explain the differences in physical formation which underlie the phonetic differences:

| | | | |
|---|---|---|---|
| voice | vice | coined | kind |
| rout | rot | cone | corn |
| call | coil | found | fond |
| loiter | lighter | mice | mouse |

2. Make a phonetic transcription of your own pronunciation of the following words; indicate your own diphthongal allophones as accurately as you can:

town, eyes, choir, handsome, whole, going, delight, royal, buckwheat, blouse, honest, aisle, switch, whisper, oysters, grown, humorous, showers, whose, everywhere, qualify, spoiled, allowed, hungry, rejoice, annihilate, thousand, whether, Ohio, humanity, invoice, anywhere, courthouse, dialogue, poisonous, choices, wharves, houses, lawyer, retired, winding, ouch.

3. Make a phonetic transcription of your own pronunciation of the following sentences; indicate your own diphthongal allophones:

The rioters crowded around the noisy orator.
A queer sound came from the whirring machinery.
The humorous policeman directed traffic politely.
Somewhere downstairs was a box of fine Havana cigars.
They had fried eggs and buckwheat cakes for breakfast.
The twilight lasted for more than an hour after dinner.

# CHAPTER 16

# Stress

Variations in the level of energy we use in speaking have an important bearing on oral communication. We are accustomed to hear some syllables pronounced with greater force than those which precede or follow them. If we do not hear such a variation, the speaking becomes monotonous, sometimes unintelligible. Occasionally, indeed, a difference in the degree of force may change the meaning: if we pronounce the syllables [ɪnsaɪt] with more energy in the first syllable than in the second, we pronounce the noun *insight* [ˈɪnsaɪt]; but if we put more energy into the second syllable than the first, we pronounce the verb *incite* [ɪnˈsaɪt]. Thus the energy level alone may have distinctive value, though ordinarily changes in the energy are accompanied by noticeable changes in the quality of the vowels as well. If, for instance, we add stress to the second syllable of *youngest* [ˈjʌŋ-gəst], we change the meaning to that of *young guest* [ˈjʌŋ ˈgɛst]. If we add stress to the normally unstressed first syllable of *occur* [əˈkɝ], we may confuse the verb with the pigment *ocher* [ˈokɚ].

Perhaps the most important single aspect of the energy level is what we shall call *stress*, the relative increase in energy during the pronunciation of the word or syllable. Other terms, such as *accent* and *emphasis*, are sometimes used, but are unsatisfactory.

*Accent* is ambiguous, since it may refer to accent marks on paper, or to regional or foreign dialects. *Emphasis* may more profitably be reserved for the total effect of various factors, of which stress is one. Emphasis properly relates to the art of speech; stress relates to the structure of the language.

Though the laboratory phonetician may discover many levels of stress, our purpose will be amply served if we distinguish three: *primary* stress, as in the third syllable of *independent* or the first syllable of *secretary*; *secondary* stress, a weaker level, as in the first syllable of *independent* or, in American speech, the third syllable of *secretary*; and *minimal* stress, as in the second and fourth syllables of these two words. When it is necessary to indicate stress, the phonetic convention is, as we have seen, to use short vertical marks before the stressed syllable, above the line for primary stress, below the line for secondary, and with minimal stress left unmarked. Thus we may transcribe *independent* [ˌɪndɪˈpɛndənt], *secretary* [ˈsɛkrəˌtɛri], *above* [əˈbʌv], and *button* [ˈbʌtn]. We may do the same to individual words, including monosyllables, in a phrase, as in *in the first place* [ˌɪn ðə ˈfɜ˞st ˌples].

Since we have defined stress in terms of relative force, it is evident that the term has only limited application to isolated monosyllables. But groups of monosyllables obviously show stress patterns: that of *in the first place* is not very different from that of *independent*. Since, however, different reasons account for the forms which these two stress patterns take, it will be convenient to distinguish them as *syllabic* stress in *independent*, and *phrasal* stress in *in the first place*.

What determines syllabic stress? No completely satisfactory answer can be given, but two historical tendencies may be noted.[1]

---

[1] Compare C. M. Lotspeich, "Romance and Germanic Linguistic Tendencies," *Journal of English and Germanic Philology*, XXIV (1925), 325–34.

In native English words, such as the series *love, lovely, lovable, loveliness, lovableness*, the stress remains on the root syllable. But in words of Greek or Latin origin, such as the series *photograph, photography, photographic*, or the series *equal, equality, equalization, equalitarian*, the stress shifts from one syllable to another as the word is lengthened. Words like *love* illustrate the so-called fixed or recessive stress of the native English and Germanic tradition. Words like *equal* and *photograph* illustrate the so-called free or variable stress of the Greco-Latin tradition. Since the vocabulary of modern English has approximately equal parts of native English and Greco-Latin origin, it is not surprising that these two tendencies should have often come into conflict with each other.

In borrowed words which have been used in English for a long time, the stress has frequently moved forward to the root syllable, as in *candle* [ˈkændəl] and *castle* [ˈkæsəl]. Later borrowings from the same roots show the survival of the Greco-Latin tradition in *chandelier* [ˌʃændəˈlɪr] and *chateau* [ˌʃæˈto]. Some verbs and nouns with one spelling have one stress pattern for the noun, another for the verb, for instance, the nouns *subject* [ˈsʌbdʒɪkt] and *object* [ˈɑbdʒɪkt] in contrast to the verbs *subject* [səbˈdʒɛkt] and *object* [əbˈdʒɛkt]. It is worth notice, in passing, that the radio announcer's [ˈsʌbˈdʒɛkt] for *subject*, which combines the first syllable of the noun with the second syllable of the verb, gives no clue as to which he intends. The continuing controversies over [əˈdrɛs] or [ˈædˌrɛs] for *address* and [ˈditel] or [diˈtel] for *detail* show, however, that the pattern has never been completely settled. In this country, *garage* is usually [gəˈrɑdʒ] or [gəˈrɑʒ]; in England, it is often [ˈgærɪdʒ], a development that parallels the earlier development of *carriage* to [ˈkærɪdʒ].

An important feature of English structure is that the stress pattern may differentiate a compound noun from a sequence of adjective plus noun. Thus *black bird* [ˌblæk¹bɝd] designates any bird of that color, regardless of species; *blackbird* [¹blækˌbɝd] designates a particular species. *Green house* [ˌgrin¹haʊs] refers to a house colored green; *greenhouse* [¹grinˌhaʊs], to a structure used for growing green plants. The shifts from [ˌaɪs ¹krim] to [¹aɪs ˌkrim] for *ice cream* and [ˌpinʌt ¹bʌtɚ] to [¹pinʌt ˌbʌtɚ] for *peanut butter* were essentially shifts from sequences of adjectives plus nouns to compound nouns. In the adjective-noun sequence the stress normally falls on the noun; in a compound noun the stress normally falls on the first element of the compound.

Rhythm also helps to determine stress patterns. Such words as *secretary*, *dictionary*, and *military* are pronounced in England with a single strong stress on the first syllable, in accordance with one rhythmic pattern: [¹sɛkrətrɪ], [¹dɪkʃənrɪ], and [¹mɪlɪtrɪ]. In America they also have a secondary stress on the third syllable, in accordance with a different rhythmic pattern: [¹sɛkrəˌtɛri], [¹dɪkʃəˌnɛri], and [¹mɪləˌtɛri]. In less definite ways, the stress patterns of individual words may vary in accordance with the rhythm of neighboring words or the need for contrast.

In sum, syllabic stress depends, in standard speech, on the conventions and traditions developed by the interplay of various forces in the history of each word. In most words the convention is fixed, and any departure from the accepted stress pattern is branded as substandard. In a few words, the convention is not fixed, and some variation occurs on the standard level. *Independent* has a fixed stress pattern; *address* does not.

Phrasal stress, on the other hand, reflects variations in the shade of meaning or emotional content to be communicated, as may be illustrated by attaching various shades of meaning to the sentence, *I am going down town.* One stress pattern will be natural in answer to the question: Who is going? Another, to the question: Where are you going? You should be able to work out still other stress patterns which will fit still other questions.

Syllabic and phrasal stresses do not conflict with each other: the former represents the relative prominence of syllables within the word; the latter, the relative prominence of words within the phrase or sentence. Syllabic stress is a part of English structure. Phrasal stress is part of the art of speech, one of the devices by means of which we make speaking effective.

All occurrences of primary stress are accompanied by a modulation of the sentence melody, or intonational pattern. In the compound *greenhouse*, for instance, the first syllable normally has a high pitch, the second a low. In the sequence *green house*, however, the pitch modulation is confined to the word *house*, and normally consists of a glide from high to low. These basic intonational patterns are used in statements, such as: *This is the greenhouse*, and in questions which contain a specific interrogative word, such as: *Where is the greenhouse?* But in a question without a specific interrogative word, such as: *Is this the greenhouse?* the low pitch will precede the high. Other variations in the intonational pattern lead us into questions of semantics and the art of speech. Those mentioned in this paragraph are fundamental to the structure of the language.

An understanding of stress is important to the student of phonetics, not only for its own sake, but also for the important changes in English vowels and diphthongs which result from changes in the stress pattern. *Subject* and *object*, as we saw earlier in this chapter, illustrate the changes in the vowel patterns which may take place under varying degrees of stress. Closer examination reveals that some English vowels are used only with primary or secondary stress, that some are used only with minimal stress, and that some are used with little or no change in quality under primary, secondary, or minimal stress.

The vowel phoneme [i] occurs with primary or secondary stress, usually in the form of the diphthongal allophone [ɪi], as in *creature* [ˈkrɪitʃɚ] and *oaktree* [ˈokˌtrɪi]. It reduces to monophthongal [i] or [ɪ] under minimal stress before a vowel, as in *create* [ˈkriˈeɪt] or [krɪˈeɪt]; or to [i], [ɪ], or [ə] before a consonant, as in *event* [iˈvɛnt], [ɪˈvɛnt], or [əˈvɛnt]. *The* is pronounced [ðɪi] only on the rare occasions when it is stressed. Its normal unstressed forms are [ðə] before consonants and [ði] or [ðɪ] before vowels.

The diphthongal [ʊu] reduces in much the same way; all four forms may be illustrated in the sentence: *They went to* [tə] *France and to* [tu] (or [tʊ]) *England too* [tʊu]. The vowels [e], [eɪ], and [ɛ] reduce to [i], [ɪ], and [ə], as in *always* [ˈɔlwiz], [ˈɔlwɪz], or [ˈɔlwəz] and *needless* [ˈnɪidlɪs] or [ˈnɪidləs]. The vowels [ɝ] and [ɜ] reduce to [ɚ] and [ə]; compare the emphatic *yes sir* [ˈjɛs ˈsɝ] or [ˈjɛs ˈsɜ] with the less emphatic [ˈjɛsɚ] or [ˈjɛsə]. In general, high front vowels reduce to [i], [ɪ], or [ə]; high back vowels, to [u], [ʊ], or [ə]; others, to [ə]. This reduction under minimal stress again emphasizes the importance of [ə] in English.

In the following table, though not all the illustrative pairs are related, and though not all the possible pronunciations are included, the relationships between stressed and unstressed syllables should be made clear.

In addition to its use in unstressed syllables, reduction takes place in a number of monosyllables whose function is to tie the sentence together structurally rather than to add to the logic or imagery. These monosyllables include auxiliary verbs, prepositions, conjunctions, and pronouns in unstressed positions in connected phrases. In the sentence: *One and one are two* [ˈwʌn ən ˈwʌn ɚ ˈtuu], the numerals carry the meaning; *and* and *are* merely hold the sentence together. If the radio announcer announces that the store will be open from *one to three* [ˈwʌn

| Stressed Vowel | | Unstressed Vowel | |
|---|---|---|---|
| [i] | *creature* [ˈkritʃɚ] | [i] | *create* [kriˈet] |
| | | [ɪ] | *create* [krɪˈet] |
| | *compete* [kəmˈpit] | [ə] | *competition* [ˌkɑmpəˈtɪʃən] |
| [ɪ] | *indicative* [ɪnˈdɪkətɪv] | [ɪ] | *indicate* [ˈɪndɪket] |
| | | [ə] | *indicate* [ˈɪndəket] |
| [e] | *today* [təˈde] | [i] | *Monday* [ˈmʌndi] |
| | | [ɪ] | *Monday* [ˈmʌndɪ] |
| | *separate* [ˈsɛpɚˌet] | [ə] | *separate* [ˈsɛprət] |
| [ɛ] | *exit* [ˈɛksɪt] | [ɪ] | *exist* [ɪgˈzɪst] |
| | | [ə] | *exist* [əgˈzɪst] |
| [æ] | *man* [mæn] | [ə] | *woman* [ˈwʊmən] |
| [a] | *ask* [ask] | [ə] | *askance* [əˈskæns] |
| [aɪ] | *oblige* [əˈblaɪdʒ] | [ɪ] | *obligation* [ˌɑblɪˈgeʃən] |
| | | [ə] | *obligation* [ˌɑbləˈgeʃən] |
| [aʊ] | *town* [taʊn] | [ə] | *Easton* [ˈistən] |
| [ɑ] | *conduct* [ˈkɑnˌdʌkt] | [ə] | *conduct* [kənˈdʌkt] |
| [ɒ] | *conduct* [ˈkɒnˌdʌkt] | [ə] | *conduct* [kənˈdʌkt] |
| [ɔ] | *author* [ˈɔθɚ] | [ə] | *authority* [əˈθɔrəti] |
| [o] | *below* [bɪˈlo] | [ʊ] | *billow* [ˈbɪlʊ] |
| | | [ə] | *pillow* [ˈpɪlə] |
| [ʌ] | *company* [ˈkʌmpəni] | [ə] | *companion* [kəmˈpænjən] |
| [ʊ] | *full* [fʊl] | [ə] | *beautiful* [ˈbjutɪfəl] |
| [u] | *fluent* [fluənt] | [ʊ] | *affluent* [ˈæfluənt] |
| | *doom* [dum] | [ə] | *freedom* [ˈfridəm] |
| [ju] | *music* [ˈmjuzɪk] | [jʊ] | *musician* [mjʊˈzɪʃən] |
| | *accuse* [əˈkjuz] | [jə] | *accusation* [ˌækjəˈzeʃən] |
| | | [ə] | *manufacture* [ˌmænəˈfæktʃɚ] |
| [ɝ] | *certify* [ˈsɝtɪˌfaɪ] | [ɚ] | *certificate* [sɚˈtɪfɪkət] |
| [ɜ] | *certify* [ˈsɜtɪˌfaɪ] | [ə] | *certificate* [səˈtɪfɪkət] |

ˡtuu ˡθrii], he sounds as if he were counting; the correct pronunciation for the information he intends to give is [ˡwʌn tə ˡθrii].

Weak forms occur for *an, as, at, but, could, from, has, must, not, of, or, should, some, than, the, us,* and about forty other words.[2] In isolation, in a series of the sort just given, and in the rare instances in which they contrast with one another, such words are pronounced with the full value of vowels and consonants. In most instances, however, their use in the sentence is incidental to other words, and the retention of the full pronunciation can have no other effect than that of obscuring the prominence of those words which carry the essential ideas. Contrast the awkward ineffectiveness of [ˡgɪv ˡhɪm ˡsʌm ˡhæm ˡænd ˡɛgz] with the normal [gɪv ɪm səm ˡhæm ən ˡɛgz]. As Chapter 6 points out, this reduction of vowel quality is not an indication of carelessness, but the normal differentiation of subsidiary from principal material. It is correct. The person who emphasizes every word, no matter how subsidiary, as far too many radio and television announcers do, speaks incorrectly and ineffectively.

Though the vowel [ə] has its counterparts in French and German, they are not normally reduced as much as English [ə], nor are they used as frequently. The peculiar unstressing pattern of English constitutes a major contrast with most other languages, especially with those in the Romance group. Unstressing is one of the most important factors in the characteristic rhythm of English speech. Foreign students do well if they master it early in their study of English. Conversely, English students must know about unstressing in order to be on their guard against it in speaking other languages.

    [2] See L. S. Hultzén, "The Pronunciation of Monosyllabic Form-Words in American English," *Studies in Speech and Drama in Honor of Alexander M. Drummond* (Ithaca: Cornell University Press, 1944), pp. 255–84.

## EXERCISES

1. Select ten of the words from the list in the second paragraph preceding of those which frequently have unstressed forms, and construct sentences or phrases in which the ten words are properly unstressed.

2. From the same list select five words, and use them in sentences or phrases in which they are properly stressed.

3. Make a phonetic transcription of your own pronunciation of the following sentences. Indicate phrasal stress:

I have to go back to give the dog his dinner.

He said he'd see you tomorrow night if he could.

He could see me tonight if he really wanted to.

What will you do with the book if I give it to you?

One of us will probably be chosen to do it for him.

Rip Van Winkle was one of those happy mortals who took life easy.

# CHAPTER 17

# The Dynamics of Consonants

One important corollary of the English stress pattern is that stops, or explosive consonants, have more energy than the corresponding phonemes of some other languages. If a native speaker of English sounds one of the voiced stops, [b], [d], or [g] in isolation, the pent-up energy of articulation normally escapes as a weak vowel; the actual pronunciation becomes [bə], [də], or [gə]. In connected speech, of course, the pent-up energy escapes into whatever vowel or consonant follows the voiced stop; normally [ə] does not intrude in such words as *ball* [bɔl], *drift* [drɪft], *dwell* [dwɛl], or *glad* [glæd]. At the end of the word, less energy is available for the voiced stop, since the peak of the stress has been passed earlier in the syllable. Hence there is normally no trace of [ə] at the end·of such words as *cab* [kæb], *red* [rɛd], *end* [ɛnd], *weld* [wɛld], or *hug* [hʌg]. Only with exaggerated articulation will [ə] occur in any of the words illustrated in this paragraph.

For voiceless stops, the situation is somewhat different. First, the articulatory energy of the voiceless stop is greater than that of its corresponding voiced stop, because none of the energy has been used in setting the vocal bands into vibration, and

156

because the vocal bands are drawn far enough apart to offer a minimum of resistance to the passage of breath. Secondly, the articulatory energy of the voiceless stop, because it is voiceless, does not blend well with a following vowel or voiced consonant. Consequently a vigorously articulated voiceless stop normally ends with an off-glide consisting of a rush of voiceless breath known as the *aspirate* ['æspərət]. In phonetic transcription the aspirate may be indicated by placing a small [ʰ] above the line, as in *pill* [pʰɪl], *till* [ʰɪl], *kill* [kʰɪl], *plow* [pʰlɑʊ], *try* [tʰraɪ], *queer* [kʰwɪr], *appear* [ə'pʰɪr], *intend* [ɪn'tʰɛnd], and *acquire* [ə'kʰwaɪr].

At the beginning of stressed syllables, corresponding voiced and voiceless stops are differentiated by three factor: the voice-less stop is strongly articulated, aspirated, and voiceless; the voiced stop is more weakly articulated, unaspirated, and voiced. When the contrast between voiceless and voiced quality is lost in whispering, the other two factors enable us to distinguish between such pairs as *pill* and *bill*, *time* and *dime*, and *come* and *gum*.

In positions other than the beginning of a stressed syllable, the voiceless stop is normally unaspirated, as in *spill* [spɪl], [stɪl], *skill* [skɪl], *upper* ['ʌpɚ], *utter* ['ʌtɚ], *aching* ['eɪkɪŋ], *rap* [ræp], *rat* [ræt], and *rack* [ræk].[1] Because of these unaspirated forms, the distinction between corresponding voiced and voice-less stops in the middle of words is often difficult to maintain. At best, *metal* ['mɛtl] and *medal* ['mɛdl] sound very alike. Furthermore, it is very easy, in careless speech, for the weak, unaspirated [t] to pick up voice from its voiced surroundings, so that both *metal* and *medal* come to be pronounced ['mɛdl]. For the socially acceptable pronunciation of words like *metal*, *butter*,

---

[1] Compare W. F. Twaddell, *On Defining the Phoneme* (Baltimore: Linguistic Society of America, 1935); Morris Swadesh, "The Phonemic Principle," *Language*, X (1934), 117–29.

and *sitting*, you should try to avoid both the careless extreme of [ˈmɛdl], [ˈbʌdɚ], and [ˈsɪdɪŋ], and the pedantic exaggeration of [ˈmɛtʰəl], [ˈbʌtʰɚ], and [ˈsɪtʰɪŋ].

Some voiced forms have, however, passed over into general speech. [ˈprɑdəstənt] is almost universal for *Protestant.* [sɪgˈnɪfəgənt] for *significant* usually passes unnoticed. Other voiced forms are still suspect. The radio and TV [kəngrædʒəˈleʃənz] for *congratulations* [kəngrætʃəˈleʃənz] still offends many listeners.

### Linking of Stop Consonants

In its complete form, a stop consonant consists of three distinct phases: a period of closure, or on-glide, in which the complete obstruction of the oral and nasal valves is established; a period of compression, in which the pressure of the breath is increased; and a final period of release, or off-glide, in which the sudden opening of either the oral or nasal valve allows the breath to escape. Schematically, this action may be represented by the following diagram, with the on-glide on the left, the period of compression in the middle, and the off-glide at the right:

When the stop occurs between vowels, as in *making* [ˈmekɪŋ] and *rigor* [ˈrɪgɚ], the complete form usually occurs as diagrammed. Often the complete form also occurs, at the beginning or end of a word, as in *make* [mek], *king* [kɪŋ], *rig* [rɪg], and *girl* [gɝl], though the off-glide does not always occur before a pause.  In other phonetic contexts, however, at least one, and often two, of the phases may be lost or modified.  If a nasal consonant precedes the stop, as in *lump* [lʌmp], *lend* [lɛnd], or *rank* [ræŋk], the oral valve closes at the beginning of the nasal [m], [n], or [ŋ], and the transition to the stop consonant is accomplished by closing the velar valve. Thus the on-glide has been modified. If a nasal consonant follows the stop, as in *Chapman* [ˈtʃæpmən], *eaten* [ˈitn], or the substandard pronunciation of *bacon* and *baking* [ˈbekŋ], the oral valve remains closed, and the velar valve opens to mark the transition from the stop to the nasal. Here the off-glide has been modified.

Minor modifications of the on-glide and off-glide occur when stops and fricatives formed in much the same part of the mouth occur in sequence. Thus in *list* [lɪst] the space between the tongue and the gum ridge is considerably reduced for [s]; very little on-glide is necessary to complete the stop for [t]. In *hits* [hɪts], the off-glide is similarly restricted by the [s] which follows. In *obvious* [ˈɑbviəs], the off-glide of [b] is restricted by the contact between the teeth and the lip needed for [v]. In all these instances the complete three-phase articulation of the stop is reduced in one way or another.

When two identical stop consonants come together in a word or phrase, we cannot represent the dynamics of the combination by a doubling of the diagram on page 158. In *bookcase*, for instance, the first [k] has lost its off-glide, the second its on-glide; the period of compression has been lengthened, and the final explosion delayed, till the resulting long consonant has taken as much time as two separate consonants. Therefore we transcribe *bookcase* [ˈbʊk: es], letting the length mark indicate the added length of the period of compression, and represent the dynamics of [k:] as follows:

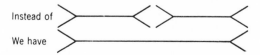

The same diagram illustrates the dynamics of the prolonged stop consonants of *that time* [ðæt: aɪm], *stop pulling* [stɑp: ʊlɪŋ], *grab bag* [græb: æg], *red dress* [rɛd: rɛs], and *big girl* [bɪg: ɝl]. Consecutive stops which are not thus linked in close juncture sound artificial in English.

The sequence of a voiced and a voiceless stop, as in *red tape* [rɛd tep] or *hot day* [hɑt de], may also be represented by the above diagram, so long as the two consonants thus brought together are homorganic, that is, formed at the same place of articulation. If the places of articulation are different, as in *act* [ækt] or *rubbed* [rʌbd], the dynamics are still substantially the same. During the period of compression, contact for the second consonant is established before release of the first. Thus in *act* the establishment of the contact between the velum and the back of the tongue constitutes the on-glide for [k]. During the period of compression, the tip of the tongue makes contact with the gum ridge, and the velar contact is released. When the final release comes, it takes the form of the off-glide for [t]. This close juncture between [k] and [t] represents a feature of English which is lacking in some other languages, where, as in French, the off-glide of [k] is complete before the on-glide of [t] begins.

In *rubbed*, the lips close for [b], the tip of the tongue makes contact with the gum ridge for [d], the lip contact is then released, and finally the tongue-gum contact is released. The successive points of contact in both *act* and *rubbed* overlap in time, and the consonants are thus linked without the instrusion of any gliding sound between them. Close juncture of consonants is often difficult for foreigners to learn, but until they do their speech will sound foreign.

The effects of linking other consonants are less noticeable, because the three phases of on-glide, hold, and off-glide are not so strongly marked as for stops. Nevertheless the linking takes place. The prolonged [n] of *penknife* [ˈpɛn : aɪf] results from the same sort of linking as the prolonged [d] of *red dress*. The long [n :] of *penknife* contrasts with the short [n] of *penny*. Similar linkings occur in *will learn* [wɪl : ɝn], in contrast to *will earn* [wɪl ɝn]; in *this sink* [ðɪs : ɪŋk], in contrast to *this ink* [ðɪs ɪŋk]; and in many other combinations.

The native speaker of English is not likely to repeat the foreigner's mistake of separating closely linked consonants unless he has picked up the false notion that close juncture represents indistinctness.   Historically, of course, the linked consonants seem to be inherently instable, with the result that simplification has often taken place.   In some words the simplification has become standard: the sequence [kg] in *blackguard* has been simplified, first to [g :], then to [g], in the pronunciation [ˈblægɝd]. The sequence [pb] in *clapboard* has been simplified, first to [b :], then to [b], in the pronunciation [ˈklæbɝd].   Since these two words have become relatively uncommon in the daily speech of the present day, the spelling-pronunciations [ˈblækgɑrd] and [ˈklæpbɔrd] have brought the pronunciation full circle.   *Cupboard*, a more familiar word, is always the simplified [ˈkʌbɝd] or [ˈkʌbəd]

Such simplified forms as [fæks] for *facts*, [kɛp] for *kept*, [aʊdɔrz] for *outdoors*, and [ˈkænədet] for *candidate* occur in casual conversation, and are apparently increasing in frequency, though they have not yet achieved the standing of generally accepted good usage.   The judicious avoidance of both the substandard and the pedantic is nowhere better illustrated than in the treatment of these linked consonants.

## EXERCISES

1. Find words and phrases which illustrate the close juncture

of each of the six English stop consonants followed by each of the others.   Arrange your illustrations systematically, in some such order as [pb], [pt], [pd], [pk], [pg], [bp], etc.

2. Trancribe your own pronunciation of the following sentences and indicate the aspirated consonants:

The tramp spilled cigarette ashes on the steps.
We had a quiet time on last Sunday's picnic.
The spruce tree sprouted on the first clear spring day.
The criminal appealed to the higher court for a new trial.
He quickly shut the top of the paper box as the bell tolled.

3. Describe the phonetic and physical details of the linking of stop consonants in the following sentences:

The actor paid eight dollars for the big poster.
What time does the night bus leave for Westport?
I can't come to Aunt Christine's party next Tuesday.
One dark day last January the old bookkeeper caught cold.

# CHAPTER 18

# Length of Sounds

In popular speech the vowel of *same* [sem] is often called "long *a*"; the vowel of *Sam* [sæm], "short *a*"; that of *psalm* [sɑm], "broad *a*". Elementary school readers, written by educationists, not by linguists, use such terms without explaining what is long, short, or broad about such sounds. As the phonetic transcriptions indicate, the actual distinctive differences between the vowels of our three illustrative words are not of length but of quality. "Long *a*" may be shortened in duration, and "short *a*" lengthened, without producing any ambiguity between *same* and *Sam*. In short, popular terminology confuses quantity with quality. To avoid confusion we must keep these two concepts distinct; hence we restrict the term *length* to relative duration. We can best illustrate relative duration by showing varying degrees of length in the same vowel or consonant.

In comparing *bee* and *beet* you will notice that the allophone of [i] in *bee* lasts for an appreciably longer time than the allophone of the same vowel phoneme in *beet*. Closer measurement reveals that the vowel of *beam* averages slightly shorter than that of *bee*, and that the vowel of *bead* averages slightly shorter than that of *beam*, but longer than that of *beet*. Degrees of length can thus be multiplied according to the nature of the following sound, as the following sound is voiced or voiceless, stopped or continuant. Variation in length also depends on other features in the phonetic context, on the speaker's habitual rate of speed, on the momentary emotional context, and the amount of stress which the syllable carries. If one were to attempt to record all the possible variations in the absolute length of speech sounds, every phonetic transcription would require the assistance of the laboratory phonetician with his instruments of exact measurement. The problem of symbolization would become virtually insoluble, and no practical benefit would result.

For practical purposes it is usually enough to record the vowel of *bee* as [biː], with the symbol [ː] to indicate relatively full length. Similarly, the vowels of *beam* and *bead* may be recorded as [iˑ], with the symbol [ˑ] above the line to indicate intermediate length. The relatively short vowel of *beet* [bit] may be left unmarked. Often, indeed, it is not necessary to indicate length at all, since, except for minor dialectal variations, length plays no part in distinguishing one English word from another. For us to recognize the word *bead*, it makes no difference whether we hear and record it as [bid], [biˑd], [biːd], or [bɪid]; such distinctions are likely to be chiefly useful to the dialect geographer.

In most forms of American speech no ambiguity results from recording *hot* as [hɑt], [hɑˑt], or [hɑːt]; all three degrees of length may be heard at one time or another. On the other hand, ambiguity may very well result in the South, in the New York City area, and to a lesser extend in eastern New England, because in these areas [hɑt] will normally be interpreted as *hot*, and [hɑːt] as *heart*.

Thus the degree of length may have distinctive value in a few pairs of words, but only in limited areas. Sometimes, moreover, such a distinction is either not heard, or is obliterated by the lengthening of [ɑ] to [ɑː]. This is especially true in the New York City area, where [hɑːt] may mean either *hot* or *heart*, and where the listener must distinguish the meaning by the context, just as all speakers of English use the context to distinguish *see* from *sea* and *guest* from *guessed*. Few Americans sense differences in length as significant, and such differences are therefore of greater stylistic than practical importance.

Various phonetic factors affect the relative length of individual vowels. In general, tense vowels are longer than lax vowels in the same contexts. The vowel of *peel* [piːl] is normally longer than that of *pill* [pɪl]; that of *pool* [puːl], longer than that of *pull* [pʊl]; *caught* [kɔːt], than *cot* [kɑt]; *sale* [seːl], than *sell* [sɛl]; and *home* [hoːm], than *hum* [hʌm]. Remember, too, that diphthongal allophones may develop from most of these long, tense vowels.

The tense vowels [ɝ] and [ɜ] are usually longer than the lax [ɚ] and [ə], but tension is not the only factor here, since greater stress works toward the same end. Individual speech habits may obscure the lengthening effect of tension, since many speakers, particularly in the New York City area and in the South, lengthen and diphthongize most vowels, tense or lax. Thus *bird*, *dog*, and *ʒlass* may be [bɜɪd], [dɔːəg], and [glæːəs] in New York City; [bɜɪd], [dɔʊg], and [glæɪs], in the Deep South.

In addition to tension, position within the word affects length. At the end of a word a vowel is usually longer than when followed by a consonant. It is likely to be longer before a voiced consonant than before a voiceless, and longer before a continuant than before a stop, as we have already seen in comparing *bee*, *beam*, *bead*, and *beet*. Similarly, the vowel is normally longer before the voiced fricative in *leave* [liːv] than before the voiceless fricative in *leaf* [lif]. Some of these differences are, of course, so slight that we usually disregard them.  We notice them chiefly when a foreigner, or an artificially speaking native, departs from the usual pattern.

Length is also affected by the number of consonants which follow, and by the presence or absence of following unstressed syllables.  Thus in *child* [tʃaɪld] the diphthong [aɪ] represents the normal development from Old English [iː]; in *children*, the extra consonant [r] and the extra syllable have kept the vowel lax and short.  The vowel of *goose* [guːs] represents the normal development of Old English [oː]; in *gosling*, the extra consonant and extra syllable have kept the vowel lax and short.  *Vineyard*, when pronounced [ˈvɪnjɚd] and not given the spelling pronunciation [ˈvaɪnjɑrd], shows the same kind of relationship to *vine* [vaɪn].

A stressed vowel followed immediately by an unstressed is usually relatively long, as in *re-enact* [ˈriːənˈækt].  Conversely, an unstressed vowel followed immediately by a stressed is usually quite short, as in *react* [riˈækt], and may also be reduced in tension, as in [rɪˈækt].  Finally, the loss of a following consonant gives added length to the vowel; it is longer when *farm* is pronounced [fɑːm] than when pronounced [fɑrm].

So many factors affect the length of vowels that no set of rules can give much help in deciding in advance what the length of a given vowel in a given word is likely to be.  In recording length, the ear is a better guide than any formula based on the facts and tendencies we have been examining.  There are too many variables, and we do not know what comparative weight to assign to each.  In the speech of foreigners, however, length of vowels may require a good deal of attention, since stylistic variations in length are greater in English than in many other languages.  So are the variations in muscular tension which so often accompany the changes in length.  Many foreigners need special practice in lengthening vowels, and in developing the characteristic diphthongal allophones of English tense vowels, and in the shortening and relaxing of English lax vowels.

Conversely, English-speaking students of other languages need to realize that distinctions between long and short vowels, and between tense and lax vowels, are characteristically less noticeable in most languages than in English. Most important of all, perhaps, the English-speaking student must avoid substituting the allophonic diphthongs [ɪi], [eɪ], [oʊ], and [ʊu] for the monophthongs [i], [e], [o], and [u] of whatever language he is studying.

Diphthongs are intrinsically long, not because of the prolongation of either element, but because of the time required for the glide. In drawling speech, the extra length is usually produced by prolonging the first element and postponing the glide, as in [tɑːʊn] for *town* and [bɔːɪl] for *boil*. Singers do the same when singing a diphthong on a long note or a series of notes.

The length of consonants varies according to the following sounds, but only slightly. Thus [n] is slightly longer before the voiced [d] of *bend* [bɛn·d] than before voiceless [t] of *bent* [bɛnt]. It is slightly longer at the end of *run* [rʌn·] than before the unstressed syllable of *runner* [ˈrʌnɚ]. Variations of this sort, though parallel to more noticeable variations in the length of vowels, are so slight that they may usually be disregarded. Only when length results from the coalescence of identical consonants, as in *bookcase* and other such words discussed in Chapter 17, does added length become meaningfully significant.

## EXERCISES

1. Make a phonetic transcription of your own pronunciation of the following sentences; indicate vowel length:

In the pool behind the barn were three white geese.
She closed the door slowly after gazing down the street.

In the great open spaces of the West the stars seem closer.
No matter what you say, I simply won't do it today.
The boys stirred and stirred and seemed unable to sleep.
The children entered the woods and saw a great big bear.

2. Indicate the places where nondistinctive diphthongs might replace the long vowels of your transcription.

# CHAPTER 19

# Phonetic Change: Assimilation

Variations in pronunciation that we have already noted should convince us that language is not static and uniform, but that it develops and changes. We notice this development even more if we read the literature of earlier periods. Shakespeare's English is noticeably different from our own, even though our present-day archaic spelling masks some of the differences. To understand Chaucer we must frequently refer to a glossary; to appreciate his rhythms and rhymes we must also know something about the language spoken in fourteenth-century London. To read Old English, of the time of King Alfred for instance, we must study it as we would a foreign language.

Changes in the language are usually imperceptible till afterward, and often seemingly capricious. Analysis of the historical changes shows, however, that the patterns of development are usually clear in retrospect, and that definite causes can be assigned to some of them. In this chapter we are going to examine one type of historical change, in order to throw light on the changeable nature of present-day speech.

169

## Assimilation

The usual pronunciation of *income* is [ˈɪnˌkʌm], with primary stress on the first syllable, secondary stress on the second syllable, and a distinct syllabic division between [n] and [k]. When we use the word as an adjective, however, in the phrase *income tax*, the pronunciation may be [ˈɪnˌkʌm ˈtæks], but often it changes to [ˈɪŋkəm ˌtæks]. The reduced vowel represents reduced stress. The change from [n] to [ŋ] illustrates what is known as *assimilation*, a type of phonetic change which occurs frequently enough to warrant detailed examination.

When *income* becomes part of the larger unit, *income tax*, we scan the details more rapidly. The succession of three stressed syllables conflicts with our normal rhythmic patterns, and we weaken the second syllable from [ʌ] to [ə]. The phrase as a whole telescopes within itself, and the amount of time available for the shift from one syllable to the next is shortened. The tongue, however, requires an appreciable amount of time to shift from the alveolar contact of [n] to the velar contact of [k]. If the time is too short, the tongue anticipates the velar contact by shifting from [n] to [ŋ], since the sequence [ŋk] can be made with a single contact of the tongue, instead of the sequence of contacts required for [nk]. Furthermore, as Kent has pointed out,[1] thought constantly outstrips utterance, and this mental anticipation is closely associated with the mechanical adjustment just described.

Assimilation may therefore be defined as the process whereby one sound is changed to a second under the influence of a third;[2] in *income tax* the alveolar [n] changes to the velar [ŋ] under the

---

[1] Roland G. Kent, "Assimilation and Dissimilation," *Language*, XII (1936), 245–58.

[2] Compare Daniel Jones, *An Outline of English Phonetics* (8th ed.; New York: E. P. Dutton & Co., 1956), pp. 217–18.

influence of the velar [k]. Another useful definition is that of Bloomfield,[3] who points out that the position of the speech agents for the production of one sound is altered to a position more like that of a neighboring sound.

All assimilations start in a manner similar to that of *income tax*. The change may take place as soon as the two original sounds come close together: we have every reason to suppose that the sequence [ŋk] formed as soon as the word *sank* was formed. On the other hand, the change may take place more slowly if, as in *income tax*, the sequence is brought gradually together in the act of compounding. That is, many assimilations start as accidental mispronunciations of an accepted sequence of sounds. Some never progress beyond this stage, for they may be noticeable enough to cause adverse criticism, and to induce speakers to avoid the assimilation.

A substandard pronunciation of *length* illustrates this accidental type of assimilation. The shift from the velar [ŋ] to the linguadental [θ] is apparently too great for some speakers' muscular control. Consequently the tongue anticipates the dental position, [ŋ] changes to [n] in anticipation of the following [θ], and we hear the new pronunciation [lɛnθ], rhyming with *tenth* [tɛnθ]. The pronunciation [lɛnθ] has never, however, risen to the standard level, because it has always been noticeable enough to provoke adverse criticism. Most people pronounce *length* as [lɛŋθ] or [lɛŋkθ], the added [k] serving as a kind of insulation against assimilation.

On the other hand, some assimilations are adopted so promptly and generally that adverse criticism is futile. For example, derivatives of the Latin preposition *cum* occur in English with all three nasal consonants. The original [m] of

[3] Leonard Bloomfield, *Language* (New York: Henry Holt & Co., Inc., 1933), p. 372.

*cum* survives in such words as *combine* [kəmˈbaɪn], *compare* [kəmˈpɛr], and *comfort* [ˈkʌmfɚt]; but it has become [n] in such words as *contact* [ˈkɑnˌtækt], *condemn* [kənˈdɛm], and *constant* [ˈkɑnstənt]; and has become [ŋ] in such words as *congress* [ˈkɑŋgrəs] and *conquer* [ˈkɑŋkɚ]. A glance at the consonant which follows the nasal shows that in every word the nasal has approximated the position of the following consonant; [m] has assimilated to [n] before alveolar consonants, and to [ŋ] before velars.    Many of these assimilations took place in the Latin period.

The assimilative process is essentially the same, whether in *length*, *income tax*, *condemn*, or *congress*, but the effect of adverse criticism has been selective.   There was probably no appreciable criticism of the assimilations based on Latin *cum*; most of them were completely established and accepted before English adopted the words from Latin or French.

Between the extremes of accidental, substandard assimilations of the type of [lɛnθ] and established, standard assimilations of the type of [ˈkɑŋgrəs] lie a few instances on which a final verdict has not yet been made.   Some people object to [ˈɪŋkəm ˌtæks]; others accept it, not only without objection, but often without even being aware that any change in pronunciation has taken place.   Some people object to the assimilated [ˈhɔrʃˌʃu] for *horse-shoe*; others accept it without noticing that they have lost the [s] of *horse* [hɔrs].   The fate of these and similar assimilations will be decided only in the future.   In and of themselves, assimilations are neither good nor bad.   General acceptance or rejection of a particular assimilation is completely irrelevant to the assimilative process.

When we consider the inherent nature of the assimilative process, we notice that in all the illustrations used thus far the preceding sound has been influenced in anticipation of the sound that follows. Though this is the most common type,[4] the direction of influence may be otherwise.

Americans who pronounce *tune* [tun] and *duty* [ˈduti] often wonder why British and Canadian speakers sometimes insert a seemingly gratuitous [ʃ] in *tune* [tʃun] and *duty* [ˈdʒutɪ]. Far from being gratuitous, these sounds represent the assimilations that sometimes develop from [tjun] and [ˈdjutɪ]. The sequences [tj] and [dj] are unstable, not because of the distance through which the tongue must move, but because of the delicacy of adjustment required. In [tʃun], the tongue has moved forward from the position of [j] to that of [ʃ], which blends more readily with [t]. In [ˈdʒutɪ], the tongue has moved forward from the position of [j] to that of [ʒ]. Thus [t] has assimilated [j] to [ʃ]; [d] has assimilated [j] to [ʒ]. The articulation of [t] and [d] is vigorous enough to move the place of articulation forward for the following sound, and the voiceless quality of [t] also carries over to the following sound. A more subtle illustration can be shown in the comparison of *rip*, *drip*, and *trip*. In *rip*, most Americans use the ordinary frictionless [r]. In *drip*, the tip of the tongue is so close to the gum ridge after [d], that a frictional allophone of [r] often results. In *trip*, the allophone of [r] may be both frictional and voiceless. In all these instances in which the preceding sound influences the sound that follows, classify the assimilation as *progressive*. When the second sound influences the first, as in *length* and *congress*, we call it *regressive*.

Finally, there is a third assimilative classification known as *reciprocal*, in which the two sounds influence each other and combine to produce a single sound which is a compromise between the two. The word *sure*, for instance, was formerly pronounced

[4] See Roland G. Kent, "Assimilation and Dissimilation." *Language*, XII (1936), 246; Leonard Bloomfield, *Language* (New York: Henry Holt & Co., Inc., 1933), p. 372; E. H. Sturtevant, *Linguistic Change* (Chicago: University of Chicago Press, 1917), p. 49.

[sjʊr]; but the sequence [sj] required a more delicate adjustment than most speakers gave it.   Consequently, the tongue slipped further back for [s] and further forward for [j], perhaps through some intermediate stage like [ʃj] or [sç], until the two sounds came together at the position for [ʃ] and gave us our present pronunciation [ʃʊr].

A similar reciprocal assimilation has taken place in *vision* [ˈvɪʒən], from earlier [ˈvɪzjən].   In *issue* and a few similar words, Americans habitually use the assimilated [ˈɪʃu]; the most frequent British pronunciation seems to be the unassimilated [ˈɪsju].[5] Similarly, the change from [hw] to [ʍ] in such a word as *when* is a reciprocal assimilation in which [ʍ] takes its adjustment of tongue and lips from [w] and its voiceless quality from [h].

### Assimilation and Voicing

From the direction of influence in the assimilative process we now turn to the nature and varieties of the physical changes. First, assimilation may produce a change in the voicing of consonants.   In *north* [nɔrθ] and *worth* [wɝθ], the final consonant is voiceless; but in *northern* [ˈnɔrðɚn] and *worthy* [ˈwɝði], the voiceless [θ] has been assimilated to the voiced [ð] by the voiced quality of the following vowels.   In *thieves* [θivz], in comparison with *thief* [θif], [v] results from an earlier assimilation to a vowel which is now no longer pronounced.

Instances of the change from a voiced to a voiceless consonant are more numerous.   The inflectional ending *-ed*, as we have seen in Chapter 6, ends in [d] so long as the ending remains a separate syllable and [d] follows either of the voiced sounds [ɪ] or [ə], as in *heated* [ˈhitɪd] or *heeded* [ˈhidɪd].   But when in-

[5] See the 1956 edition of Daniel Jones, *An English Pronouncing Dictionary.*

flectional -ed becomes nonsyllabic, it remains [d] after voiced sounds, as in *begged* [bɛgd], but assimilates to the voiceless [t] after voiceless consonants, as in *baked* [bekt].

Similarly, inflectional -es continues to end in [z] when the ending is syllabic, as in *guesses* ['gɛsɪz]. When reduced to non-syllabic status, inflectional -es and -s remain [z] after voiced sounds, as in *begs* [bɛgz], but assimilate to the voiceless [s] after voiceless consonants, as in *bakes* [beks].

A double assimilation takes place in the phrase *used to*. The verb *used* [juzd] has been assimilated to [just] by the following [t], and has acquired the meaning "formerly accustomed." The unassimilated pronunciation, with looser juncture, has been kept for the meaning "utilized." Thus, *the pen he used to* ['just:ə] *write with* means the pen he was accustomed to write with; *the pen he used to* [juzd tə] *write with* means the pen he utilized for writing.

Something similar occurs in the phrases *have to* and *has to* when they denote compulsion. *That is all I have to* ['hæftə] *do* means that that is all I am compelled to do. *That is all I have to* [hæv tə] *do* means that that is all I have on hand at the moment to do. In the sentence, *That is all he has to do,* ['hæstə] and [hæz tə] indicate the same distinction in meaning. The form ['just:ə] is fully established in standard speech; the assimilated ['hæftə] and ['hæstə], despite their usefulness, still impress some conservatives as substandard.

A few minor instances, such as the occasional assimilation of *width* [wɪdθ] to [wɪtθ] and *breadth* [brɛdθ] to [brɛtθ], complete the list of changes from voiced to voiceless consonants. There is an element of unvoicing in the assimilation of [sj] to [ʃ] in *sure* and of [tj] to [tʃ] in *tune*, but these assimilations are primarily positional, and we shall examine them next.

## Positional Assimilation

The substitution of a voiceless consonant for a voiced, or vice versa, involves, of course, a change in the position of the vocal bands. Ordinarily, however, we think of positional change in terms of the speech mechanism in the mouth. Under this category we find several important classes.

One class consists of assimilations which often occur when [j] follows certain consonants. As arleady noted in Chapter 14, [j] is stable in the initial position, as in *unit* ['junɪt]; after labial consonants, as in *pew* [pju], *beauty* ['bjuti], and *music* ['mjuzɪk]; after labiodentals, as in *few* [fju] and *view* [vju]; after velars, as in *cube* [kjub], and *argue* ['ɑrgju]; and after [h], as in *human* ['hjumən]. [j] may be partly or completely unvoiced after voiceless consonants, as in *pew*, *few*, *cube*, and *human*, but in none of the illustrative words of this paragraph is the position of the tongue affected by neighboring sounds, all of which are far enough away in the mouth to prevent interference.

After alveolar consonants, however, the shift to [j] is delicate and difficult. *Tune* [tjun] is likely to assimilate to [tʃun]; *duke* [djuk], to [dʒuk]; *assume* [ə'sjum], to [ə'ʃum]; and *presume* [prɪ'zjum], to [prɪ'ʒum]. The sequence [nj] is likely to assimilate to [ɲ], a palatal nasal intermediate between English [n] and [ŋ] which has phonemic status in the Romance languages. Thus *onion* ['ʌnjən] may, by reciprocal assimilation, change to ['ʌɲən], and *news* [njuz] to [ɲuz]. The reciprocal nature of this assimilation may be observed in the fact that [ɲ] takes its nasal quality from [n] and its palatal articulation from [j].

Similarly, the sequence [lj] is likely to assimilate to [ʎ], a palatal lateral which has phonemic status in Italian and Castilian Spanish. Thus *million* may, by reciprocal assimilation, change from ['mɪljən] to ['mɪʎən]; *lunatic*, from ['ljunətɪk] to ['ʎunətɪk].

The reciprocal nature of this assimilation may be observed in the fact that [ʎ] takes its lateral quality from [l] and its palatal articulation from [j].

In the Romance languages, the characteristic formation of [ɲ] and [ʎ] is the contact of the front, not the tip, of the tongue with the hard palate; the tip remains lowered. When used in English, these sounds sometimes have the tip lowered, as in the Romance languages, but sometimes have the tip, blade, and front of the tongue in contact with the roof of the mouth all the way from the gum ridge to the fore part of the hard palate. [ʎ] requires a delicate contact between tongue and hard palate, in order to assure adequate space at the sides for the sound to get out. If this delicate contact is broken, as it often is, the tongue is then in the position for a simple [j]. Hence *million*, when pronounced ['mɪʎən], is likely to change to ['mɪjən].⁶ The reduction of [ʎ] to [j] is not assimilative, but a by-product of assimilation.

The assimilations based on the instability of [j] may, of course, be avoided if the speaker considers avoidance worth while. If, in common with most Americans, he pronounces the instable words without [j], as in *tune* [tun], *duke* [duk], *lunatic* ['lunətɪk], *news* [nuz], *assume* [ə'sum], and *presume* [prɪ'zum], the assimilative problem does not arise. The unassimilated forms with [j], in *tune* [tjun], *duke* [djuk], and *news* [njuz] are common in natural speech only in the South; elsewhere in the United States they are largely limited to artificial speech. The sequence [lj], as in *lunatic*, does not occur in the United States except in artificial speech.

In unstressed syllables, however, the assimilated forms are normal.   Present-day speech has *nature* ['netʃɚ] from earlier

⁶ The change from [ʎ] to [j] is also a characteristic of American Spanish, in contrast to Castilian. See T. Navarro Tomas, *El Idioma Español en el Cine Parlante*, Madrid, 1930.

[ˈnetjɚ], *grandeur* [ˈgrændʒɚ] from earlier [ˈgrændjɚ], *pressure* [ˈprɛʃɚ] from earlier [ˈprɛsjɚ], and *measure* [ˈmɛʒɚ] from earlier [ˈmɛzjɚ].

### Assimilation of Nasal Consonants

Another class consists of those assimilations which involve a change in the place of articulation of nasal consonants. We have already seen this class illustrated in such derivatives of Latin *cum* as *compound* [ˈkɑmˌpɑʊnd], *combine* [kəmˈbaɪn], and *comfort* [ˈkʌmfɚt], which retain the unassimilated [m] before labials and labiodentals; and *content* [kənˈtɛnt], *condemn* [kənˈdɛm], *constant* [ˈkɑnstənt], *conquer* [ˈkɑŋkɚ], and *congress* [ˈkɑŋgrəs], which illustrate assimilation of the nasal to the place of articulation of the following consonant.

Other illustrations in this class usually depend on the loss of an "insulating" sound. After the loss, an instable sequence results, and assimilation is likely to take place. Thus if *open* [ˈopən] loses [ə] and becomes [ˈopn], it is likely to assimilate to [ˈopm], the alveolar [n] giving way to the labial [m] under the influence of the labial [p]. Similar assimilations may take place in *ribbon*, which may change from [ˈrɪbən] to [ˈrɪbn], and then assimilate to [ˈrɪbm]; in *bacon*, which may change from [ˈbekən] to [ˈbekn], and then assimilate to [ˈbekŋ]; in *wagon*, which may change from [ˈwægən] to [ˈwægn], and then assimilate to [ˈwægŋ]; in *grandpa*, which may change from [ˈgrændpɑ], to [ˈgrænpɑ], and then assimilate to [ˈgræmpɑ]; and in *pumpkin*, which may change from [ˈpʌmpkɪn] to [ˈpʌmkɪn], and then assimilate to [ˈpʌŋkɪn].

### Partial Assimilations

Most of the assimilations discussed thus far are readily audible, even to speakers with little or no phonetic training.

Most of them involve shifts from one phoneme to another. There remain some minor assimilations in which the change is slight enough not always to be audible to the untrained listener. Most of these changes involve only a shift from one allophone to another. Thus the [g] of *goose* has the normal contact of the back of the tongue with the soft palate. The [g] of *geese*, however, is a different allophone, partially assimilated to the front vowel [i] which follows it, and articulated farther forward in the mouth, sometimes as far forward as the back part of the hard palate. In *sing*, [ŋ] is similarly assimilated to a more forward allophone by the preceding front vowel [ɪ]; in *song*, a more backward allophone of [ŋ] follows the back vowel [ɔ]. The [t] of *eighth* [etθ], the [d] of *width* [wɪdθ], the [n] of *tenth* [tɛnθ], and the [l] of *health* [hɛlθ] are not ordinarily the usual alveolar allophones, but are usually assimilated to the dental position in anticipation of the dental [θ].

In initial sequences of voiceless consonants followed by voiced semivowels, the voicing of the semivowel may be slightly delayed by assimilation to the preceding voiceless consonant. This assimilation is most noticeable after voiceless fricatives. *Sweet* [swit] may become [sʍwit] or [sʍit]; *thwart* [θwɔrt] may become [θʍwɔrt] or [θʍɔrt]. *Sled, frame, flame, throw,* and *shred* may have voiceless or partly voiceless [l] and [r] instead of the usual voiced allophones.

After voiceless stops, the assimilative unvoicing is a little less noticeable, but *twice* [twaɪs] may become [tʍwaɪs] or [tʍaɪs]; *quart* [kwɔrt] may become [kʍwɔrt] or [kʍɔrt]; and *play, pray, tray, clay,* and *crane* may have partly or completely unvoiced allophones of [l] or [r]. *Smell* and *snail* may have partly unvoiced [m] or [n].

Except for the idiomatic phrases *used to, have to,* and *has to,* single words have been used to illustrate the assimilative process.

But assimilation may also take place at the junction of words, whenever the words are spoken without a pause. Thus we may hear such assimilations as *Miss Shaw* [mɪʃ ˈʃɔ], *Miss Young* [mɪʃ ˈjʌŋ] or [mɪʃ ˈʃʌŋ], *did you?* [ˈdɪdʒə], *was sure* [wəʒ ˈʃʊr] or [wəʃ ˈʃʊr], and *in court* [ɪŋ ˈkɔrt]. Though the social status of some of these illustrations is not secure, it must be realized that they look stranger than they sound.

The question of standard speech is, as we have seen, quite distinct from that of assimilation. The latter is a phonetic process, continually taking place, and restricted at times by conservative opinions. Many of the results of the assimilative process have been accepted on the standard level, immediately or eventually. Some of the assimilated forms characterized in this chapter as substandard may come to be accepted as standard in the future. Others may continue indefinitely to carry the stigma of sub-standard usage. The classification of particular assimilations as standard or substandard is therefore but one aspect of the question of standard or substandard speech in general. Questions of standards involve the judgments of speakers and critics of the language; they must not be confused with the "natural history" of the language itself.

## EXERCISES

1. The following phonetic transcriptions include one or more examples of assimilation in each word. Analyze the assimilations by stating, in each case, the sound which has been changed by assimilation, (2) the sound to which it has been changed, (3) the sound responsible for the change, (4) the reason why this sound was able to effect the change, and (5) the direction of influence: progressive, regressive, or reciprocal:

strɛnθ, ˈprɛʃɚ, ˈsʌðɚn, dɪˈsɪʒən, ˈkʌbɚd, ˈkɑŋkɚ, brɛtθ, nɪ ˈjɔrk, ˈnuspepɚ, ˈhɔrʃʃu, ˈpʌŋkɪn, ˈræzbɛri, ˈɛdʒəket, ˈgræmmɑ, ˈhæŋkətʃɪf, mɪsɪʒ ˈʃɛldən, ˈgɑzlɪŋ, lovz, ˈkrɪtʃɚ.

2. Make a phonetic transcription of your own pronunciation of the following words and phrases, and comment on any assimilations you find:

McGregor, paths, in case of fire, questionable, sweater, five dollars, buckwheat, cash sales, immature, soldier.

# CHAPTER 20

# Other Phonetic Changes

## Dissimilation

Though the terms assimilation and dissimilation suggest parallel processes,[1] there are differences, and dissimilation affects fewer sounds than assimilation. Dissimilation may be defined as the process by which the awkward repetition of a sound is obviated by the omission or change of the sound in one of its occurrences. Thus most Americans pronounce *survive* [sɚˈvaɪv], but many of those who retain [ɚ] in this word also pronounce *surprise* [səˈpraɪz]. This apparent inconsistency in the pronunciation of the first syllables indicates dissimilation; the [r]-coloring of [ɚ] in *surprise* may be lost by the dissimilative effect of [r] in the second syllable. Since the second syllable of *survive* has no [r], no dissimilation occurs. Of course if a speaker pronounces *survive* [səˈvaɪv] and *surprise* [səˈpraɪz], we are justified in inferring

---

[1] See Roland G. Kent, "Assimilation and Dissimilation," *Language*, XII (1936), 245–58; E. H. Sturtevant, *Linguistic Change* (Chicago: University of Chicago Press, 1917), pp. 52–54. The best account is that of Albert J. Carnoy, "The Real Nature of Dissimilation," *Transactions of the American Philological Association*, Vol. XLIX (1918), pp. 101–13.

that his speech derives from eastern New England, the New York City area, or the South, and that his consistent loss of [r]-coloring before consonants is a regional feature.

Other common illustrations of the dissimilative loss of [r] or the dissimilative change from [ɚ] to [ə] may be found on both the standard and substandard levels, as in the pronunciations *governor* [ˈgʌvənɚ], *thermometer* [θəˈmɑmətɚ], *particular* [pə-ˈtɪkjələ], *library* [ˈlaɪbɛri], *secretary* [ˈsɛkətɛri], *stenographer* [stəˈnɑgəfɚ], *professor* [pəˈfɛsɚ], and *February* [ˈfɛbjuɛri] or [ˈfɛbuɛri].[2]

Other consonants may occasionally be lost by dissimilation: [n], as in [ˈgʌvɚmənt] for *government* and [ənˈvaɪrəmənt] for *environment*; [l], as in [fuˈfɪl] for *fulfill*; and [d], as in [ˈkænədet] for *candidate*. By dissimilation, one sound may be substituted for another: [l] for [r], as in *pilgrim*, derived ultimately from Latin *peregrinum*; and in *turtle*, from Latin *turtur*. In *colonel* [ˈkɚnəl], [ɚ] results from the dissimilation of the first [l], which now survives only in the spelling; the second [l], which effected the dissimilation, survives in both spelling and pronunciation. French *colonel* [kɔlɔnɛl] is not dissimilated; Spanish *coronel* [kɔrɔˈnɛl] is dissimilated. English *colonel* combines the dissimilated pronunciation with the spelling which represents the un-dissimilated form.

Illustrations which combine more than one instance of dissimilation in a single word are uncommon, but may be found. Thus Latin *marmor* became *marbre* in French, with the second [m] dissimilated to [b]; and became *marble*, with the second [r] dissimilated to [l] when the word was taken from French into English. English *particularly* is sometimes [pəˈtɪkjɚli], with dis-

[2] For additional illustrations see George Hempl, "Loss of *R* in English through Dissimilation," *Dialect Notes*, I (1893), 279-81.

similation of both [ɚ] and [l]. *Antarctic* is sometimes [ænˈɑrtɪk], with dissimilation of both [t] and [k].

Many of the instances of dissimilation are substandard, like those noted for *secretary, stenographer,* and *library.* Others, like those noted for *pilgrim, marble,* and *turtle,* are not only standard, but have been accepted so long that present-day spelling hides the historical evidence of the dissimilative process. The more usual direction of dissimilation, like that of assimilation, is regressive; that is, the first occurrence of the sound in the word is more likely to be dissimilated than the second.

## Metathesis

Metathesis [məˈtæθəsɪs] is a reversal of the order of sounds. Historical instances have usually had the spelling altered to conform to the phonetic change, as in *bird,* from Old English *bridd.* English *ask* had two forms of the infinitive in Old English, *ascian* and *acsian,* one a metathesized form of the other. *Ascian* leads to present-day [æsk]; *acsian,* to present-day [æks].

Metathesis is relevant to present-day speech chiefly because of its dubious occurrence in prefixes which include *r*: [prɛspɚˈleʃən] for *perspiration* from earlier [pɛrspəˈreʃən]; [priˈfɔrm] for *perform*; [pɚˈnɑʊns], from earlier [pərˈnɑʊns], for *pronounce.*

In *pretty* [ˈprɪti], the stressed vowel sometimes changes to the central vowel of [ˈprəti], which may then metathesize to [ˈpɚti] and then simplify to [ˈpɝti]. In [ˈhɪmpətɪzəm] for *hypnotism* we have a combination of metathesis and assimilation. Occasionally the metathesized sounds are separated by intervening sounds, as in *tradegy* for *tragedy.* Though metathesis does not occur with great frequence, it is sometimes the clue to sound changes which would otherwise baffle the analyst.

## Miscellaneous Loss of Sounds

Sounds are added or lost in a variety of ways. The history of English shows a complete loss of some sounds. The spelling *gh* in *thought* is the orthographic survival of a voiceless velar fricative [x], now heard only in such regional words as Irish *lough* [lɒx] and Scotch *loch* [lɒx]. In *light*, *gh* is the orthographic survival of the corresponding voiceless palatal fricative [ç], which survives in Scotch *licht* [lɪçt]. Elsewhere in present-day English, [ç] occurs only as an occasional result of reciprocal assimilation between [h] and [j], as in [ˈçumən] for *human* [ˈhjumən]; or as a weakened and probably dissimilated allophone of [k], as in [ˈtɛçnɪkəl] for *technical* [ˈtɛknɪkəl]. Otherwise in American and southern British English the earlier [x] and [ç] have gone completely, as in *thought* and *light*; or have changed to [f], as in *cough* and *laugh*. In rare instances they have changed to [g], as in *Pittsburgh*; or to a vowel, as in *borough*; both of which represent derivatives of Old English *burh* [burx].

The development of English [ŋ] as an independent phoneme also results from the loss of a sound. *Sing* was originally [sɪŋg], and [ŋ] was originally the allophone of [n] used before velar consonants. The loss of [g] left [ŋ] as the phoneme which differentiates *sing* from *sin*. Similarly, the final cluster [-mb] has been simplified by the loss of [b], as in *climb* and *tomb*.

The inflectional endings *-es* and *-ed* originally had a vowel in all phonetic contexts. Today the vowel has been lost in all contexts except where a cluster of consonants unpronounceable in English would result, as in *heated* [ˈhitɪd], *needed* [ˈnidɪd], *faces* [ˈfesɪz], *phases* [ˈfezɪz], *dishes* [ˈdɪʃɪz], *ditches* [ˈdɪtʃɪz], and *bridges* [ˈbrɪdʒɪz]. In short, the loss of sounds, which inevitably seems like unwarranted carelessness at the time the loss is taking place, may come later to be considered perfectly normal.

In present-day speech, complex consonant clusters often simplify: [sts] often loses [t], leaving a single prolonged [s] in place of the cluster, as in [lɪs:] for *lists* and [tɛs:] for *tests*, the latter a significant contrast with *Tess* [tɛs]. When [t] occurs between consonants it may weaken and drop out, as in the successive stages in the eroding of *mountain* from [ˈmɑʊntən] to [ˈmɑʊntn], [ˈmɑʊnˀn], and eventually to [mɑʊn:].

When [θ] comes between consonants it often drops out, as in [ˈɪsməs], which is now the standard pronunciation of *isthmus*; and as in [mʌns] for *months*, [fɪfs] for *fifths*, and [ets] for *eighths*, in which the social status of the simplified forms is debatable. Other simplified clusters may be illustrated by [æst] or [æsk] for *asked* [æskt], [fæks] for *facts* [fækts], [twɛlθ] for *twelfth* [twɛlfθ], [læn] for *land* [lænd], and [filz] for *fields* [fildz]. The speaker needs to be on the alert when pronouncing such clusters. Sometimes the simplification may pass unnoticed, but frequently it may attract unfavorable attention.

### Miscellaneous Addition of Sounds

To bring a final continuant consonant to a more definite termination, speakers sometimes add a final stop. English *sound* from Latin *sonare* illustrates the addition of a [d] which has become standard; the same addition in *drownd* for *drown* is still considered substandard. The pattern of sound development is the same in *sound* and *drownd*; the reaction of the populace is different. The [t] of *against* is intrusive in the same way, but has become acceptable; the [t] of [wʌnst] for *once* and of [əˈkrɔst] for *across* is likewise intrusive, but has never been accepted on the standard level. Why the public should have accepted some added sounds and not others is unknown. Intrusion in the middle of a cluster is ordinarily not noticeable; consequently it often passes readily into standard usage, as in [wɔrmpθ] for *warmth* and [lɛŋkθ] for *length*.

Comparison of *sense* with *cents*, and *false* with *faults*, illustrates the falling together of originally distinct clusters. As the clusters [-nts] and [-lts] of *cents* and *faults* have weakened, [t] has intruded into the clusters [-ns] and [-ls] of *sense* and *false*, so that homophonous pairs have developed. Only the laboratory phonetician, with instruments more sensitive than the human ear, can rightly decide whether to record both *sense* and *cents* as [sɛns] or both as [sɛnts]; whether to record both *false* and *faults* as [fɔls] or both as [fɔlts]. For the practical purposes of daily speaking we distinguish *sense* from *cents*, and *false* from *faults*, in the same way that we distinguish *see* from *sea*, by context, not by sound.

On the whole, the addition of sounds creates fewer problems than the omission. Added sounds are usually obvious, and are consequently likely to be normalized in terms of contemporary standards. The omission of sounds is less likely to be noticed, and less likely to be changed. [drɑund] for *drown* is more likely to be noticed than [sɑun] for *sound*.

## Isolative Changes

The phonetic changes thus far discussed are sometimes grouped under the heading of *combinative changes*, since all depend on the presence of other particular sounds in the context for the changes to become effective. In contrast, we have certain changes in the history of English which are independent of neighboring sounds, and which consequently are known as *isolative changes*. The principal type, and the only one we need to consider here, is the series of modifications of the long tense vowels from the Old English period to the present. The essential modifications may be summarized in the accompanying table:

| Old English Vowel | Old English Word | Modern English Vowel or Diphthong | Modern English Word |
|---|---|---|---|
| [æ:] | sæ | [i] | sea [si] |
| [e:] | seon | [i] | see [si] |
| [ɑ] | nama | [e] | name [nem] |
| [ɑ:] | stan | [o] | stone [ston] |
| [o:] | gos | [u] | goose [gus] |
| [i:] | is | [aɪ] | ice [aɪs] |
| [u:] | mus | [ɑʊ] | mouse [mɑʊs] |

The changes illustrated in this table have taken place very gradually, and no completely satisfactory explanation of the causes has yet been made. The most satisfactory explanation is that of C. M. Lotspeich,[3] in essentially the following chain of reasoning:

1. The English linguistic tendency is to move the stress forward, in word, syllable, and sound. Hence the English tendency to diphthongize is a stressing of the beginning, rather than the ending, of a vowel.

2. When the muscles which open the jaw relax, as they do at the end of a long vowel, the angle of the jaw becomes narrower, and the tongue assumes a higher position.

3. In accordance with these two principles, English vowels tend to be diphthongized by gliding into a higher tongue position.

[3] "The Cause of Long Vowel Changes in English," *Journal of English and Germanic Philology*, XX (1921), 208–12. For less satisfactory explanations, see Janet R. Aiken, *Why English Sounds Change* (New York: The Ronald Press Co., 1929); and George K. Zipf, "Relative Frequency as a Determinant of Phonetic Change," *Harvard Studies in Classical Philology*, Vol. XL (1929), pp. 1–95.

As English recessive accent pushes the higher tongue position further forward in the word, the whole vowel tends to be raised into a high tongue position.

4. As the jaw and tongue moved upward to reach the Old English high vowels [i] and [u], voice tended to begin before the full height had been achieved; thus [i] and [u] might be diphthongized as [ɪi] and [ʊu]. If the subsequent development of these sounds carried them, as we have reason to believe it did, from [ɪi] to [eɪ], [ɜɪ], and [aɪ], and from [ʊu] to [oʊ], [ɜʊ], and [ɑʊ], such developments can be considered a continuation of the same tendency.

Lotspeich's explanation has much to recommend it. The development within the last century or so of new sets of favored allophones suggests that the process is continuing in present-day speech. During this period [ɪi] has developed at the expense of [i], [eɪ] at the expense of [e], [oʊ] at the expense of [o], and [ʊu] at the expense of [u]; it requires no great feat of imagination to envisage a period in which the monophthongal allophones will have died out completely, and when the stage will be set for a new shift.

The sound changes discussed in this and the preceding chapter should have given you a new perspective on language, and a willingness to accept the fact of change. School training in foreign languages, and even in your native language, usually fails, for understandable and practical reasons, to give you this perspective. In the high-school study of Latin, for instance, limitations of time made it essential that one particular type of Latin should be studied: the sophisticated literary type of the late republican and early imperial period. There was no time to study the development of Latin before Cicero and Vergil, nor to study the development of literary Latin into the medieval and modern Latin of the Roman Catholic Church, nor to study the development of popular Latin into Italian, French, and the other modern Romance languages.

Similarly, the school teaching of English must be limited to that of a particular type and time. There are not enough hours in the curriculum to study the changes in patterns of sounds, grammatical structure, and vocabulary from King Alfred to the present. Nor are most high-school teachers, whose training has been more literary than linguistic, capable of guiding you in such a study.

The result is that you, as a student, often gain the impression that language is something fixed and immutable, that the study of language consists in learning certain rules of linguistic behavior, rather than of understanding the patterns of something that is alive and changing. If this has been your impression, it is to be hoped that these two chapters have helped you overcome it.

*CHAPTER 21*

# Regional Variations
# in American Pronunciation

In the growth of the United States from the few sparsely inhabited settlements on the Atlantic seaboard in the seventeenth century to the continental size and population of the twentieth, some factors have worked for uniformity in pronunciation, others for variety. In contrast to the great national languages of Europe, even in contrast to the English of the British Isles, American English shows surprising uniformity. Differences which indicate social level, education, or wealth may show in vocabulary and grammatical usage, but less so than in the corresponding segments of the British population.

Regional differences in pronunciation are less marked than in the much smaller territory and smaller population of the British Isles. Alabama and Maine can usually understand each other without much trouble, though each may think the other a bit quaint. Up and down the Atlantic coast we may observe striking differences in pronunciation,[1] but further inland the

---

[1] See my article, "The Sound of US 1," *Town & Country Magazine*, January, 1954.

differences become blurred.  Over large areas, from the Connecticut valley to the Oregon coast, for instance, differences are so slight that casual listeners rarely notice them at all.  For variations in American pronunciation we must think in terms of regional standards, and only occasionally in terms of narrowly localized dialects.

During the Colonial period, the foundations of most of the later diversities in American pronunciation were laid.[2]  Though the details are complex and obscure, we know that the early settlers of the New England coast and the Virginia Tidewater came largely from the south of England, and that those who settled Pennsylvania and southern New Jersey came in larger proportions from the north of England.  Thus some differences in American speech represented differences in British speech from the outset.  Later settlers reflected later usage in the British Isles.  We know that the stream of migration westward from Pennsylvania and the southern coastal settlements was supplemented by the arrival of the Scotch and Scotch-Irish, whose speech was similar to that of the north of England.  Greet[3] has traced the migrations from western New England through upper New York, Ohio, Michigan, and Iowa, to the farming communities of the great plains; the migrations from Pennsylvania down the Ohio valley and, in a different stream, through the Shenandoah valley to the southern mountains, the plains of

[2] For greater detail, see Hans Kurath, "The Origin of the Dialectal Differences in Spoken American English," *Modern Philology*, XXV (1928), 385–95; his *Handbook of the Linguistic Geography of New England* (Providence: Brown University, 1939), chap. iii; and his *Word Geography of the Eastern United States* (Ann Arbor: University of Michigan Press, 1949). See also G. P. Krapp, *The English Language in America*, 2 vols. (New York: The Century Co., 1925); and Norman Eliason, *Tarheel Talk* (Chapel Hill: University of North Carolina Press, 1956).

[3] W. C. Greet, "A Standard American Language?" *New Republic*, XCV (1938), 68–70.

Texas, and the cattle country to the north; and the migrations from the coastal South[4] across the Gulf States to eastern Texas.

During the century in which these migrations were filling the west, the original settlements maintained a contact with the British Isles which the western settlers lost. Ships which arrived in Boston, Baltimore, and Charleston brought new fashions from across the Atlantic, and new fashions in speech arrived on the tongues of travelers. The pioneer in Ohio or Tennessee heard virtually nothing of this. New fashions in speech rarely reached him, and such changes as he made in his pronunciation were the unconscious gradual kind that always take place in a living language. Some of the present differences between the speech of the Atlantic Coast and that of the inland areas can be attributed to the greater rate of change which took place along the coast.

Even so, the changes brought about in the coastal types of pronunciation were by no means uniform, though a certain substratum represents the earlier coastal uniformity.[5] The New England coast changed most. The South and the area which had New York City for its cultural and commercial center changed somewhat less. The Middle Atlantic area, from central New Jersey to Baltimore, changed least, and has remained the closest of any of the coastal types to the speech of the interior.

Substantial Scotch and Scotch-Irish immigration to western Pennsylvania produced pronunciations which can be heard to this day.[6] Immigration of Scotch and Scotch-Irish into the

[4] From here on, references to points of the compass will be geographical if they begin with lower-case letters, but will refer to speech areas if they begin with capital letters. Thus references to the south or to eastern New England are geographical; references to the South or to Eastern New England refer specifically to speech areas.

[5] See W. C. Greet, "A Record from Lubec, Maine, and Remarks on the Coastal Type," *American Speech*, VI (1931), 397–403, especially 401–3.

[6] See I. C. C. Graham, *Colonists from Scotland* (Ithaca: Cornell University Press, 1956), especially the section which begins on p. 18.

southern mountains, and the relative isolation of the mountain communities, produced a type of pronunciation akin to that of western Pennsylvania. Immigration from western Pennsylvania down the Ohio valley and across the Mississippi established the Central Midland type of pronunciation. The whole complex of Midland types, ranging from Middle Atlantic through Western Pennsylvania, Southern Mountain, and Central Midland, to the Northwest, represents a mixture of northern and southern features which will be discussed later. The South also represents a number of separate types; Norfolk and Mobile, for instance, are different in speech, though both are demonstrably Southern. Similarly, the Northern areas, from Eastern New England through the North Central area, have some features in common, with other distinguishing differences.

Other areas require special mention. New York City and its tributary territory comprise a large population in a small area. As described later, its speech will be found to combine features characteristic of all the other areas, though its kinship with the South is the more notable for its geographical separation. One trap into which careless analysts of New York City speech regularly fall is the confusion of foreign pronunciations—English spoken in accordance with the phonemic patterns of the immigrant's native language—with the native regional pattern.[7] Confusion between [ŋ] and [ŋg], for example, is not a feature of New York City English, but of the imperfect English of those immigrant groups who do not have [ŋ] as an independent phoneme in their native languages.

The Southwest Coastal area is mixed, but has close ties with the North Central area, as does the Oregon coast, though the rest of Oregon is part of the Northwest. In the South, the Virginia

---

[7] See my article, "Jewish Dialect and New York Dialect," *American Speech*, Vol. 7 (1932), pp. 321–326.

Tidewater, the Outer Banks of North Carolina, the Charleston area, and the New Orleans area are important subareas. Florida is mixed. North and west Florida are Deep South. Central Florida represents an extension of Southern Mountain. The Miami area has strong overtones of New York City. The other resort areas in Florida represent the North Central area more than any other. Both Florida and southern California represent large growths of population at the expense of other areas. There has not yet been time either for the new population to become assimilated to the local type, or for the development of a compromise type.

## Phonetic Criteria of Regional Types
### [r], [ɝ], and [ɚ]

The most striking difference between the various regional pronunciations, and the difference around which the most lively, though inconclusive, arguments have revolved, is the nature of the sounds which correspond to the letter *r*. In many words, of course, all regions agree: in the pronunciation of [r] in words like *red, green, crow, pray, break, shred, through*, and *from*.[8] In most American speech [r] may be heard between vowels within a word, as in *very* [ˈvɛri] and *Carolina* [kærəˈlaɪnə], but in some parts of the South [ˈvɛːɪ] and [kæəˈlaɪnə], [kæːˈlaɪnə], or [kəˈlaɪnə] may often be heard. With this exception, we pronounce *r* as [r], in all parts of the country, when a vowel follows immediately in the same word.

When, however, *r* comes at the end of a word, or before a consonant, wide differences in pronunciation exist. In *far* and

---

[8] Loss of [r] from *through* and *from* is, however, a feature of the illiterate speech recorded in such books as Julia Peterkin's *Black April* and DuBose Heyward's *Porgy*. Some Southerners maintain, moreover, that such pronunciations may be heard on all levels of Southern speech.

*farm*, Eastern New England and the South customarily omit [r], and pronounce *far* as [fɑ:] and *farm* as [fɑ:m].⁹ The normal pronunciations in the New York City area are also [fɑ:] and [fɑ:m], but [fɑr] and [fɑrm] have more currency than in Eastern New England or the South.¹⁰ In the rest of the country, [fɑr] and [fɑrm] are normal.

In words like *fear* and *fierce*, *scare* and *scarce*, *sure* and *surely*, the predominant pronunciations in the South and in Eastern New England replace [r] with [ə]: *fear* [fɪə], *fierce* [fɪəs], *scare* [skɛə], *scarce* [skɛəs], *sure* [ʃuə], and *surely* [ˈʃuəli]. The New York City area usually follows this pattern, but sometimes pronounces these words [fɪ:], [fɪ:s], [skɛ:], [skɛ:s], [ʃu:], and [ˈʃu:li]. The New York City area sometimes retains [r]; the Southern Mountain area sometimes loses it. In the rest of the country, the almost universal pronunciations are [fɪr], [fɪrs], [skɛr], [skɛrs], [ʃur], and [ˈʃurli].

In words of the type of *for* and *form*, Eastern New England and the South usually have [fɔ:] and [fɔ:m], occasionally [fɔə] and [fɔəm]. The New York City area has [fɔə] and ]fɔəm] most frequently, [fɔ:] and [fɔ:m] almost as frequently, [fɔr] and [fɔrm] least frequently. Elsewhere [fɔr] and [fɔrm] are almost universal.

In words like *four*, *force*, and *board*, the same regional variation in the use of [r] occurs. In these words, moreover, there is a regional variation in the choice of vowel phonemes, a variation which will be discussed later in this chapter.

When [r], [ɚ], and [ɚ] come at the end of a word, before a following word which begins with a vowel, and where there is no pause between words, Eastern New England and the New

⁹ No account has been taken here of differences in vowel quality, which will be discussed later in this chapter.

¹⁰ Here, as elsewhere in this chapter, undocumented statements about regional usage are based on my private files, which hold detailed data about the speech of over 14,000 speakers from all parts of the country.

York City area normally retain the [r]-coloring, as in *far, far away* [ˈfɑːˈfɑrəˈwe] and *better and better* [ˈbɛtɚənˈbɛtə], but omit the [r]-coloring at the end of a phrase or before a consonant. These same pronunciations may be heard in the South, but the more usual Southern pronunciations are [ˈfɑːˈfɑːəˈwe] and [ˈbɛtəənˈbɛtə]. Eastern New England and the New York City area characteristically use [r]-coloring as a link between vowels; the South does so less frequently. Similarly, Eastern New England and the New York City area frequently use intrusive [r]-coloring, as in [lɔr] for *law* and [aɪˈdiɚ] for *idea*; the South rarely does. Most speakers in the area in which intrusive [r]-coloring is frequent regard it as substandard.

The [r]-colored vowels [ɝ] and [ɚ] follow much the same regional pattern as [r]. In Eastern New England, [ɜ] and [ə] characteristically replace [ɝ] and [ɚ], except before vowels, as in [ˈmɜmə] for *murmur*. In the South, [ˈmɜmə] is normal, but in the Deep South, from Savannah to New Orleans, and occasionally as far west as eastern Texas, it may give way to [ˈmɜɪmə]; in the upper South the diphthongal allophone is much less frequent. In the New York City area, [ˈmɜɪmə] is frequent,[11] but seems to be giving way to [ˈmɜmɚ] and [ˈmɜmə] because in the last generation many New Yorkers have come to regard the diphthong as comically substandard. No such emotional attitude exists in the Deep South, where the diphthong is taken for granted.

The diphthong [ɜɪ] is restricted to preconsonantal positions in root words. It occurs before the [d] in *third*, but not in the final position in *purr*, nor before the inflectional [d] of *purred*.

---

[11] See A. F. Hubbell, "'Curl' and 'Coil' in New York City," *American Speech*, XV (1940), 374–76; Henry Alexander, "Soiving the Ersters," *American Speech*, I (1926), 294–95; see also the table in my article, "Pronunciation in Downstate New York," *American Speech*, XVII (1942), 150–51.

## Vowels before r

Several regional variations involve differences in the quality of the vowels which precede *r*. Perhaps the most characteristic feature of Eastern New England speech is the use of [a:] in such words as *far* [fa:] and *farm* [fa:m]. Along the Maine coast the variation may be almost as extreme as [fæ:] and [fæ:m], reflecting the eighteenth-century [fær] and [færm]. For much of Eastern New England, [a] is an independent phoneme, corresponding to the phoneme [ɑ] of other areas. In the North Central area, [a] also occurs with some frequency, generally as an allophone of [ɑ], as in *far* [far] and *farm* [farm].

In the New York City, Midland, and Southern areas, [ɑ] and [ɒ] are usual in such words, with more frequent use of [ɒ] as one goes further south. Thus *far* and *farm* may have [ɑr] or [ɒr] in the New York City and Midland areas. They may have [ɑ:] and [ɒ:] in the New York City area and the South. The western half of the United States generally has [ɑr], though there are local outcroppings of [ɒr], and along the Oregon coast there is some use of [ar].

The historical distinction between [ɔ] and [o] before [r], as in *horse* [hɔrs] and *hoarse* [hors] and similar pairs, has survived in some parts of the United States, but not in others. In words like *hoarse, four,* and *force,* Eastern New England usually has [hoəs], [foə], and [foəs], with [ə] almost prominent enough to form a second syllable. The South has [hoəs], [foə], and [foəs], with a much less prominent [ə] that sometimes drops out althogether, leaving [ho:s], [fo:], and [fo:s].[12] Some Southerners consider the omission of [ə] substandard. The various Midland areas generally

[12] See Hans Kurath, "*Mourning* and *Morning*," *Studies for William A. Read,* ed. N. M. Caffee and T. A. Kirby (Baton Rouge: Louisiana State University Press, 1940), pp. 166–73. See also Chapter 11 of the present volume.

retain the distinction between the two classes of words. In the Middle Atlantic area, especially in southeastern Pennsylvania, the contrast may go as far as [hɔrs] for *horse* and [hʊrs] for *hoarse*.

The New York City area usually has [hɔəs] for both *horse* and *hoarse*; [hɔːs] is somewhat less frequent; [hɔrs] is rare. The New York City area, like the south of England, has virtually lost the distinction between [ɔr] and [or]. The North Central and Southwest Coastal areas have largely lost the distinction too; characteristically they use [ɔr] for both *horse* and *hoarse*. Usage in the Northwest is mixed; some speakers retain the distinction; others have lost it.

In words like *barren*, *narrow*, and *marry*, the characteristic stressed vowel of the stretch of Atlantic and Gulf Coast is [æ]. In the North Central area the characteristic vowel is [ɛ], making *marry* homophonous with *merry*. Western Pennsylvania, except for the northern tier of counties bordering on New York, has [æ], but West Virginia, to the south, shows a strong infiltration of [ɛ]. In the rest of the Southern Mountains, as in the South, the predominant vowel is [æ], which infiltrates as far west as New Mexico. Throughout the rest of the Midland areas, and the rest of the territory beyond the Mississippi, as far south as Oklahoma, [ɛ] is characteristic, and in most places predominant. In Pennsylvania and the South, [a] occurs frequently, and [ɑ] occasionally, in words like *barren*, *narrow*, *marry*, and *barrel*.

In the South, words like *area*, *various*, and *Mary* characteristically have [e] in the stressed syllable, where the rest of the country has [ɛ] or [ɛː]. Thus the South may distinguish *merry* [ˈmɛrɪ], *marry* [ˈmærɪ], and *Mary* [ˈmerɪ]. The New York City area distinguishes *marry* [ˈmærɪ] from *merry* and *Mary* [ˈmɛrɪ]. The North Central area, much of the Central Midland, and most of the west use [ˈmɛri] for all three words. A narrow band of territory running west from southern New Jersey and south-eastern Pennsylvania, and a small area in and around Norfolk, Virginia, occasionally have [æ] in *various*. The Northwest has occasional traces of [ˈveriəs].

Before [r] and a following vowel, such words as *forest, foreign, horrid, orange*, and *warrant* illustrate a regional variation which is as clearly defined as any in American speech. Eastern New England, the New York City area, the Middle Atlantic area, and the South show a strong predominance of [ɑ], as in [ˈfɑrəst], [ˈɑrɪndʒ], and [ˈwɑrənt]. The Southern Mountain area, except for West Virginia, characteristically uses [ɑ], but there is some infiltration of [ɔ]. In the rest of the country, including West Virginia, [ˈfɔrəst], [ˈɔrɪndʒ], and [ˈwɔrənt] predominate. For this variation it is possible to draw a continuous line on the map from central Vermont to western Texas, separating [ɑ] on the east from [ɔ] on the west;[13] [ɒ] occurs sporadically, especially along the seam, but nowhere predominantly. In *borrow, sorrow, sorry*, and *tomorrow*, [ɑ] has superseded [ɔ] except for a few scattered speech islands. [təˈmɔro], for instance, predominates only in Vermont, the northernmost part of New York State, part of western Pennsylvania, and scattered areas in Minnesota and the Dakotas.[14]

A similar variation has developed in words like *hurry, worry*, and *courage*, in which the older forms [ˈhɜri], [ˈwɜri], and [ˈkɜ-rɪdʒ][15] survive in the west; and [ˈhʌri], [ˈwʌri], and [ˈkʌrɪdʒ] occur chiefly in the east and south. Though the evidence is not clear for

---

[13] See my article, "The Dialectal Significance of the Non-Phonemic Low-Back Vowel Variants before *R*," *Studies in Speech and Drama in Honor of Alexander M. Drummond* (Ithaca: Cornell University Press, 1945), pp. 244–54.

[14] See also Albert H. Marckwardt, "Middle English *o* in American English of the Great Lakes Area," *Papers of the Michigan Academy of Science, Art*, and *Letters*, Vol. XXVI (1940), pp. 561–71.

[15] [ɝ] may replace [ɜr] in any of these words.

all words of this type, [ˈhʌri] seems to predominate in Eastern New England, the New York City area, the Middle Atlantic area, Western Pennsylvania, and the South. Usage is divided in the Southern Mountains and the Central Midland. In the rest of the country, [ɜr] predominates. The line marking the boundary between predominant types agrees fairly closely with the western boundary of [ˈfɑrəst], except that it swings west of Western Pennsylvania, in which *forest* is predominantly [ˈfɔrəst], and *hurry*, predominatnly [ˈhʌri].[16] Elsewhere, [ˈhʌri] is the usual pronunciation of the speaker who habitually pronounces *forest* [ˈfɑrəst].

### The "Broad A"

In a group of about 150 words, usage varies among [æ], [a], and [ɑ].[17] In most of them the letter *a* precedes a voiceless fricative, [f], [θ], or [s], but not [ʃ], as in *glass*, *path*, and *staff*; or a nasal followed by a stop or a voiceless fricative, as in *example*, *demand*, *dance*, and *plant*; *aunt* and *laugh*, with *au* spellings, follow the same pattern of variation. In such words, Southern British normally has [ɑ]. Eastern New England sometimes has [ɑ] or, more frequently, [a]; many New Englanders, however, now use [æ].[18] Eastern Virginia also uses [ɑ] or [a], but, except in the Norfolk area, [æ] seems to be rapidly gaining in use.

For those in eastern Virginia or eastern New England who

[16] See my article, "Notes on the Pronunciation of *Hurry*," *American Speech*, XXI (1946), 112–15.

[17] See J. S. Kenyon, "Flat A and Broad A," *American Speech*, V (1930), 323–26; M. L. Hanley, "Observations on the Broad A," *Dialect Notes*, V (1925), 347–50; C. H. Grandgent, "Fashion and the Broad A," in his *Old and New* (Cambridge: Harvard University Press, 1920).

[18] My own data show [a] to be more frequent along the Maine coast than elsewhere. See also Virginia Rogers Miller, "Present-Day Use of the Broad A in Eastern Massachusetts," *Speech Monographs*, Vol. XX (1953), pp. 235–46.

consistently use [ɑ] or [a], there is a clear distinction between words like *path* [paθ] and those like *pat* [pæt]; the two vowels represent separate phonemes. The New York City area makes no such consistent distinction. The minority in New York City that uses [a] in *glass, path,* and *dance* also uses [a] in *bad, land, thanks,* and *fancy*; here [a] is a subordinate member of the [æ] phoneme.[19]

In the South, a diphthongal allophone frequently develops, as in *glass* [glæɪs], *dance* [dæɪns], and *bad* [bæɪd]. Increasing the tension and raising the tongue lead from [æɪ] to [eɪ], as in the Southern [keɪnt] for *can't.*

In the rest of the country, [æ] is normal for all such words. Scattered individuals have, however, cultivated [a] or [ɑ], the "broad *a*", usually inconsistently, for its supposed prestige value, a value which is wholly absent from its use in Eastern New England or Southern British.[20]

The word *rather* shows a wide variety of pronunciations, some of which have regional significance. Penzl's analysis[21] of the variations reported in the *Linguistic Atlas of New England* indicates that among older speakers [æ] is the predominant vowel of the stressed syllable. My own case records, mostly of college students, suggest that [ɑ] is frequent in the neighborhoods of Boston, New York City, and Philadelphia, and moderately frequent in the South; elsewhere [æ] predominantes. Occasional pronunciations with [ɛ] and [ʌ], rhyming with *feather* and

[19] See my articles, "Pronunciation in Downstate New York," *American Speech*, XVII (1942), especially pp. 32–34; "The Place of New York City in American Linguistic Geography," *Quarterly Journal of Speech*, XXXIII (1947), 314–20. See also Lois Strong, "Voyelles et Consonnes de New-York," *Revue de Phonétique*, Vol. V, p. 74.

[20] See C. H. Grandgent, "Fashion and the Broad A," *Old and New* (Cambridge: Harvard University Press, 1920); Herbert Penzl, "The Vowel-Phonemes in *Father, Man, Dance* in Dictionaries and New England Speech," *Journal of English and Germanic Philology*, XXXIX (1940), 13–32.

[21] Herbert Penzl, "The Vowel in *rather* in New England," *Publications of the Modern Language Association*, LIII (1938), 1186–92.

*brother*, probably represent patterns of restressing rather than regional variations.

## Vowels Before Velar Consonants

When the letter *o* comes before velar consonants, as in *log*, *mock*, *gong*, *honk*, and *donkey*, variation ranges between the limits of [ɑ] and [ɔ]. In *log*, [ɑ] predominates along the east coast from Boston to Philadelphia, and is all but universal in New York City. In the South, [ɔ] generally predominates over [ɒ] and [ɑ]; the South also has its diphthongal variants, [lɔʊg] and [lɒʊg]. Throughout most of the rest of the country, [lɔg] predominates. For *frog*, *hog*, and *fog*, the use of [ɑ] extends into western New England and upstate New York, where [a] is a common variant. *Bog* and *clog* have [ɑ] more often than *log*; *dog* has [ɔ] more often than *log*.

The vowel in *mock* and its derivatives is the only instance of a wide-range variation in a monosyllable before [k]. Other [k] words, such as *lock*, *rock*, and *stock*, have [ɑ] except as noted later in this chapter. In *mock*, however, [ɑ], [ɒ], and [ɔ] may all be heard in the North Central area; [ɔ] predominates in the South. *Mockingbird* has [ɔ] in all those regions in which the bird itself is common.

Before the velar nasal [ŋ], as in *gong* and *tongs*, variation is much the same as for *log*; [ɑ] is normal along the north Atlantic seaboard, [ɔ] elsewhere. Other orthographically similar words, like *song*, *wrong*, and *long*, have [ɔ] except as noted later in this chapter.

In general, *honk* and *donkey* follow the pattern of *log*, but with an added variation. In *donkey*, the older [ˈdʌŋki] predominates in southeastern Pennsylvania and southern New Jersey; it is frequent in the rest of New Jersey, in New York City, and in western Pennsylvania; and occasional in the Central Midland area and the South. For *honk*, an occasional [hʌŋk] occurs in the same areas as [ˈdʌŋki]. Elsewhere [ˈdɑŋki] and [hɑŋk] usually occur in the speech of those who say [lɑg]; [ˈdɔŋki] and [hɔŋk], in the speech of those who say [lɔg].

Other vowels occasionally vary before [g] or [ŋ]. Thus [æ], though normally lax, may become tense before [g] or [ŋ], and the tension may induce a higher tongue position, as in [beg] for *bag*, [ˈeŋgri] for *angry*, and [ˈeŋkɚ] for *anchor*. The same increase in tension may be noticed in the change of [ɛ] to [e] in such words as *egg*, *beg*, and *leg*.

### Vowels before [l]

The vowels of such words as *doll*, *solve*, *involve*, and *golf* vary between the limits of [ɑ] and [ɔ]. In *doll*, [ɔ] and [ɒ] are frequent in Eastern New England, except for Rhode Island and eastern Connecticut. [dɔl] predominates in Western Pennsylvania, and has a limited currency in the areas derived from Pennsylvania settlement. In the New York City area, the Middle Atlantic area, the South, and the Southwest Coastal area, [dɑl] is almost universal. In the North Central area, it may be [dɑl] or [dal].

In *solve* and *involve*, [ɔ] is less frequent in Eastern New England than in *doll*, but predominant in Western Pennsylvania. In *golf*, [ɔ] is frequent in upstate New York and Western Pennsylvania. In all these words, [ɒ] occurs occasionally in those areas in which [ɔ] predominates, less frequently in those in which [ɑ] predominates.

Before [l], [æ] occasionally shifts to [a], as in [ˈvali] for *valley* and [ˈaləs] for *Alice*. Sometimes the shift may go as far as [ɑ], as in [hɑloˈlin] for *Halloween*. The shift toward [a] and [ɑ] before [l] occurs mostly in the Middle Atlantic, Western Pennsylvania, and North Central areas, but scattered instances occur elsewhere.

## "Short o" Variants

The use of [ɑ] in such words as *hot, stop, shock, odd, on,* and *college* derives from a seventeenth-century unrounding of [ɒ].[22] Southern British [ɑ] subsequently rounded again to [ɒ]; today it seems to be undergoing a second unrounding. [23]  In America, [ɑ] has remained predominant, but [ɒ] occurs with some frequency in Eastern New England and Western Pennsylvania, and with a somewhat lesser frequency in the areas derived from Pennsylvania settlement.  In these areas, both [ɑ] and [ɒ] occur; elsewhere [ɒ] occurs only as a conscious imitation of Eastern New England or the traditional speech of the south of England.  In the North Central area, all such words have either [ɑ] or [a].

In the word *on,* however, there is a clear regional variation. South of a line drawn from southern Pennsylvania to New Mexico, the predominant pronunciation is [ɔn], with the diphthongal [ɔʊn] and [ɒʊn] frequent in the South.  Some Southerners report [oʊn], making *on* homophonous with *own,* but my own records do not include this extreme variant.  North of the line, the predominant pronunciation is [ɑn], with [ɒn] occasional in Eastern New England and along the seam between north and south, and [an] frequent in the North Central area.

## Variants of [ɔ]

Two classes are involved here.  Words like *north, caught, brought, lawn,* and *law* traditionally have [ɔ], and are compara-

---

[22] See William Matthews, "Two Notes on Seventeenth Century Pronunciation," *Journal of English and Germanic Philology,* XXXII (1933), 296–300.

[23] Daniel Jones, *An English Pronouncing Dictionary* (11th ed.; New York: E. P. Dutton and Co., Inc., 1956), records only the rounded [ɒ] for the Southern British type, but the practice of many southern British speakers, in their radio speeches to this country, indicates a very considerable use of the unrounded [ɑ].

tively stable. Words like *toss, cough, broth, soft, cost,* and *long* are more variable. Some dictionaries use diacritic markings to distinguish the vowels, or at least the categories of variation, of such representative words as *hot, soft,* and *north*. The category represented by *hot* usually has [ɑ], as we have seen. The two categories represented by *soft* and *north* have [ɔ] in most parts of the United States. In Eastern New England, however, [ɒ] may occur in all three categories. In Western Pennsylvania, the Central Midland, and the Northwest, [ɒ] may replace [ɔ] in all the categories except that typified by *north*.

Whenever a speaker uses [ɒ] instead of either [ɑ] or [ɔ], he eliminates the distinctive difference between numerous pairs of words. Thus in Western Pennsylvania, and to a lesser extend in Eastern New England, [ɒd] may represent either *odd* or *awed*; [kɒt], either *cot* or *caught*. Meaning can be determined only from context. In other parts of the country, the distinction is normally kept: *caught, bought, lawn,* and *law* normally have [ɔ], rarely [ɒ]; *broth, soft,* and *cost* probably have [ɔ] more frequently than [ɒ]; *cot, odd, stop,* and *rock* normally have [ɑ].

The South has developed diphthongal allophones for both [ɔ] and [ɒ]; *walk* may be [wɔk], [wɒk], [wɔʊk], or [wɒʊk]. Other words in the same category, like *dog, log, cost,* and *water,* do likewise; *laundry* may be [ˈlɑndrɪ] or [ˈlaʊndrɪ] in addition to the four variations which parallel those of *walk*.

## Tense Vowel Variants

The tense vowels [i], [e], [o], and [u] show a considerable range of allophonic variation, some of it regional. Diphthongal variants have become so frequent that some investigators have analyzed them as phonemic diphthongs. As a pedagogical device for teaching the pronunciation of English to foreigners, the treatment of these four syllabic elements as diphthongs is undoubtedly useful.[24]    But for the analysis of American speech, such a procedure is not satisfactory.

The phonemic contrast between *pound* [pɑʊnd] and *pond* [pɑnd], or between *boil* [bɔɪl] and *ball* [bɔl], is obvious. But the difference between [geɪt] and [get] is not phonemic; both pronunciations mean *gate*, and are phonemically distinct from *get* [gɛt]. The distinction between [geɪt] and [gɛt] is audible from the beginning of the vocalic element; only in the comparatively rare pronunciation [gɛɪt] must the listener wait for the second part of the diphthong to identify the word as *gate*. In other phonetic contexts, as in *gay*, *game*, *gale*, and *gaze*, the diphthongal allophones are, of course, more frequent, but even such lengthened allophones may sometimes be [e:] instead of [eɪ].

The monophthongal [e] occurs in contexts in which the vowel is short, as in *gate*, *cape*, *rake*, *chaotic*, and the first syllable of *vacation*. The diphthongal varieties are more likely to occur when the vowel is longer, as illustrated in the previous paragraph. The most frequent diphthongal variety is [eɪ]; less frequent is [ɛɪ]; in extreme cases the variation may go as far as [æɪ], an allophone which my records show sporadically in Texas and Oklahoma.

In some areas, notably the North Central, the monophthongal [e] occurs in a wider variety of phonetic contexts. In the northern part of this area, in Minnesota, Wisconsin, northern Michigan, and northern New York, the vowel is regularly monophthongal, and may be raised part way toward [i], a variation recorded in this book as [ê]. A similar variation sometimes occurs in the neighborhood of Charleston, South Carolina, and in the Northwest as far west as Spokane. Allophonic variations in these areas include [e], [eɪ], [ê], and [êɪ].

---

[24] They are presented as diphthongs in my *Handbook of Speech Improvement* (New York: The Ronald Press Co., 1956).

Monophthongal allophones of [i] occur regularly in *beet*, *keep*, *seek*, and *create*, and in a wider variety of contexts in the North Central area.    The chief diphthongal allophone is [ɪi], which occurs in all parts of the country.    In unstressed final positions, with or without inflectional endings, as in *sandy* [sændi], *coffee* [ˈkɔfi], and *monkeys* [ˈmʌŋkiz], [i] is normally monophthongal.    In the southeastern third of the country, from southern Pennsylvania and the Ohio valley down, the older [ɪ] survives, though by no means universally, as in *sandy* [ˈsændɪ]. Final unstressed [ɪ] also survives in Eastern New England and among older people in other parts of the country, but has become rare outside the southeastern third.

Monophthongal allophones of [o] occur regularly in *hope*, *boat*, *soak*, and *obey*, and in a wider range of contexts in the North Central area.    The chief diphthongal allophone is [ou], which occurs in all parts of the country.    When [o] is used before *r*, as in *hoarse*, it is regularly monophthongal.

Several regional variations occur.    In Eastern New England there are about fifty words, including *home*, *whole*, *road*, *toad*, *coat*, and *stone*, in which [o] traditionally shifts almost to [ʌ]; *home* and *hum* become very close.    When this variation was carried westward into the North Central area, it shifted all the way to [ʌ], so that where it survives west of New England *home* and *hum* are both [hʌm].    In both areas, however, the variation has become rare.

In the Middle Atlantic and Western Pensylvania areas, a noticeably fronted allophone, here symbolized by [ö] or [öu],[25] is characteristic, except before [l] and [r].    In extreme cases, both elements of the diphthong may be fronted, as in [röüd] for *road*.

---

[25] The dieresis [¨] represents partial centralization; used as a diacritical mark with back vowels, it represents a partial fronting; with front vowels, a partial retraction.

The monophthongal [ö] is perhaps most frequent in Delaware and Eastern Shore Maryland. The allophones [ö] and [öʊ] occur sporadically in New York City, parts of the Central Midland, and parts of the South, but [öü] is extremely rare outside the Middle Atlantic area. These variations are audibly different from the South British fronted allophone, affected, incidentally, by a few individuals in New York City, which is nearer to [ɛʊ].

The most characteristic allophone in the South is a raised variety, here symbolized as [ôʊ], and which may occur in all positions except immediately before *r*, as in *hoarse*. In extreme cases the second element may be intensified from [ʊ] to [u], as in *roll* [rôul] and *go* [gôu].

In weakly stressed syllables, [o] may shift to [ə] or [ʊ], sometimes to [u], as in *potato* [pəˈtetə] and *window* [ˈwɪndʊ] or [ˈwɪndu]. The shift toward [ə] is perhaps most noticeable in the South; toward [ʊ] and [u], in the North Central area.

Monophthongal allophones of [u] occur regularly in *stoop*, *boot*, and *Luke*, and in a wider range of contexts in the North Central area. The chief diphthongal allophone is [ʊu], which occurs in all parts of the country. The chief regional variation is a centralized enunciation which takes the various forms of [ü], [ʊü], and, in extreme cases, [üü]. Centralized allophones are most characteristic of the South. Less noticeable centralizing characterizes the New York City, Middle Atlantic, Western Pennsylvania, and Central Midland areas. Sporadic centralizing may also be found in the Northwest and Southwest Coastal areas.

### Miscellaneous Vowel Variants

The phonemic distinction between [ɪ] and [ɛ] is sometimes lost before nasals, chiefly in the South, but also to some extent in the southern parts of the various Midland areas. Here *pin* cannot be distinguished in isolation from *pen*, since either word may have a vowel ranging between the limits of [ɪ] and [ɛ]. Similarly, the vowels of *him* and *hem*, *string* and *strength*, may be confused.

Other miscellaneous vowel variants, such as [ɛ] in *catch* and [ɪ] in *get*, show no clear regional pattern, and are likely to be dismissed as substandard whenever they occur.

### Diphthongal Variants

The three phonemic diphthongs show a wide range of regional variation. For [aɪ], the variant [ɑɪ] occurs throughout New York State, and occasionally in other areas. In eastern Virginia, in Canada, and along the Canadian border in New York and New England, an older allophone, variously recorded as [ɜɪ] or [ʌɪ], may occur, chiefly before voiceless consonants, as in [prɜɪs] or [prʌɪs] for *price*. This allophone has little currency today.[26]

In the South, [aɪ] frequently simplifies to [a:], as in [fa:n ta:m] for *fine time* and [faə] or [fa:] for *fire*. Some Southerners regard simplification of the diphthong before voiceless consonants as substandard, but such a pronunciation as [ra:t] for *right* is widespread. In the Southern Mountain and Central Midland areas, simplification also occurs, especially before [r], as in [far] or [fɑr] for *fire*.

In the Middle Atlantic area, and to some extent in the Western Pennsylvania and Central Midland areas, [ɔɪ] often changes to [oɪ], as in [boɪ] for *boy*, [tʃoɪs] for *choice*, and [oɪl] for *oil*. In the South and the Southern Mountains, [ɔɪ] is usually stable when

---

[26] I have heard it only along the Canadian border; for Virginia, see Edwin F. Shewmake, *English Pronunciation in Virginia*, University of Virginia dissertation, 1920; privately printed, 1927, p. 26; see also Shewmake's "Laws of Pronunciation in Eastern Virginia," *Modern Language Notes*, XL (1925), 294–95.

final, as in *boy* [bɔɪ], but often simplified to a long monophthong before consonants, as in [ɔ:l] for *oil*.

In the New York City area, [ɔɪ] used to be frequently replaced by [ɜɪ], but today this usage is rare. The current allophone is an [ɔɪ] with the first part of the diphthong lengthened and intensified. When both *oil* and *earl* have been reduced to [ɜɪl] in traditional New York speech, people from other areas sometimes think they hear *oil* as [ɝl] and *earl* as [ɔɪl]. Actually, as Alexander has pointed out,[27] they are overcompensating in hearing. A real interchange of *oil* and *earl*, or of *voice* and *verse*, is extremely rare except in imitations of New York speech.

The older substitution of [aɪ] for [ɔɪ], as in [baɪl] for *boil* and [ˈpaɪzn] for *poison*, is now extremely rare, and is characteristic of remote areas rather than of particular regions.[28]

The principal allophones of the phonemic diphthong in *pound* are [ɑʊ] and [aʊ]. [aʊ] is more frequent along the Atlantic and Gulf Coasts, and in the Southern Mountain and Central Midland areas. [ɑʊ] is more frequent to the north and west of these areas. The variant [æʊ] occurs frequently in the New York City and Middle Atlantic areas, and in the South; somewhat less frequently in Eastern New England, the Central Midland, and the Southern Mountains. There is a trace of [æʊ] in the St. Lawrence valley in northern New York. Except in the South, [æʊ] is usually considered substandard. In the South, [aʊ] and [æʊ] sometimes become [a:] and [æ:] in word-final position before a following vowel, as in the phrase *now and then* [næ: ən ðɛn].

In eastern Virginia, Canada, and along the Canadian border in New England, New York, Michigan, and Minnesota, an older

---

[27] Henry Alexander, "Soiving the Ersters," *American Speech*, I (1926), 294–95. See also A. F. Hubbell, "'Curl' and 'Coil' in New York City," *American Speech*, XV (1940), 374–76.

[28] See also James W. Abel, "The Phonetic Contexts of [ɔɪ]," *Speech Monographs*, Vol. XX (1953), pp. 247–52.

allophone, variously recorded as [ʌʊ] or [ɜʊ], survives, chiefly before voiceless consonants, as in [hɑʊs] or [hɜʊs] for *house*, in contrast to [ˈhɑʊzɪz], [ˈhaʊzɪz], or [ˈhæʊzɪz] for *houses*.[29] Like the similar allophones of [aɪ], the use of [ʌʊ] and [ɜʊ] represents a survival from the eighteenth century.

In Virginia, the second element of the diphthong may also vary, by being fronted. *House* may be [hɜüs]; *houses*, [ˈhaüzɪz]. The fronting is also evident in eastern Maryland and eastern North Carolina, where *house* is sometimes [haüs]; and *out* [aüt], almost [aɪt]. Fronting of the second element of the diphthong does not occur along the Canadian border.

### Consonantal Variations

Except for [r], there are few consonantal variations that can be traced to a regional base. Variation between [s] and [z] in *desolate* and *discern* seems to be personal rather than regional. In *absorb* and *absurd*, [z] seems to be slightly more frequent in the north than in the south, but there is no clear predominance.

The noun *grease* always has [s], but the verb *grease* and the adjective *greasy* show a regional variation, though the variation is not as clearly marked as some. For the verb *grease*, a line drawn from Atlantic City to Philadelphia, thence westward to the neighborhood of Wheeling, West Virginia, thence to the west and southwest through the Ohio valley, and on to New Mexico, marks the approximate seam between [s] to the north and [z]

[29] See Shewmake's *English Pronunciation in Virginia* (Privately printed, 1927), and his "Laws of Pronunciation in Eastern Virginia," *Modern Language Notes*, XL (1925), 489–92. See also G. S. Lowman, "The Treatment of aʊ in Virginia," *Proceedings of the Second International Congress of Phonetic Sciences*, Cambridge, England, 1936, pp. 122–25; Argus Tresidder, "The Sounds of Virginia Speech," *American Speech*, XVIII (1943), 268–69.

to the south.  For *greasy*, the eastern end of the line swings north to include most of New Jersey in [z] territory.  In the New York City area more older people than younger use [z] in these two words; [s] seems to have been gaining ground at the expense of [z].  Furthermore, there is more variation in the neighborhood of the seam than for a more sharply regionalized word like *forest*, and a wider seam.[30]

Some regional variations occur in the choice among the clear, dark, and velar allophones of [l].[31]  All varieties of American and South British speech use a relatively clear [l] before vowels, as in *let* and *clean*.  A relatively dark allophone, [ɫ], occurs finally, as in *feel* or *battle*, or before a consonant, as in *field*.  When, however, the phoneme occurs between vowels, as in *village* and *hollow*, South British and the American South use the clear [l]; other American regions use the dark [ɫ].  The intervocalic clear [l] is one of the most striking features of the speech of the South.

In certain phonetic contexts, chiefly before labial or velar consonants, as in *help*, *self*, *milk*, *vulgar*, and *Elmira*, a velar allophone [L] sometimes replaces the usual dark [ɫ].  The back of the tongue comes lightly in contact with the velum along the midline, to permit lateral emission, and the tip of the tongue loses its contact with the gum ridge.  When the tenuous velar contact fails to maintain itself, the velar [L] gives way to a vowel, and such pronunciations as [mɪuk] for *milk*, [hɛəp] and [hɛ:p] for *help*, result.  There are traces of this velarizing and vocalizing everywhere, but the tendency is most clearly in the South.

The South also makes greater use of [j] than other regions.  In such words as *tune*, *due*, and *new*, the traditional Southern

[30] See George Hempl, "Grease and Greasy," *Dialect Notes*, I (1896), 438–44; Hans Kurath, "American Pronunciation," *Tract* No. 30 New York: Society for Pure English, pp. 279–97); Argus Tresidder, "The Sounds of Virginia Speech," *American Speech*, XVIII (1943), 270–71.

[31] See Chapter 4 for descriptions of these allophones.

pronunciations are [tjun], [dju], and [nju], with more frequent use of the centralized [ü] than in such a word as *cool*. Sometimes [j] relaxes to [ɪ], as in [tɪün], [dɪü], and [nɪü]; the allophonic [ʊu], [ʊü], and [üü], with and without a preceding [ɪ] or [j], also occur.

In the various Midland areas, [j] and [ɪ] are rare in such words, but the diphthongized and centralized allophones of [u] are frequent. Eastern New England makes some use of [ju] and [jʊu]. Elsewhere [tun] and [tʊun], [du] and [dʊu], and [nu] and [nʊu] are normal, with [ju] and [jʊu] largely the result of conscious effort rather than of habit. Many radio and TV announcers have trained themselves to say [tjun] for *tune*, [dju] for *due*, [nju] for *new*, and even [sjut] for *suit*, the latter a pronunciation which is nowhere normal in unaffected American speech.

In the *wh* words, like *whistle* and *whisper*, the substitution of [w] for [hw] or [ʍ] is most frequent in the larger cities, less frequent in smaller cities and rural areas.[32] The use of [w] seems to be growing with the growth of our cities.

Loss of consonants, as in [læs] for *last* and [læn] for *land*, seems to be personal and contextual, not regional. Addition of sounds, as in ['draʊndɪd] for *drowned*, [ə'krɔst] for *across*, and ['æθəlɪt] for *athlete*, seem to be purely personal, and are usually considered substandard.

No clear summary of these types of variation can be made at present. Some of the boundary lines between different pronunciations of individual words can be indicated with fair exactness, ['fɑrəst] and ['fɔrəst], for instance. Other boundary lines are broader and less definite, ['grisi] and ['grizi], for instance; they await the collection of additional data for further verification.

---

[32] See my articles, "Pronunciation in Upstate New York (VII)," *American Speech*, XII (1937), 123; and "Pronunciation in Downstate New York (II)," *American Speech*, XVII (1942), 154.

Still others remain so obscure that no attempt has been made here to explain them. Generally, however, the variations in individual words group themselves into large regional patterns, and the boundary lines group themselves in bundles. The resulting speech regions, still tentative in some instances and some details, constitute the subject matter of the following chapter.

# CHAPTER 22

# The Speech Areas

Geographical divisions in American speech are most clearly defined along the Atlantic coast, the area of earliest settlement. To the west, the boundaries between one speech area and another are harder to delimit, because the streams of westward migration during the nineteenth century often crossed and intermingled. The relative isolation of the coast settlements in the seventeenth and eighteenth centuries was never quite matched in the westward march. Along the Atlantic coast, therefore, we find three well-defined, major areas: Eastern New England, the Middle Atlantic area, and the South. To these must be added the New York City area, which is anomalous because its speech resembles both the Middle Atlantic and Southern types, and because its type was never reflected further west.

### Eastern New England

The western boundary of Eastern New England may be marked by a line running south from the Canadian border along the summits of the Green Mountains in central Vermont. In Massachusetts the boundary arcs southeastward to the Connecticut valley east of the Connecticut River, and then swings southward to Long Island Sound.

Eastern New England speech is characterized by the loss of [r] in the final and preconsonantal positions, as in *far* [fa:] and *farm* [fa:m]; by the substitution of [ə] for [r], as in *fierce* [fɪəs], *scarce* [skɛəs], and *poor* [pʊə]; and by the substitution of [ɜ] for [ɝ] and of [ə] for [ɚ], as in *murmur* [ˈmɜmə] and *perverse* [pəˈvɜs]. It has the linking [r] of *far away* [ˈfar əˈwe], the linking [ɚ] of *better and better* [ˈbɛtɚ ən ˈbɛtə], and frequently the intrusive [r] of *law* [lɔr] and the intrusive [ɚ] of *ideas* [aɪˈdiɚz].

The prolonged [a] of such words as *far, farm, farther, calm,* and *Harvard* is perhaps the most striking feature of the regional type, the shibboleth by which the outsider recognizes the Eastern New Englander. In extreme cases, notably along the coast of Maine, this variation may shift almost as far as [fæ:m] for *farm.*

Eastern New England makes a phonemic distinction between *cart* [ka:t] and *cot* [kɒt], *calmer* [ˈka:mə] and *comma* [kɒmə], *balm* [ba:m] and *bomb* [bɒm]; but not always between *cot* and *caught,* each of which may be [kɒt]. Other variations, such as [kɑ:t] for *cart,* [kɑt] for *cot,* and [kɔt] for *caught,* represent newer speech habits, chiefly in the larger cities, and are less typical than the main phonemic distinction between [a] and [ɒ].

In such words as *ask, dance, path,* and *aunt,* [a] is traditional and phonemically distinct from [æ], though the use of [æ] is growing, especially in the more heavily populated areas.[1] Along the coast of Maine, however, [a] remains in frequent use.

In *forest, horrid, orange, warrant,* and *borrow,* [ɑ] predominates. [ˈhʌri] is normal for *hurry,* and [ˈkæri] for *carry.* For *hoarse,* the traditional [hoəs] is still current, especially in the northern part of the area, but [hɔəs] has made some inroads in the southern part. *Horse* is usually [hɔ:s], rarely [hɔəs].

---

[1] See Virginia Rogers Miller, "Present-Day Use of the Broad A in Eastern Massachusetts," *Speech Monographs,* Vol. XX (1953), pp. 235–46.

The most frequent vowel in *log, frog, mock, gong, honk*, and *donkey* is [ɑ], though [ɒ] and [ɔ] occur sporadically, especially in the northern part of the area. The most frequent vowel in *doll* and *involve* is also [ɑ], though [ɒ] and [ɔ] occur more frequently than in the previous list. The traditional New England "short *o*," by which *coat* and *home* came to be almost identical with *cut* and *hum* is now almost obsolete except in the most remote areas. There are some traces of final unstressed [ɪ] in such words as *sandy*, *coffee*, and *donkey*, especially along the Maine coast, but [i] predominates throughout the area.

The diphthongs [aɪ], [ɔɪ], and [ɑʊ] are relatively stable, though some traces of [aʊ] and [æʊ] remain in rural areas, and such pronunciations as [hɜʊs] for *house* and [ɜʊt] for *out* are common in the norther half of the area.

*Tune, due*, and *new* sometimes have [jʊu], more often [ʊu]. *Absorb, absurd*, and *desolate* may have either [s] or [z]; *greasy* and the verb *grease* usually have [s]. The distinction between [hw] and [w], as in *whale* [hweɪl] and *wail* [weɪl], has been retained in some parts of the area, but largely lost in the larger cities, where both words are commonly pronounced [weɪl].

In general, whatever is typical of the speech of Eastern New England becomes more striking as one proceeds further up the coast. Further inland, transitional types occur more frequently, as in Orleans County, Vermont, and Hampshire County, Massachusetts. The most striking divergence from the general pattern occurs in Aroostook County, in northern Maine, where such North Central pronunciations as [ˈfɔrəst] for *forest*, [fɑrm] for *farm*, and [ˈkɛri] for *carry* frequently occur.[2]

[2] Writings on New England speech go back to the late years of the nineteenth century. The most complete account of the area will be found in the *Linguistic Atlas of New England*, edited by Hans Kurath, Providence, Brown University, 1939–1943, and its accompanying *Handbook*, 1939. Other references will be found in the bibliography at the end of this volume.

## The New York City Area

This area includes not only the five counties which comprise New York City itself, but also the two remaining counties on Long Island; most of Westchester County, directly north of New York City on the east bank of the Hudson River; Rockland County, northwest of New York City across the Hudson River from Westchester County; the New Jersey counties of Hudson and Bergen, directly across the Hudson River from New York City; and commuting areas in Fairfield County, southwestern Connecticut.

There are traces of New York City speech in the lower Hudson valley, directly north of this area, but except for the city of Hudson, which in earlier days was a whaling port in close contact with New York City, the speech rapidly gives way to the type of North Central speech current in upstate New York.

In the New York City area, speech is characterized by a frequent, but by no means universal, loss of [r] in the final and preconsonantal positions, as in *far* [fɑ:] and *farm* [fɑ:m]. In *fierce*, *scarce*, and *poor*, [r] usually gives way to [ə] or drops out entirely, as in [fɪəs] or [fɪ:s], [skɛəs] or [skɛ:s], and [pʊə] or [pʊ:]. *Horse* and *hoarse* are both usually [hɔəs], sometimes [hɔ:s], but with no distinction between the traditional [ɔr] and [or].

[ɝ] is somewhat more stable that it was a generation ago, but often gives way to [ɜ] and [ɜɪ]; [ɚ] usually gives way to [ə]. *Murmur* and *perverse* may be [ˈmɜmə] and [pəˈvɜs] or [ˈmɜɪmə] and [pəˈvɜɪs]. New York has the linking [r] of *far away* [ˈfɑr əˈweɪ], the linking [ɚ] of *better and better* [ˈbɛtɚ ən ˈbɛtə], the intrusive [r] of *law* [lɔr], and the intrusive [ɚ] of *ideas* [aɪˈdiɚz].

New York City contrasts *cart* and *cot* most frequently by lengthening the vowel of *cart* [kɑ:t] and retaining the short vowel of *cot* [kɑt]. This distinction may, however, be lost by a lengthening of the vowel of *cot* to [ɑ:]. Less frequently the contrast is between [kɑrt], [kɒrt] or [kɒ:t] for *cart* and [kɑt] for *cot*. In the New York City phonemic pattern, unlike that of Eastern New England, *cot* goes with *cart*, not with *caught*, which is normally [kɔt].

In *forest, horrid, orange, warrant, borrow, log, mock,* and *gong,* [ɑ] is all but universally the stressed vowel. In *donkey,* the older [ʌ] occurs somewhat more often than [ɑ]; in *honk,* [ɑ] is usual, but [ʌ] occurs occasionally. This use of [ʌ] links New York City with the Middle Atlantic area.

[ˈhʌri] is all but universal for *hurry.* [ˈwʌri] and [ˈnʌrɪʃ] are frequent for *worry* and *nourish,* but [ˈwɜri] and [ˈnɜrɪʃ] may also be heard. *Barren, narrow,* and *marry* normally have [æ]. *Mary* is either [ˈmɛri] or [ˈmɛ:ri], and is rarely distinguishable from *merry.* In *ask, dance, aunt,* and *path,* [a] occurs occasionally, but since it occurs about as frequently in *bad, land, thanks,* and *fancy,* and almost never in *command, plant,* and *example,* there is no phonemic contrast between [æ] and [a] as there is in Eastern New England. *Rather* may have [æ], [a], or [ɑ], with [ɑ] somewhat more frequent here than in most other areas. The only other "broad *a*" word in which [ɑ] occurs with any frequency is *aunt.* The final unstressed vowel in *sandy, coffee,* and *donkey* is normally [i].

In *nice* and *time,* the normal diphthong is [aɪ], but [ɑɪ] occurs frequently, especially before voiced consonants and at the ends of words. In *boil* and *noise,* the traditional substitution of [ɜɪ] for [ɔɪ] is now rare; current usage includes an overtense [ɔ] at the beginning of the diphthong. In *out* and *town,* [aʊ] is normal; [æʊ], frequent; [ɑʊ], rare; and [ɜʊ], unknown.

*Tune, due,* and *new* sometimes have [j], but less frequently than in either Eastern New England or the South; [tʊun], [dʊu], and [nʊu] are normal. In the artificial speech of the elocution schools and the radio studios, the use of [j] sometimes extends to words like *suit* and *lucid*, where all unaffected American speech uses [u] or [ʊu] without [j], and to words like *noon*, in which there is no historical precedent for [j]. Such affectations are regional only in the sense that the New York City area seems to have more than its share of them.

The New York area regularly replaces [hw] and [ʍ] with [w], so that *whale* and *wail* must be distinguished by context. *Absorb*, *absurd*, and *desolate* have [z] in a proportion somewhat above the national average. Among older New Yorkers, [z] occurs somewhat more frequently in *greasy* and the verb *grease* than among the younger generation, but [s] is now the characteristic regional consonant.[3]

In considering the pronunciation of any metropolitan area, one must not confuse remnants of foreign-language habits confined to foreign-language enclaves with the native idiom. This warning is equally applicable to such other large cities as Boston, Providence, and Los Angeles. In New York, the Irish and Germans of a hundred years ago have been largely assimilated. The speakers of Yiddish, Italian, and languages of eastern Europe, who constituted the bulk of the incoming stream of immigration before World War I, still retain some features of the European languages in their backgrounds, and the speakers of Spanish from Puerto Rico constitute a serious problem in the New York schools at present. In at least two phonetic details the speech of relatively recent arrivals differs from that of the native New York tradition. One is the dental articulation of [t], [d], [n],

[3] For further details on New York City speech, see my articles, "Pronunciation in Downstate New York," *American Speech*, XVII (1942), pp. 30–41, 149–57; and "The Place of New York City in American Linguistic Geography," *Quarterly Journal of Speech*, XXXIII (1947, pp. 314–20. See also Allan Forbes Hubbell, *The Pronunciation of English in New York City* (New York: King's Crown Press, 1950).

and [l], as in the word *dental*, which contrasts with the native alveolar articulation, and which is noticeable because these four consonants themselves are so frequent in English speech. The other is the confusion of the [ŋ] of *singer* with the [ŋg] of *finger*. Both these features are foreignisms, and should not be confused with the native tradition of American English.[4]

Although the geographical area of the New York City type of speech is limited, the population approximates ten million, or more than that of the Eastern New England area. New York cannot, therefore, be considered a subarea, like Charleston, South Carolina, or the Oregon coast, but must be considered a major American speech area with its own patterns and standards.

### The Middle Atlantic Area

The Middle Atlantic area includes all New Jersey except the northernmost part. It includes the southeastern third of Pennsylvania and all Delaware. In Maryland the speech is mixed, and, in some areas, confused. The western panhandle goes with Western Pennsylvania; some sections of the Potomac valley and some of the eastern shore show Southern influences. The District of Columbia and its Virginia suburbs are largely Middle Atlantic in speech; so is the eastern shore from Ocean City, Maryland, down to Cape Charles, Virginia.

The Middle Atlantic is the only east-coast area which consistently uses [ɝ], [ɚ], and final and preconsonantal [r]. There is rarely an intrusive [r] in *law*, or an intrusive [ɚ] in *idea*. *Cart* may be [kɑrt] or [kɒrt]; the use of [ɒ] relects an east-coast characteristic extending all the way from New York City to the Deep South. *Cot* is normally [kɑt]; *caught*, normally [kɔt]; there is no confusion between the [ɑ] and [ɔ] phonemes.

---

[4] See my article, "Jewish Dialect and New York Dialect," *American Speech*, VII (1932), 321–26.

In *forest*, *horrid*, *orange*, *warrant*, and *borrow*, the coastal [ɑ] predominates, perhaps more strongly along the New Jersey coast than anywhere else in the country.	In *hurry* [ˈhʌri] and *carry* [ˈkæri], coastal vowels also predominate.	*Various* is usually [ˈvɛriəs], but from New Jersey westward through southern Pennsylvania, [ˈværiəs] is frequent.	In central New Jersey and central Pennsylvania, *for* and *four*, *horse* and *hoarse*, all have [ɔr].	In southern New Jersey, south of the northern boundary of Burlington County, in southeastern Pennsylvania, and areas to the south, the historical distinction between *for* and *horse* with [ɔr], and *four* and *hoarse* with [or], begins to be noticeable.	In southeastern Pennsylvania and parts of Maryland, the distinction may go as far as [ʊr] in *four*, *hoarse*, and similar words.

*Ask*, *dance*, *aunt*, and *path* have [æ] throughout the area. *Rather* is usually [ˈræðɚ], but there are numerous instances of [ˈrɑðɚ] in Philadelphia and towns nearby.	*Log* varies greatly in New Jersey; in the Philadelphia area it is predominantly [lɑg]; in Delaware and Maryland, predominantly [lɔg].	Throughout the area, *gong* usually has [ɑ]; *mock*, *doll*, and *involve*, almost invariably [ɑ].	Southeastern Pennsylvania is the focal area for [ʌ] in *donkey*; from here the vowel thins out in frequency in other areas, traces of it occurring in New York City, the South, Western Pennsylvania, and occasionally points further west. Though [ʌ] predominates throughout the Middle Atlantic area, [ɑ] occurs occasionally.	In *honk*, [ɑ] predominates; [ʌ] occurs occasionally.

Fronted allophones of [u] and [o] characterize the Middle Atlantic area.	The principal allophones of [u] are [ü], [ʊü], and [üü]; [ü] occurs chiefly before voiceless stops, as in *stoop* [stüp] and *mute* [mjüt]; [ʊü] and [üü], in all contexts.	The principal allophones of [o] are [ö], [öʊ], and [oʊ].	[ö] occurs sometimes before voiceless stops, as in *hope* [höp] and *boat* [böt], and in a wider variety of contexts on the Delmarva peninsula.[5] [öʊ] may occur in all contexts except before [l], in which [oʊ] is normal, as in *old* [oʊld]; and before [r], in which [o] is normal, as in *board* [bord].   The allophone [oʊ] may occur in all contexts except before [r].

The final unstressed vowel in *sandy, coffee,* and *donkey* is variable.   Roughly speaking, [i] shows a slight preponderance north of the latitude of Philadelphia; [ɪ], a slight preponderance south of that latitude.   But the seam is wide and irregular, and a clear predominance of [ɪ] does not develop for some distance south of Philadelphia.

The diphthong [aɪ] occasionally shifts to [ɑɪ], most often before voiced consonants and finally, as in New York State. Before [r] it often simplifies, as in [far] or [fɑr] for *fire*.   [ɔɪ] frequently becomes [oɪ] as in *noise* [noɪz], a variation which may be heard only occasionally in the South, and which is otherwise limited to the Middle Atlantic area.   As in New York City, [aʊ] is standard, as in *out* and *town*; [æʊ] is frequent; [ɑʊ] is rare.   The second element of the diphthong is sometimes fronted, especially in Maryland, and usually before voiceless consonants, as in [aüt] or [æüt] for *out*.

The use of [j] in *tune, due,* and *new* is somewhat more frequent than in the New York City area.   [tjuün], [djʊü], and [njʊü] are frequent; so are [tuün], [duü], and [nuü]; forms with [ʊu] and [üü], with or without [j], are somewhat less frequent.

In *absorb, absurd,* and *desolate,* [z] occurs less frequently than in the New York City area; here [s] is usual.   For *greasy* and the verb *grease,* [s] is usual north of the latitude of Philadelphia;

[5] Delmarva [dɛl'mɑrvə] is a local word made from abbreviations of the names of the three states—Delaware, Maryland, and Virginia—which occupy the peninsula between the Delaware and Chesapeake Bays.   For details of the speech of the region, see W. C. Greet, "Delmarva Speech," *American Speech*, VIII (1933), no. 4, pp. 57–63.

[z], to the south; along the seam, which is wide and irregular, usage varies greatly. In southern New Jersey there is an occasional substitution of [t] for [d] in the inflectional -*ed*, as in [ˈwetɪt] or [ˈwetət] for *waited*. Substitution of [w] for [hw] or [ʌ] is frequent throughout the Middle Atlantic area.

## The South

The South represents a sweep of coastal country from southern Maryland to east Texas. Within it are many subareas which require further analysis; and gradations of social status, as reflected in speech, to be found nowhere else in the country. The principal subareas are the Virginia Tidewater, centering on Norfolk; the "outer banks" of North Carolina, essentially the area east of U.S. highway 17; the area around Charleston, South Carolina; and the New Orleans area. Florida is a mixture: north Florida is Deep South, like southern Georgia and Alabama, to which it is contiguous; peninsular Florida shows Southern Mountain settlement in the central ridge, and infiltration from the north in the coastal resort areas.

Generally speaking, the speech of the South is limited to the coastal plain and the piedmont; in the higher country of western Virginia, the western Carolinas, and the northern parts of Georgia, Alabama, and Mississippi, we find a transition to Southern Mountain speech; and in northwestern Louisiana and western Arkansas, a transition to Central Midland speech. Despite the local subareas, however, the speech of the entire area contains enough Southern flavor to be recognizable as Southern to people from other parts of the country.

Except for the subareas, the South generally adheres to the following pattern. Normally [ɜ] and [ə] replace the [ɝ] and [ɚ] of other areas, as in *murmur* [ˈmɜmə]. In the Deep South, [ɜ] may be diphthongized as [ɜɪ] when another consonant follows in the same syllable, as in *murmur* [ˈmɜɪmə] and *first* [fɜɪst].    This diphthongization is most noticeable in the New Orleans area and in southern Mississippi, but may be heard elsewhere throughout the Deep South, and occasionally as far north as Chattanooga, Tennessee, and North Carolina.    The popular attitude toward the diphthong is quite different from the New York attitude; in the South [ɜɪ] carries no social stigma.

The South usually omits final and preconsonantal [r], as in *far* [fɑː] or [fɒː] and *farm* [fɑːm] or [fɒːm], though some use of [r] has recently infiltrated the area.    Intervocalic [r] frequently drops out, as in [ˈvɛːɪ] for *very* and [kəˈlaːnə] for *Carolina*.    The linking and intrusive [r] and [ɚ] are rare; *far away* is usually [ˈfɑː əˈweɪ]; *ideas*, [ˈaːdɪəz] or [aɪˈdɪəz].

*Fierce* and *scarce* are usually [fɪəs] and [skɛəs]; in the Deep South [ə] occasionally drops out, as in New York City, leaving [fɪːs] and [skɛːs], but this simplification occurs much less frequently than in New York City.    *Poor* may be [pʊə], less frequently [poə] or [poː].    The South retains the distinction between [ɔ] and [o] before *r*, as in *horse* [hɔːs] and *hoarse* [hoəs].    In *hoarse, mourn, four, more*, and similar words, the usual forms include [oə] and [oː], though some Southerners consider the absence of [ə] substandard.

*Cart* [kɑːt], *cot* [kɑt], and *caught* [kɔt] are usually clearly differentiated; the lengthened vowel of *cart* serves the same function as [r] in other areas.    *Cart* often shifts to [kɒːt], sometimes almost to the extreme of [kɔːt], approaching ambiguity with *caught*.    On the other hand, *caught* sometimes diphthongizes as [kɔʊt], approaching ambiguity with *coat* [koʊt].    The shift to [ɒː] characterizes the whole class of words illustrated by *cart, barn, far, father*, and *calm*.    The shift to [ɔʊ], less frequently to [ɒʊ], characterizes the whole class of words illustrated by *caught*,

*walk, cost, log, on,* and *law*.  The diphthongal extreme is best illustrated by *laundry*, which may have [ɔ], [ɒ], [ɑ], [ɔʊ], [ɒʊ], or [ɑʊ].

In *forest, horrid, orange, warrant,* and *borrow*, the coastal [ɑ]
predominates, except for the "outer banks" of North Carolina,
where [ɒ] and [ɔ] are more frequent than elsewhere in the coastal
South.  *Hurry* is predominantly [ˈhʌrɪ]; *carry*, predominantly
[ˈkærɪ], with [ˈkarɪ] occasional.  The stressed vowel of *area,
various,* and *Mary* is usually [e], occasionally [eɪ].  Only in the
South can we find a three-way contrast between *merry* [ˈmɛrɪ],
*marry* [ˈmærɪ], and *Mary* [ˈmerɪ].

Except for some surviving use of [a] and [ɑ] in Tidewater
Virginia, the South normally has [æ] in *ask, dance, path,* and
*aunt*.  *Rather* is usually [ˈræðə], but [ˈraðə] and [ˈrɑðə] occur
occasionally throughout the entire area.  A diphthongal allophone [æɪ] is frequent, as in [æɪsk] for *ask*.  This diphthong is an
intermediate form between [æ] and the [eɪ] of Southern [keɪnt]
for *can't*.

The Charleston area has [ê] and [êɪ], raised allophones of [e]
which we also find in the North Central area.  Interchanges
between [e] and [ɛ] occur sporadically throughout the South in a
few words: [grɛt] for *great*, [ˈnɛkɪd] for *naked*, [hed] for *head*; the
social status of these interchanges remains in some doubt.
Variation between the limits of [ɪ] and [ɛ] before nasals indicates
that the normal phonemic contrast has broken down in this
context.  Either *pin* or *pen* may be [pɛn], [pɪn], or something in
between.  *Length* ranges from [lɛŋθ] to [lɪŋθ]; *them*, from [ðɛm] to
[ðɪm].  The final unstressed vowel of *sandy, coffee,* and *donkey* is
usually [ɪ], though there has been some infiltration of [i], especially in the upper South.

*Log* and *mock* usually have [ɔ]; for *log*, variants with [ɒ],
[ɒʊ], and [ɔʊ] also occur.  *Donkey* ranges between [ˈdɑŋkɪ] and
[ˈdɔŋkɪ], with [ɔ] somewhat more frequent, and with [ɒʊ] and

[ɔʊ] occasional. In the neighborhood of Norfolk, Virginia, [ˈdʌŋkɪ] predominates, but this form is rare elsewhere in the South. In all words in which [ɔ] predominates, [ɒ] occurs occasionally; [ɒ] is less frequent in words in which [ɑ] predominates.

The diphthong [aɪ] commonly simplifies to [a:] before voiced consonants, as in *fine* [fa:n], and finally, as in *high* [ha:]. Before voiceless consonants, as in [ra:t] for *right*, some Southerners regard the substitution as substandard. The use of [ɑ:] for [aɪ] is rare except before [l], where both [a:] and [ɑ:] are frequent, as in *mile*; and before *r*, where various simplifications occur, as in [faə] and [fa:] and, less commonly, [fɑə] and [fɑ:] for *fire*.

The diphthong [ɔɪ] commonly simplifies to [ɔ:], as in [ɔ:l] for *oil*. Occasionally in Virginia one may hear [oɪ], an infiltration from the Middle Atlantic area. Although the Deep South parallels New York City in using [ɜɪ] for [ɝ], it does not parallel the traditional New York use of [ɜɪ] for [ɔɪ].

In *out* and *town*, the characteristic Southern diphthong is [aʊ]; [æʊ] is frequent; [ɑʊ] is rare. In Tidewater Virginia, and to some extent in the Charleston area, [ɜʊ] is a normal variation before voiceless consonants, as in *out* [ɜʊt] and *house* [hɜʊs], but not before voiced consonants, as in *town* [taʊn] or [tæʊn] and *houses* [ˈhaʊzɪz] or [ˈhæʊzɪz]. This use of [ɜʊ] extends from Tidewater Virginia over into northeastern North Carolina. Fronting of the second element of the diphthong also occurs: *out* may be [æüt], [aüt], or [ɜüt].

Characteristic diphthongal allophones of [o] and [u] occur. In Virginia, an occasional [öʊ] indicates infiltration from the Middle Atlantic area. Further south, the more characteristic variation is a raised allophone, here symbolized as [ôʊ]. The most characteristic allophone of [u] is fronted as [ʊü], in extreme cases as [üü].

Retention of [j] in *tune*, *due*, and *new* is more characteristic of the South than of any other area. *Tune* may be [tjʊun] or [tjʊün], less frequently [tɪun], [tɪün] or [tün]. *Absorb*, *absurd*, and *desolate* have [s] more frequently than further north. *Greasy* and the verb *grease* regularly have [z].

The greater use of diphthongal allophones, the wider range of pitch in sentence melody, and a somewhat slower rate of utterance, in comparison with other areas, constitute what is commonly called the Southern drawl. But, like most generalizations, the drawl must be taken with some skepticism. Speech in the Virginia Tidewater and in up-country South Carolina is crisp. The pitch range in sentence melody is wider in the "outer banks" of North Carolina and in the Yazoo delta in Mississippi than elsewhere in the South. Actually the variations in the so-called drawl reflect the wide variety in all aspects of Southern speech.[6]

## The North Central Area

The speech of this area derives ultimately from the Long Island Sound settlements in colonial Connecticut. Separated at first from Boston and Plymouth, the western Connecticut settlers expanded up the Housatonic valley into western Massachusetts, and the Champlain valley into western Vermont. Eventually their type of speech expanded into upstate New York, the northern tier of counties in Pennsylvania; into northern Ohio, Illinois; into all of Michigan, Wisconsin, and Minnesota; and into the northern two thirds of Iowa and the eastern two thirds

[6] For additional details, see W. C. Greet, "Southern Speech," in *Culture in the South*, ed. W. T. Couch (Chapel Hill: University of North Carolina Press, 1935), pp. 594–615; W. A. Read, "The Vowel System of the Southern United States," *Englische Studien*, Vol. XLI, pp. 70–78; C. M. Wise, "Southern American Dialect," *American Speech*, VIII (1933), No. 2, 37–43.

of the Dakotas. The area is almost cut in two by the extension of Pennsylvania speech to Lake Erie, at Erie, Pennsylvania, but reinforced and connected by a very similar type of speech extending through the southern part of the Canadian province of Ontario along the north shore of Lake Erie.

Speech characteristics of the North Central area include the retention of [r], [ɝ], and [ɚ], as in *far* [fɑr], *farm* [fɑrm], and *murmur* ['mɝmɚ]. A characteristic allophone of [ɑ] is [a], which occurs both in *cart* [kɑrt] or [kart] and in *cot* [kɑt] or [kat]. *Caught* is usually [kɔt], occasionally [kɒt]; [ɒ] occurs most frequently in those areas in which [a] is also most frequent in *cot*, so that there is rarely any danger of ambiguity.

*Forest*, *orange*, *horrid*, and *warrant* normally have [ɔ]; the ratio of [ɔ] to [ɑ] runs as high as nine to one in such a typical North Central city as Cleveland, Ohio, in contrast to coastal New Jersey, where the ratio is about nine to one in favor of [ɑ]. In the North Central area, however, *borrow*, *sorry*, and *tomorrow* have [ɑ] predominantly except in limited subareas which include western Vermont, the St. Lawrence valley in northern New York, and local areas in Minnesota and North Dakota, where [ɔ] predominates as it does in *forest*. In this smaller group of words, [ɑ] seems to have spread at the expense of [ɔ].[7]

*Hurry* is normally ['hɝi] or ['hɝri]; similar forms occur in related words like *worry*, *courage*, and *nourish*. *Carry* is usually ['kɛri], though ['kæri] is frequent in the eastern part of the area; similar forms occur in such words as *barren*, *marry*, and *narrow*. *Mary*, *various*, and *area* generally have [ɛ] or [ɛ:]; *Mary*, *marry*, and *merry* are often identical in pronunciation. *Four*, *mourn*, and *hoarse* usually have [ɔr]; [or] is rare.

[7] See A. H. Marckwardt, "Middle English *ŏ* in American English of the Great Lakes Area," *Papers of the Michigan Academy*, Vol. XXVI (1940), pp. 561–71.

*Log, gong, donkey,* and *honk* normally have [ɔ]; [ɒ] and [ɑ] are occasional. *Doll, solve, involve,* and *on* usually have [ɑ] or [a]. *Ask, dance, path,* and *aunt* always have [æ] in unaffected speech; *rather* usually has [æ], but may occasionally have [a], or even [ɑ]. The final unstressed vowel of *sandy, coffee,* and *donkey* is [i] except among older people, who sometimes use [ɪ].

In Michigan, Wisconsin, and to some extent in other northern parts of the area, [e] has raised allophones which take the form of [ê] and [êɪ], so that *rainy day* [ˈrêɪni ˈdêɪ] and *lake* [lêɪk or lêk] almost reach the level of [ˈriɪni ˈdɪi] and [lɪik] or [lik]. This raised allophone has already been noted in Charleston, South Carolina, and will be noted later in the Northwest. Throughout the North Central area, the phonemes [i], [e], [o], and [u] have more monophthongal allophones than elsewhere in the country.

The diphthong [aɪ] is stable throughout the area, except in New York State, where [ɑɪ] is a frequent allophone. [ɔɪ] is stable throughout the area. In the northern part of the area, [ɑʊ] frequently has the allophone [ɜʊ], especially before voiceless consonants, as in [ɜʊt] for *out*; occasionally the allophone may be heard before voiced consonants, as in [tɜʊn] for *town*, a context in which [ɜʊ] rarely occurs in Canada, northern New England, or eastern Virginia. Otherwise, [ɑʊ] is the normal allophone; [aʊ] and [æʊ] are rare except in the St. Lawrence valley in northern New York.

*Tune, due,* and *new* normally have some allophone of [u], and omit [j]. *Absorb* and *absurd* have [s] and [z] in about equal proportions; there is a slight preponderance of [s] over [z] in *desolate.* *Greasy* and the verb *grease* have [s] almost universally. The distinction between *whale* and *wail* is generally maintained except in the larger cities; [hw] and [ʍ] occur more frequently here than in most areas.

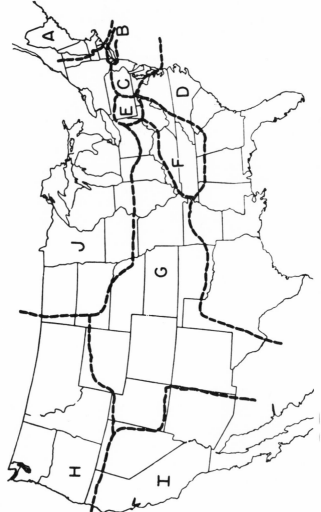

Map showing the major regional speech areas: A: Eastern New England; B: New York City; C: Middle Atlantic; D: Southern; E: Western Pennsylvania; F: Southern Mountain; G: Central Midland; H: Northwest; I: Southwest; J: North Central.

### Western Pennsylvania

This area has Pittsburgh as its cultural and economic center. It is cut off from eastern Pennsylvania by the southwestward arch of the mountains in central Pennsylvania. Scotch and Scotch-Irish migrants formed a larger proportion of the early settlers than were to be found in the Philadelphia area. On the north, Western Pennsylvania is bounded by the area of settlement from western New England and upstate New York, roughly the northern tier of counties. The forks of the Susquehanna represent transitional territory, where Middle Atlantic, North Central, and Western Pennsylvania come together. The northwest corner of Pennsylvania represents another transitional area, where expansion from eastern Pennsylvania met expansion from upstate New York. On the west, Western Pennsylvania includes the northern panhandle of West Virginia and some adjacent territory in Ohio. On the south, it includes part of northern West Virginia and the westernmost tip of Maryland.

The speech characteristics of Western Pennsylvania include [ɝ], [ɚ], and final and preconsonantal [r]. *Cart* is usually [kɑrt], but with some traces of [kɒrt] in the southern parts of the area. *Cot* and *caught*, however, represent a breakdown of the phonemic contrast between [ɑ] and [ɔ]. Either word may have [ɑ] or [ɔ] or, more frequently, [ɒ]. The same range of variation may be found in *cost*, *coffee*, *mock*, *stop*, *law*, and many other words. Here [lɑst] means *lost*, not *last*. *On* ranges from [ɑn] near the New York area to [ɔn] throughout most of the area. In *doll, solve*, and *involve*, Western Pennsylvania uses [ɔ] more frequently than any other part of the country. For *donkey*, [ʌ] is somewhat less frequent, and [ɔ] much more frequent, than in the Middle Atlantic area. In *forest, horrid, orange*, and *warrant*, [ɔ] predominates. In *borrow, sorry*, and *tomorrow*, [ɔ] predominates only in Pittsburgh and its immediate neighborhood; elsewhere, [ɑ] predominates. *Log* is normally [lɔg].

In *four*, *mourn*, and *hoarse*, [ɔr] and [or] vary, with [ɔr] in the northern part gradually giving way to [or] in the southern. *Hurry* [ˈhʌri] and *carry* [ˈkæri] agree with coastal types rather than with the contiguous North Central area. *Various* is usually [ˈvɛriəs], but [ˈværiəs] is frequent in a thin wedge along the southern boundary of the area. As in the Middle Atlantic area, [ɪ] begins to replace the northern [i] in such words as *sandy*, *coffee*, and *donkey*, along the southern boundary of the area.

*Ask*, *dance*, *path*, and *rather* normally have [æ]. Occasional fronted allophones of [o] and [u] occur, but not as frequently as in the Middle Atlantic area. *Home* and *moon* are usually [houm] and [muun], less frequently [höum] and [muün]. [aɪ] is usually stable. [ɑu] is a little less stable, since [au] and even [æu] occasionally occur. [ɔɪ] sometimes gives way to [oɪ], but not as frequently as in the Middle Atlantic area.

*Tune*, *due*, and *new* usually have allophones of [u], including fronted allophones; inclusion of [j] is rare except along the southern boundary. *Absorb* and *absurd* show no clear preponderance of either [s] or [z]. *Greasy* and the verb *grease* have [s] along the northern boundary, [z] throughout most of the area. [hw] and [ʍ] have little currency.

### The Southern Mountain Area

This area includes the high country extending from West Virginia, western Virginia, and eastern Kentucky down through western North Carolina, northwestern South Carolina, northern Georgia, northern Alabama, most of the eastern two thirds of Tennessee, and most of Kentucky south of the Ohio valley. Pennsylvanian in origin, it has been influenced by the speech of the South. On the north, the boundary between it and Western Pennsylvania and the Central Midland is transitional rather than sharp. The long isolation of the mountain settlements favored the retention of older linguistic forms, and has provided plentiful material for students of folklore. Consequently the speech of the area has been studied more completely on the folk level than on the standard.[8]

The Southern Mountain area usually retains [ɝ], [ɚ], and final and preconsonantal [r], as in Pennsylvania, but there is enough loss of [r]-coloring to warrant further investigation. Hall reports the intrusive [r] in both medial and final positions.[9] *Cart* [kɑrt], *cot* [kɑt], and *caught* [kɔt] are usually differentiated; the occasional use of [ɒ] in words of these three types does not produce the degree of ambiguity found in Western Pennsylvania. In *forest, horrid, orange,* and *warrant,* usage varies: [ɑ] is more frequent toward the south; [ɔ] predominates in West Virginia. *Borrow, sorry,* and *tomorrow* normally have [ɑ]. For *hurry,* [ʌ] predominates throughout the southern part of the area; Kentucky and West Virginia divide between [ʌ] and [ɜ]. For such words as *barren, narrow,* and *carry,* [æ] predominates except in West Virginia, where usage divides between [æ] and [ɛ]. Throughout the entire area, such words occasionally have [a], and even [ɑ], as in [ˈnarə] or [ˈnɑrə] for *narrow.*

*Four, mourn,* and *hoarse* have [or], and are distinct from *for, morn,* and *horse,* which have [ɔr]. *Ask, dance, path,* and *aunt* normally have [æ], occasionally [æɪ]. *Log, mock, donkey,* and *gong* normally have [ɔ]. *Doll* and *involve* have [ɑ] more often than [ɔ]. Fronted allophones of [u] are frequent, but less notice-

[8] See, however, Joseph S. Hall, "The Phonetics of Great Smoky Mountain Speech," *American Speech,* XVII (1942), Sec. 2 of the April issue, 1–110; Argus Tresidder, "The Speech of the Shenandoah Valley," *American Speech,* XII (1937), 284–88. These articles discuss pronunciation on both levels.
[9] J. S. Hall, *op. cit.,* 94–95.

ably so than in the lowland South. Fronted allophones of [o] are rare. Final unstressed [ɪ] predominates in such words as *sandy*, *coffee*, and *donkey*.

The diphthong [aɪ] regularly simplifies to [a:], especially before [r]; *fire* is predominantly [far] or [fa:r], occasionally [fɑr]. In West Virginia there are a few traces of the Pennsylvania [oɪ], but elsewhere in the area, [ɔɪ] regularly simplifies to [ɔ:]. [aʊ] and [æʊ] predominate over [ɑʊ], as in the South. *Tune*, *due*, and *new* usually retain [j], as in the South. *Absorb*, *absurd*, and *desolate* usually have [s]; *greasy* and the verb *grease* usually have [z]. *Whale* and *wail* are usually distinct; the area retains [hw] or [ʍ].

## The Central Midland

This is a large area in the heart of the country, originally populated largely by migration down the Ohio valley, and transitional in speech. Its boundaries are ill defined, and the accumulation of more data may force a revision in our concept of its extent, since its speech is by no means uniform throughout. In the east it is represented by the Ohio valley, with Western Pennsylvania at its easternmost point. The Southern Mountain area borders it on the southeast, and the North Central to the north. Further west it spreads out, including southern Iowa, northern and western Arkansas, much of Nebraska and Oklahoma, parts of the Texas panhandle and the El Paso area, of New Mexico, and of Utah. In the southwest, the boundary between Central Midland and Southwest Coastal comes approximately at the border between New Mexico and Arizona. In the northwest, the boundary between the Central Midland and the Northwest is ill defined, but probably runs from northeast Nevada to southwest South Dakota.

Speech characteristics of the Central Midland area are most closely allied with Western Pennsylvania and Southern Mountain, with some infiltration from both north and south. Final and preconsonantal [r], [ɝ], and [ɚ] occur regularly, with some loss of [r] and [r]-coloring along the southern seam. The distinction between *horse* [hɔrs] and *hoarse* [hors] survives predominantly through most of the area. *Various* is predominantly ['vɛriəs], but there are traces of both ['veriəs] and ['væriəs]. *Cart* may be [kɑrt] or [kɒrt]. *Forest, horrid, orange,* and *warrant* regularly have [ɔ]. *Hurry, worry,* and *courage* regularly have [ɜr] or [ɝ]. *Carry, marry, parrot,* and similar words usually have [ɛ], as in the North Central area.

Before velars, [ɔ] is somewhat more frequent than the national average. *Fog, frog, log, donkey,* and *honk* regularly have [ɔ]. Before [l], [ɔ] is also frequent, as in *solve* [sɔlv] and *revolve* [rɪ'vɔlv], but [ɒ] and [ɑ] also occur. The pronunciation of *water* shifts, from predominantly ['wɔtɚ] in the east to predominantly ['watɚ] further west.

*Cot* may be [kɑt] or [kɒt]; *caught* may be [kɔt] or [kɒt]. The distinction between this and similar pairs of words is frequently lost. [ɒ] also occurs frequently in such words as *swamp, laundry, beyond, cross,* and *cloth. On* varies from [ɑn] to [ɔn], the latter more frequent. *After, aunt, glass, rather,* and other "broad a" words have [æ]. The final unstressed vowel of such words as *sandy, coffee,* and *donkey* is usually [i], though [ɪ] occurs with some frequency near the southern seam.

Among the phonemic diphthongs, [aʊ] is the usual allophone in *out* and *town*; [æʊ] is frequent; [ɑʊ], rare. [aɪ] is the usual allophone in *night* and *line,* but [ɑɪ] occasionally occurs in *line*. Before [r], [aɪ] sometimes simplifies to [a], especially along the southern seam, as in *fire* [far] or [faɪr]. [ɔɪ] is usually stable, but with some infiltration of [oɪ] as in [oɪl] for *oil* near the Western

Pennsylvania boundary, and some use of [ɔ:] as in [ɔ:l] for *oil* in the southern part of the area. For [i], [e], [o], and [u], the diphthongal allophones [ɪi], [eɪ], [oʊ], and [ʊu] are usual. Fronted allophones of [u] occur occasionally; fronted allophones of [o] are rare.

In *desolate, absorb,* and *absurd,* [s] is usual; [z] is rare. *Greasy* and the verb *grease* are transitional; [z] is probably more frequent than [s] throughout the entire area, but [s] is more frequent in the northern part than elsewhere. [j] is rare in *tune, due,* and *new,* but fronted allophones of [u] occur somewhat more frequently in this class of words than in such words as *goose* and *moon,* which have no historical [j]. The higher proportion of fronted allophones suggests that at least part of the cause of the fronted [u] is assimilation to [j].

### The Northwest

This area includes everything from the central Dakotas westward to the Pacific Coast, and down the coast to include part of northern California. The area is not as clearly defined as those in the east, and much of the Oregon coast represents an extension of the North Central area. Nevertheless the Northwest has regional features in speech to mark it off from the other areas.

These features include the retention of [ɝ], [ɚ], and final and preconsonantal [r]. [ɑr] is usual, as in *cart* [kɑrt], but scattered occurrences of [ɒr] throughout the area represent infiltration from the Central Midland, and [ar] on the Oregon coast, from the North Central. Words of the type of *forest, horrid, orange,* and *warrant* regularly have [ɔ]. Those like *barren, narrow,* and *parrot* regularly have [ɛ]. *Various* usually has [ɛ], but the occasional use of [e] represents infiltration from the Central Midland.

Words like *hurry*, *worry*, and *courage* regularly have [ɝ] or [ɜr]; [ʌr] is extremely rare. As in the North Central area, the distinction between [ɔr] and [or] has been largely lost; *horse* and *hoarse* are both regularly [hɔrs].

Before velars, [ɔ] is frequent, but not as frequent as in the Central Midland area. *Fog, frog, log, donkey*, and *honk* usually have [ɔ], but [ɒ] is also frequent. [ɔ] is also frequent before [l], as in *doll, involve*, and *solve*, but [ɒ] and [ɑ] are relatively more frequent than in the Central Midland area. [æ] is all but universal in *ask, aunt, glass, rather*, and similar words. The final unstressed vowel in such words as *sandy, coffee*, and *donkey* is normally [i].

*Cot* may be [kɑt] or [kɒt], the latter somewhat less frequently than in the Central Midland area; [kat] occurs occasionally along the Oregon coast. *Swamp, laundry*, and *beyond* usually have [ɑ]; [ɒ] is less frequent. *Water* is frequently [ˈwatɚ]. *Cross* and *cloth* usually have [ɒ], but occasionally [ɔ]. *On* is usually [ɑn], with scattered occurrences of [ɒn] and [ɔn] throughout the area, and occasional use of [an] on the Oregon coast. Throughout the area the phonemic distinction between [ɑ] and [ɔ] is maintained more consistently than in the Central Midland area to the south or in western Canadian speech to the north.

The phonemic diphthongs [ɑʊ], [aɪ], and [ɔɪ] are relatively stable, though there is some use of [ɜʊ] for [ɑʊ] before voiceless consonants, as in *out* [ɜʊt], in the northern part of the area. Monophthongal [i], [e], [o], and [u] often occur before voiceless stops, but the diphthongal allophones [ɪi], [eɪ], [oʊ], and [ʊu] are more frequent. The raised allophones [ê] and [êɪ] have spread from the North Central area, and are occasionally heard as far west as Spokane. Fronted allophones of [o] and [u] are rare.

In *absorb, absurd*, and *desolate*, usage varies between [s] and [z]. The verb *grease* usually has [s]; *greasy*, usually [s], but ['grizi] occasionally infiltrates from the Central Midland area. *Tune, due,* and *new* almost universally have [u], not [ju].

## The Southwest Coastal Area

The Southwest Coastal area includes most of Nevada and Arizona, and all California except the northern tier of counties. In localities with a tradition of cattle ranching, there has been some infiltration from the Central Midland.    Among the metropolitan centers, San Francisco shows some infiltration from the various Midland areas, and traces of an earlier stratum of New England influence.    Los Angeles shows some infiltration from the North Central and New York City areas; Phoenix, from the Central Midland.    Infiltration is characteristic of all areas to which shifts of population in the twentieth century have brought large increases in population.    Mixture of speech is at present most noticeable in Florida, but it is also noticeable in the Southwest Coastal area.

Speech characteristics of the area include the retention of [ɝ], [ɚ], and final and preconsonantal [r].    In words like *cart,* [ɑr] is all but universal; [ar] and [ɒr] are extremely rare variants. In words like *forest, horrid, orange,* and *warrant,* [ɔ] predominates; but in *borrow, sorry,* and *tomorrow,* [ɑ] predominates.    In such words as *barren, narrow,* and *parrot,* [ɛ] is somewhat more frequent than [æ], but is not as strongly predominant as in the North Central area.    *Various* normally has [ɛ]; both [e] and [æ] are rare.    Words like *hurry, worry,* and *courage* regularly have [ɝ] or [ɝr].    The distinction between [ɔr] and [or] has been almost completely lost; both *horse* and *hoarse* are regularly [hɔrs].

Before velars, as in *frog, log, donkey,* and *honk,* [ɔ] is frequent; [ɒ], occasional.    In *fog* [ɒ] is slightly more frequent than [ɔ]. *Doll, involve, revolve,* and *solve* regularly have [ɑ].    *Stop, cot, shock, swamp,* and *beyond* usually have [ɑ]. *Laundry* varies between the extremes of [ɑ] and [ɔ], with [ɒ] most frequent. *Along, cross, cloth,* and similar words usually have [ɔ], occasionally [ɒ]. *On* is usually [ɑn]. *After, aunt, glass,* and *rather* normally have [æ]. Final unstressed [i] is normal in *sandy, coffee, donkey,* and similar words.

The phonemic diphthongs [ɑʊ], [aɪ], and [ɔɪ] are stable. Monophthongal [i], [e], [o], and [u] occur sometimes before voiceless stops, but the diphthongal allophones [ɪi], [eɪ], [oʊ], and [ʊu] are more frequent. Raised allophones of [e] and fronted allophones of [o] and [u] are extremely rare.

*Absorb, absurd, desolate, greasy,* and the verb *grease* usually have [s]; [z] is rare. *Tune, due,* and *new* have [u]; [ju] occurs only under elocutionary influence. In the larger cities [w] occurs more frequently than [hw] in words like *wheat,* and still more frequently in unstressed positions, as in *anywhere.*

As an area of comparatively recent growth in population, with its residents drawn from many other areas, the Southwest Coastal type has a more nearly neutral flavor in its speech than most of the other major areas. The neutral flavor is evident even in the speech of lifelong residents on whom this section is based.

In general, as we have already seen, diversity of speech is most marked on the Atlantic coast, in areas which have been continuously occupied by native speakers of English for the longest time. Elsewhere the differences have been maintained by differences in the migration routes, but have been blurred by the crossing and mingling of migration routes, and by the more recent shifts in population. It is probably unlikely that the speech of the country will ever be reduced to dead uniformity; it is equally unlikely that the divergences will become greater than they are at present.

# CHAPTER 23

# Regional Transcriptions

The phonetic transcriptions which make up this chapter represent the predominant pronunciations of certain subareas within the major areas discussed in the previous chapter. No single individual ever speaks exactly like the regional type he uses; he has his personal peculiarities. By tabulating a large number of individual pronunciations of individual words, however, we can eliminate the purely personal, and establish the predominant forms, for the area under consideration. Although some characteristic, but not predominant, features may be likewise eliminated, the resulting transcription will be at once more general and more typical than a transcription of the speech of a single individual.

Many of the words in the transcribed passage, though essential to the sense, are of no regional significance. I have therefore made no attempt to collect statistics for such words as *an*, *at*, *in*, *the*, *finished*, or *windmill*, but have transcribed all such words in what seems to me to be a reasonably normal fashion. Since phrasal stress patterns vary according to the interpretation of individual speakers, I have reduced stress marks to a minimum.

Nor have I burdened the transcriptions with minor allophonic subtleties unless they seemed to throw light on the regional type being illustrated; I have stayed as close to phonemic transcription as faithfulness to the regional type permitted. Each transcription may therefore be taken as a general presentation of the predominant pronunciations of regionally significant words used by the number of speakers indicated for the given area.

### 1: Eastern New England: 150 speakers from Maine

wʌn hɑrɪd reɪni deɪ, ræðə let ɪn fɛbjuɛri, wi sta:tɪd sɑʊθ, əlɔŋ ə dɛsələt roʊd θru ðə farəst. naʊ ən ðɛn wi həd frɑgz ɪn ðə swamps ɑn ðə pənɪnsələ. letɚ ə gus haŋkt, ən fɑg roʊld ɪn frəm ðə wɒtə. æftə θri ə foə maɪlz, ðə roʊd keɪm ɜut ɑntu ə bærən sændi strɛtʃ. hɪr ən ðɛə wəz ə ba:nja:d, wɪð ə dɒŋki ɚ ə fju hɑgz. səm arɪndʒ flaʊəz gru bɪsaɪd ðə roʊd. sʌdn̩li ðə reɪn keɪm daʊn ɪn tarənts, ən ðə ruf əv ðə ka: bɪgæn tə lik. wi wə sɑri ðət wi hædn̩ fɪkst ɪt bifoə livɪŋ hoʊm, bət ɑʊə plænz əd ɪnvalvd so mɛni ˈdɹitelz ðət wi hædn̩ bɒðəd. ɑ: klouz əbsɒ:bd so mʌtʃ dæmpnɪs ðət wi fɛlt koʊld, so wi hʌrid tə ðə nɛkst vɪlɪdʒ. æftə livɪŋ ðə ka: tə bi grist ət ə gəradʒ, wi faʊnd ə rɛstrənt, hwɛə wi ɒ:dəd kɒfi ən pænkeks wɪð mepəl sɪrəp. wi wetɪd fə lʌntʃ baɪ ə hjudʒ faɪəples, hwɛr ə tʃɪəfəl lɔg faɪə wəz bənɪŋ. ðə wɒlz ən floə wə meɪd wɪð hɛvi paɪn boədz, hwɪtʃ wə blæk wɪð sʊt. wi wə səpraɪzd tə si vɛriəs kwɪə θɪŋz ɪn ɒd kɔ:nəz. ðɛə wəz ə glæs keɪs fɪld wɪð dɒlz, sʌm əv hwɪtʃ wə frəm farən lændz. nɛks tə ðə tʃɪmni wəz ə kæləndə ðət ædvətaɪzd ə lɑndri, ən bijɒnd ɪt wəz ə harəbəl old pærət ɑn ə pətʃ. wi watʃt ðɪs əbsəd sin əntɪl ə wetə brɒt ɑ: lʌntʃ θru ə næro sɔ:t əv karɪdə frəm ðə kɪtʃɪn. hwaɪl wi et wi traɪd tə salv ə krɒswəd pʌzəl, bət ɑ hændz wə soʊ grisi ðət wi hæd tə waʃ ən rɪns ðəm fɜst. hwɛn wi fɪnɪʃt wi faʊnd ðət ðə reɪn əd kliəd ʌp ɪnʌf tə warənt ɑ goʊɪŋ ɑn. wi barəd ə klɒθ tə

klin ðə ka: wɪndoz, ən hopt ðət təmaro wəd brɪŋ gʊd wɛðə. ðə
ruut nʌmbə simd tə karɪspand wɪð ðə wʌn an aʊə roʊd mæp,
ən wi falod ɪt pæst ði oʊld stoʊn kwari nɪə ði arɪgan stet laɪn.
ðæt naɪt wi slɛpt ɪn ə turɪst kæbɪn, ənd lɪsnd tu ə wɪndmɪl hwɪtʃ
rivalvd sloʊli ən nɔɪzəli aʊtsaɪd a: doə.

## 2: New York City: 500 speakers

wʌn harɪd reɪni deɪ, raðə leɪt ɪn fɛbrueri, wi sta:tɪd saʊθ, əlɔŋ
ə dɛsələt roʊd θru ðə farəst.   naʊ ən ðɛn wi hɜˑd fragz ɪn ðə
swamps an ðə pənɪnsələ.   letə ə gʊs haŋkt, ən fag roʊld ɪn frəm
ðə wɔ:tə.   æftə θri ɔ fɔə maɪlz, ðə roʊd keɪm aʊt antu ə bærən
sændi strɛtʃ.   hɪr ən ðɛ: wəz ə ba:nja:d, wɪð ə daŋki ɔr ə fju
hagz.   səm arɪndʒ flaʊəz gru bisaɪd ðə roʊd.   sʌdn̩li ðə reɪn keɪm
daʊn ɪn tarənts, ən ðə ruf əv ðə ka: bɪgæn tə lik.   wi wə sari
ðət wi hædn̩ fɪkst ɪt bifɔ: livɪŋ hoʊm, bət aʊə plænz həd ɪnvalvd
so mɛni ᶦditelz ðət wi hædn̩t baðəd.   aʊə kloʊz əbzɔ:bd so mʌtʃ
dæmpnəs ðət wi fɛlt koʊld, so wi hʌrid tə ðə nɛkst vɪlɪdʒ.   æftə
livɪŋ ðə ka: tə bi grist ət ə gəradʒ, wi faʊnd ə rɛstrant, wɛ: wi
ɔ:dəd kɔfi ən pænkeks wɪð meɪpəl sɪrəp.   wi weɪtɪd fə lʌntʃ baɪ
ə hjudʒ faɪəples, wɛr ə tʃɪəfəl lag faɪə wəz bənɪŋ.   ðə wɔlz ən
flɔə wə meɪd wɪð hɛvi paɪn bɔ:dz, wɪtʃ wə blæk wɪð sʊt.   wi wə
səpraɪzd tə si vɛriəs kwɪə θɪŋz ɪn ad kɔ:nəz.   ðɛ wəz ə glæs keɪs
fɪld wɪθ dalz, sʌm əv wɪtʃ wə frəm farən lændz.   nɛks tə ðə
tʃɪmni wəz ə kæləndə ðət ædvətaɪzd ə lɔndri, ən biand ɪt wəz ə
harəbəl oʊld pærət an ə pɜtʃ.   wi watʃt ðɪs əbsɜˑd sin əntɪl ə weɪtə
brɔt aʊə lʌntʃ θru ə næro sɔ:t əv karɪdə frəm ðə kɪtʃən.   waɪl wi
eɪt wi traɪd tə salv ə krɔswɜˑd pʌzəl, bət aʊə hændz wə so grisi
ðət wi hæd tə waʃ ən rɪns ðəm fɜˑst.   wɛn wi fɪnɪʃt wi faʊnd ðət
ðə reɪn əd klɪəd ʌp ɪnʌf tə warənt aʊə goʊɪŋ an.   wi barəd ə
klɔθ tə klin ðə ka: wɪndoz, ən hoʊpt ðət təmaro wəd brɪŋ gʊd
wɛðə.   ðə ruut nʌmbə simd tə karɪspand wɪθ ðə wʌn an aʊə

roʊd mæp, ən wi fɑləd ɪt pæst ði oʊld stoʊn kwɑri nɪə ði ɑrɪgɑn
stet lɑɪn.   ðæt nɑɪt wi slɛpt ɪn ə tʊrɪst kæbɪn, ənd lɪsn̩d tu ə
wɪndmɪl wɪtʃ rɪvɑlvd sloʊli ən nɔɪzəli aʊtsɑɪd ɑr dɔə.

## 3: The Philadelphia Area: 266 speakers from Bucks, Delaware, Montgomery, and Philadelphia Counties, Pennsylvania, and Camden County, New Jersey

wʌn hɑrɪd reɪni deɪ, rɑðɚ let ɪn fɛbrʊɛri, wi stɑrtəd saʊθ,
əlɔŋ ə dɛsələt röʊd θru ðə fɑrəst.   naʊ ən ðɛn wi hɚd frɑgz ɪn
ðə swɑmps ɔn ðə pənɪnsələ.   letɚ ə güis haŋkt, ən fɑg roʊld ɪn
frəm ðə wɔtɚ.   æftɚ θri ɚ fɔr mɑɪlz, ðə röʊd keɪm aʊt ɔntu ə
bærən sændi strɛtʃ.   hɪr ən ðɛr wəz ə bʊrnjɑrd, wɪð ə dʌŋki ɚ ə
fju hɑgz.   səm ɑrɪndʒ flaʊɚz gru bisɑɪd ðə röʊd.   sʌdn̩li ðə reɪn
keɪm daʊn ɪn tɑrənts, ən ðə ruf əv ðə kɑr bɪgæn tə lik.   wi wɚ
sɑri ðət wi hædn̩ fɪkst ɪt bifɔr lɪvɪŋ hoʊm, bət ɑr plænz həd ɪnvɑlvd
so mɛni ˈditelz ðət wi hædn̩t bɑðɚd.   ɑr kloʊz əbzɔrbd so mʌtʃ
dæmpnəs ðət wi fɛlt koʊld, so wi hʌrid tə ðə nɛkst vɪlɪdʒ.   æftɚ
lɪvɪŋ ðə kɑr tə bi grist ət ə gərɑdʒ, wi faʊnd ə rɛstrɑnt, wɛr wi
ɔrdɚd kɔfi ən pænkeks wɪð mepəl sɪrəp.   wi wetɪd fɚ lʌntʃ bɑɪ ə
hjʊudʒ fɑɪrples, wɛr ə tʃɪrfəl lɑg fɑɪr wəz bɚnɪŋ.   ðə wɔlz ən flor
wɚ meɪd wɪð hɛvi pɑɪn bordz, wɪtʃ wɚ blæk wɪð sʊt.   wi wɚ
səpraɪzd tə sii vɛriəs kwɪr θɪŋz ɪn ɑd kɔrnɚz.   ðɛr wəz ə glæs
keɪs fɪld wɪð dɑlz, sʌm əv wɪtʃ wɚ frəm fɑrən lændz.   nɛks tə
ðə tʃɪmni wəz ə kæləndɚ ðət ædvɚtaɪzd ə lɔndri, ən bijɑnd ɪt
wəz ə hɑrəbəl oʊld pærət ɔn ə pɚtʃ.   wi wɑtʃt ðɪs əbsɚd siin əntɪl
ə wetɚ brɔt ɑr lʌntʃ θru ə næro sɔrt əv kɑrədɚ frəm ðə kɪtʃən.
wɑɪl wi eɪt wi trɑɪd tə salv ə krɔswɚd pʌzəl, bət ɑr hændz wɚ
söʊ griisi ðət wi hæd tə waʃ ən rɪns ðəm fɚst.   wɛn wi fɪnɪʃt wi
faʊnd ðət ðə reɪn əd klɪrd ʌp ɪnʌf tə warənt aʊr goʊɪŋ ɔn.   wi
barəd ə klɔθ tə kliin ðə kɑr wɪndöʊz, ənd höʊpt ðət təmaro wəd
brɪŋ gʊd wɛðɚ.   ðə rʊut nʌmbɚ simd tə kɑrɪspɑnd wɪð ðə wʌn

ɔn aʊr röʊd mæp, ən wi fɑləd ɪt pæst ði oʊld stoʊn kwɑri nɪr
ði ɑrigɑn stet lɑɪn.  ðæt naɪt wi slɛpt ɪn ə tʊrɪst kæbən, ən lɪsn̩d
tu ə wɪnmɪl wɪtʃ rivɑlvd slöʊli ən nɔɪzəli aʊtsaɪd ar dɔr.

## 4: The South: 207 speakers from Alabama

wʌn hɑrɪd reɪnɪ deɪ, rɑðə leɪt ɪn fɛbjuɛri wi stɑːtɪd sæʊθ əlɔŋ
ə dɛsələt roʊd θru ðə fɑrɪst.  næː ən ðɛn wi hɜd frɑgz ɪn ðə
swɑmps ɔn ðə pənɪnʃələ.  leɪtə ə güʊs hɔŋkt, ən fɑg roʊld ɪn
frɑm ðə wɔtə.  æftə θri ə foə mɑːlz, ðə roʊd keɪm aʊt ɔntu ə
bærən sændɪ strɛtʃ.  hɪə ən ðɛə wəz ə bɑːnjɑːd wɪð ə dɑŋkɪ ɚ
ə fju hɑgz.  səm arɪndʒ flaʊəz gruʊ bɪsaɪd ðə roʊd.  sʌdn̩lɪ ðə
reɪn keɪm dæʊn ɪn tarənts, ən ðə ruʊf əv ðə kɑː bɪgæn tə lïik.  wi
wə sɑrɪ ðət wi hædn̩ fɪkst ɪt bəfoː lïivɪŋ hoʊm, bət aː plænz həd
ɪnvɑlvd so mɛnɪ ˈditeɪlz ðət wi hædn̩ bɑðəd.  aʊə kloʊz əbsɔːbd so
mʌtʃ dæmpnɪs ðət wi fɛlt koʊld, so wi hʌrɪd tə ðə nɛkst vɪlɪdʒ.
æftə lïivɪŋ ðə kɑː tə bi grïizd ət ə gərɑdʒ, wi fæʊnd ə rɛstrənt,
hwɛə wi ɔːdəd kɔfɪ ən pænkeks wɪð meɪpəl sʌrəp.  wi weɪtɪd baː
ə hjuʊdʒ faəpleɪs hwɛə ə tʃɪəfəl lɔg faə wəz bənɪŋ.  ðə wɔlz ən floə
wə meɪd wɪð hɛvi pɑːn boədz, hwɪtʃ wə blæk wɪð sʊt.  wi wə
səprɑːzd tə sïi veriəs kwɪə θɪŋz ɪn ɑd kɔːnəz.  ðɛə wəz ə glæs keɪs
fɪld wɪð dɑlz, sʌm əv hwɪtʃ wə frɑm farən lændz.  nɛks tə ðə
tʃɪmnɪ wəz ə kæləndə ðət ædvətɑːzd ə lɑndrɪ, ən bijɑnd ɪt wəz
ə harəbəl oʊld pærət ɔn ə pɜtʃ.  wi wɔtʃt ðɪs əbsɜd sïin əntɪl ə
weɪtə brɔt aʊə lʌntʃ θru ə nærə sɔːt əv karədə frəm ðə kɪtʃɪn.
hwɑl wi eɪt wi traːd tə salv ə krɔswɜd pʌzəl, bət aə hændz wə
soʊ grïizi ðət wi hæd tə waʃ ən rɪntʃ ðəm fɜst.  hwɛn wi fɪnɪʃt
wi fæʊnd ðət ðə reɪn əd klïəd ʌp ɪnʌf tə warənt aʊə goʊɪŋ ɔn.
wi barəd ə klɔθ tə klïin ðə kɑː wɪndəz, ənd hoʊpt ðət təmarə
wəd brɪŋ gʊd wɛðə.  ðə ruʊt nʌmbə sïimd tə karəspand wɪθ ðə
wʌn ɔn aʊə roʊd mæp, ən wi fɑləd ɪt pæst ði oʊld stoʊn kwɑrɪ
nïə ði arəgən steɪt laːn.  ðæt naːt wi slɛpt ɪn ə tʊrəst kæbɪn, ən

lısn̩d tu ə wınmıl hwıtʃ rıvalvd sloʊlı ən nɔːzəlı aʊtsaːd aʊə doə.

## 5: The North Central Area: 360 speakers from Wisconsin

wʌn hɔrıd reɪni deɪ, ræðɚ let ın fɛbjʊɛri, wi startəd saʊθ, əlɔŋ ə dɛsələt roʊd θru ðə fɔrəst. naʊ ən ðɛn wi hɚd frɔgz ın ðə swamps an ðə pənınsələ. letɚ ə gus hɔŋkt, ən fɔg roʊld ın frəm ðə watɚ. æftɚ θri ɚ fɔr maɪlz, ðə roʊd kem aʊt antu ə bɛrən sændi strɛtʃ. hır ən ðɛr wəz ə barnjard, wıð ə dɔŋki ɚ ə fju hɔgz. səm ɔrındʒ flaʊəz gru bisaɪd ðə roʊd. sʌdn̩li ðə reɪn keɪm daʊn ın tɔrənts, ən ðə ruf əv ðə kar bıgæn tə lik. wi wɚ sɔri ðət wi hædn̩ fıkst ıt bifɔr livıŋ hoʊm, bət ar plænz əd ınvalvd so mɛni ˈditelz ðət wi hædn̩ baðɚd. aʊr kloʊz əbzɔrbd so mʌtʃ dæmpnəs ðət wi fɛlt koʊld, so wi hɚrid tə ðə nɛkst vılıdʒ. æftɚ livıŋ ðə kar tə bi grist ət ə gəradʒ, wi faʊnd ə rɛstrənt, hwɛr wi ɔrdɚd kɔfi ən pænkeks wıð mepəl sırəp. wi wetəd fɚ lʌntʃ baɪ ə hjudʒ faɪrples, hwɛr ə tʃırfəl lɔg faɪr wəz bɚnıŋ. ðə wɔlz ən flɔr wɚ med wıð hɛvi paın bɔrdz, hwıtʃ wɚ blæk wıð sʊt. wi wɚ səpraɪzd tə si vɛriəs kwır θıŋz ın ad kɔrnɚz. ðɛr wəz ə glæs kes fıld wıð dalz, sʌm əv hwıtʃ wɚ frəm fɔrən lændz. nɛks tə ðə tʃımni wəz ə kæləndɚ ðət ædvɚtaɪzd ə lɔndri, ən bijand ıt wəz ə hɔrəbəl old pɛrət an ə pɚtʃ. wi watʃt ðıs əbzɚd sin əntıl ə wetɚ brɔt ar lʌntʃ θru ə nɛro sɔrt əv kɔrıdɚ frəm ðə kıtʃən. hwaɪl wi et wi traɪd tə salv ə krɒswɚd pʌzəl, bət ar hændz wɚ soʊ grisi ðət wi hæd tə waʃ ən rıns ðəm fɚst. hwɛn wi fınıʃt wi faʊnd ðət ðə reɪn əd klırd ʌp inʌf tə wɔrənt ar goɪŋ an. wi barəd ə klɒθ tə klin ðə kar wındoz, ən hoʊpt ðət təmaro wəd brıŋ gud wɛðɚ. ðə raʊt nʌmbɚ simd tə kɔrıspand wıθ ðə wʌn an ar roʊd mæp, ən wi faləd ıt pæst ði oʊld stoʊn kwɔri nır ði ɔrıgan stet laın. ðæt naɪt wi slɛpt ın ə tʊrəst kæbın, ən lısn̩ tu ə wındmıl hwıtʃ rıvalvd sloʊli ən nɔızəli aʊtsaɪd ar dɔr.

## 6: Western Pennsylvania: 264 speakers from Pittsburgh (Allegheny County) and contiguous counties

wʌn hɔrɪd reɪni deɪ, ræðɚ let ɪn fɛbjuɛri, wi startəd saʊθ,
əlɔŋ ə dɛsələt röud θru ðə fɔrəst. naʊ ən ðɛn wi hɚd frɒgz ɪn
ðə swamps ɑn ðə pənɪnsələ. letɚ ə güs hɔŋkt, ən fɒg roʊld ɪn
frɑm ðə wɒtɚ. æftɚ θri ɚ for maɪlz ðə röud kem aʊt ɑntu ə
bærən sændi strɛtʃ. hɪr ən ðɛr wəz ə barnjard, wɪθ ə dɔŋki ɚ
ə fju hagz. səm ɔrɪndʒ flaʊɚz gru bisaɪd ðə röud. sʌdn̩li ðə
reɪn keɪm daʊn ɪn tɔrənts, ən ðə ruf əv ðə kar bigæn tə lik.
wi wɚ sari ðət wi hædn̩ fɪkst ɪt bifɔr lïivɪŋ hoʊm, bət ar plænz
həd ɪnvɒlvd so mɛni ˈditeɪlz ðət wi hædn̩t bɒðɚd. aʊr kloʊz
əbzɔrbd so mʌtʃ dæmpnəs ðət wi fɛlt koʊld, so wi hʌrid tə ðə
nɛkst vɪlɪdʒ. æftɚ lïivɪŋ ðə kar tə bi griizd ət ə gəradʒ, wi faʊnd
ə rɛstrant, wɛr wi ɔrdɚd kɒfi ən pænkeks wɪθ mepəl sɪrəp. wi
wetɪd fɚ lʌntʃ baɪ ə hjʊudʒ faɪrpleɪs, wɛr ə tʃɪrfəl lɔg faɪr wəz
bɚnɪŋ. ðə wɔlz ən flor wɚ meɪd wɪð hɛvi paɪn bordz, wɪtʃ wɚ
blæk wɪð sʊt. wi wɚ sɚpraɪzd tə sii vɛriəs kwɪr θɪŋz ɪn ɒd kɔrnɚz.
ðɛr wəz ə glæs keɪs fɪld wɪθ dɔlz, sʌm əv wɪtʃ wɚ frəm fɔrən
lændz. nɛks tə ðə tʃɪmni wəz ə kæləndɚ ðət ædvɚtaɪzd ə lɒndri,
ən bijɒnd ɪt wəz ə hɔrəbəl oʊld pærət ɑn ə pɚtʃ. wi watʃt ðɪs
əbsɚd siin əntɪl ə weɪtɚ brɒt ar lʌntʃ θru ə næro kɔrɪdɚ frəm
ðə kɪtʃən. waɪl wi eɪt wi traɪd tə sɔlv ə krɒswɚd pʌzəl, bət ar
hændz wɚ söʊ griizi ðət wi hæd tə wɔʃ ən rɪns ðəm fɚst. wɛn
wi fɪnɪʃt wi faʊnd ðət ðə reɪn əd klɪrd ʌp ɪnʌf tə wɔrənt ar goʊɪŋ
ɑn. wi bɔrəd ə klɒθ tə klïin ðə kar wɪndəz, ən höʊpt ðət təmaro
wəd brɪŋ gʊd wɛðɚ. ðə ruut nʌmbɚ siimd tə kɔrɪspand wɪθ
ðə wʌn ɑn ar röud mæp, ən wi fɒlod ɪt pæst ði oʊld stoʊn kwɔri
nɪr ði ɔrɪgən steɪt laɪn. ðæt naɪt wi slɛpt ɪn ə turɪst kæbən, ən
lɪsn̩d tu ə wɪndmɪl wɪtʃ rivɒlvd sloʊli ən nɔɪzəli aʊtsaɪd ar dor.

## 7: Southern Mountain: 165 speakers from West Virginia

wʌn hɔrəd reɪni deɪ, ræðɚ let ɪn fɛbjuɛri, wi stɑrtəd saʊθ,
əlɔŋ ə dɛsələt röud θru ðə fɔrəst. naʊ ən ðɛn wi hɚd frɔgz ɪn
ðə swɑmps ɔn ðə pənɪnʃələ. letɚ ə güs hɔŋkt, ən fɔg roʊld ɪn
frəm ðə wɔtɚ. æftɚ θri ɚ for ma:lz, ðə röud keɪm aʊt ɔntu ə
bærən sændɪ strɛtʃ. hɪr ən ðɛr wəz ə bɑrn jɑrd, wɪð ə dɔŋkɪ ɚ
ə fju hɔgz. səm ɔrɪndʒ flauəz gru bɪsaɪd ðə röud. sʌdn̩li ðə
reɪn keɪm daʊn ɪn tɔrənts, ən ðə ruf əv ðə kɑr bɪgæn tə lik. wi
wɚ sɑrɪ ðət wi hædn̩ fɪkst ɪt bəfor lɪivɪŋ hoʊm, bət ar plænz əd
ɪnvɑlvd so mɛnɪ ᴵditeɪlz ðət wi hædn̩ baðɚd. ar kloʊz əbsɔrbd
so mʌtʃ dæmpnəs ðət wi fɛlt koʊld, so wi hʌrid tə ðə nɛkst vɪlɪdʒ.
æftɚ lɪivɪŋ ðə kɑr tə bi grɪizd ət ə gərɑdʒ, wi faʊnd ə rɛstrənt
wɛr wi ɔrdɚd kɔfɪ ən pænkeks wɪð mepəl sɪrəp. wi wetɪd fɚ
lʌntʃ baɪ ə hjuudʒ farpleɪs, wɛr ə tʃɪrfəl lɔg far wəz bɚnɪŋ. ðə
wɔlz ən flor wɚ meɪd wɪð hɛvɪ pa:n bordz, wɪtʃ wɚ blæk wɪð
sʊt. wi wɚ səpraɪzd tə sɪi vɛriəs kwɪr θɪŋz ɪn ɑd kɔrnɚz. ðɛr
wəz ə glæs keɪs fɪld wɪð dɑlz, sʌm əv wɪtʃ wɚ frəm fɔrən lændz.
nɛks tə ðə tʃɪmnɪ wəz ə kæləndɚ ðət ædvɚtaɪzd ə lɑndrɪ, ən bijɑnd
ɪt wəz ə hɔrəbəl oʊld pɛrət ɔn ə pɚtʃ. wi wɑtʃt ðɪs əbsɚd sɪin
əntɪl ə wetɚ brɔt ar lʌntʃ θru ə nɛrə sɔrt əv kɔrədɚ frəm ðə kɪtʃən.
waɪl wi et wi traɪd tə sɑlv ə krɔswɚd pʌzəl, bət ar hændz wɚ
söu grɪizɪ ðət wi hæd tə woʃ ən rɪns ðəm fɚst. wɛn wi fɪnɪʃt wi
faʊnd ðət ðə reɪn əd klɪrd ʌp ɪnʌf tə wɔrənt ar goʊɪŋ ɔn. wi
bɑrəd ə klɔθ tə klɪin ðə kɑr wɪndəz ən hoʊpt ðət təmɑrə wəd
brɪŋ gʊd wɛðɚ. ðə rüt nʌmbɚ sɪimd tə kɔrɪspɑnd wɪθ ðə wʌn
ɔn ar röud mæp, ən wi fɑləd ɪt pæst ði oʊld stoʊn kwɑrɪ nɪr
ði ɔrɪgən stet la:n. ðæt naɪt wi slɛpt ɪn ə turəst kæbɪn, ən lɪsn̩d
tu ə wɪndmɪl wɪtʃ rɪvɑlvd sloʊlɪ ən noɪzlɪ aʊtsaɪd ar dor.

## 8: The Central Midland Area: 206 speakers from Kansas

wʌn hɔrəd reɪni deɪ, ræðɚ let ɪn fɛbjuɛri, wi stɑrtɪd sauθ, əlɔŋ ə dɛsələt roʊd θru ðə fɔrəst. naʊ ən ðɛn wi hɚd frɔgz ɪn ðə swɒmps ɑn ðə pənɪnsələ. letɚ ə güs hɔŋkt, ən fɔg roʊld ɪn frəm ðə wɒtɚ. æftɚ θri ɚ for maɪlz, ðə roʊd keɪm aʊt ɑntu ə bɛrən sændi strɛtʃ. hɪr ən ðɛr wəz ə bɑrnjɑrd, wɪθ ə dɔŋki ɚ ə fju hɔgz. səm ɔrɪndʒ flauɚz gru bɪsaɪd ðə roʊd. sʌdņli ðə reɪn keɪm daʊn ɪn tɔrənts, ən ðə ruf əv ðə kɑr bɪgæn tə lik. wi wɚ sɑrɪ ðət wi hædņ fɪkst ɪt bɪfor livɪŋ hoʊm, bət ar plænz əd ɪnvɑlvd so mɛni ¹diteɪlz ðət wi hædņt baðɚd. ar kloʊz əbsɔrbd so mʌtʃ dæmpnəs ðət wi fɛlt koʊld, so wi hɚid tə ðə nɛkst vɪlɪdʒ. æftɚ livɪŋ ðə kɑr tə bi griist ət ə gəradʒ, wi faʊnd ə rɛstrənt, wɛr wi ɔrdɚd kɔfi ən pænkeks wɪð mepəl sɪrəp. wi wetəd baɪ ə hjuudʒ faɪrpleɪs, wɛr ə tʃɪrfəl lɔg faɪr wəz bɚnɪŋ. ðə wɔlz ən flor wɚ meɪd wɪð hɛvi paɪn bordz, wɪtʃ wɚ blæk wɪð sʊt. wi wɚ səpraɪzd tə si vɛriəs kwɪr θɪŋz ɪn ɑd kɔrnɚz. ðɛr wəz ə glæs keɪs fɪld wɪθ dɑlz, sʌm əv wɪtʃ wɚ frəm fɔrən lændz. nɛks tə ðə tʃɪmni wəz ə kæləndɚ ðət ædvɚtaɪzd ə lɒndri, ən bijɒnd ɪt wəz ə hɔrəbəl oʊld pɛrət ɒn ə pɚtʃ. wi wɑtʃt ðɪs əbsɚd siin əntɪl ə wetɚ brot ar lʌntʃ θru ə nɛro sɔrt əv kɔrɪdɚ frəm ðə kɪtʃɪn. waɪl wi et wi traɪd tə sɔlv ə krɒswɚd pʌzəl, bət ar hændz wɚ so griisi ðət wi hæd tə wɔʃ ən rɪns ðəm fɚst. wɛn wi fɪnɪʃt wi faʊnd ðət ðə reɪn əd klɪrd ʌp ɪnʌf tə wɔrənt ar goʊɪŋ ɒn. wi bɑrəd ə klɒθ tə kliin ðə kɑr wɪndoz, ən hoʊpt ðət təmɑrə wəd brɪŋ gʊd wɛðɚ. ðə raʊt nʌmbɚ siimd tə kɔrɪspɒnd wɪθ ðə wʌn ɒn ar roʊd mæp, ən wi fɑlod ɪt pæst ði oʊld stoʊn kwɛri nɪr ði ɔrɪgən stet laɪn. ðæt naɪt wi slɛpt ɪn ə turəst kæbɪn, ən lɪsņd tu ə wɪndmɪl wɪtʃ rivɒlvd sloʊli ən nɔɪzəli aʊtsaɪd ar dor.

## 9: The Northwest: 130 speakers from Washington state

wʌn hɔrəd reɪni deɪ, ræðɚ let ɪn fɛbjuɛri, wi stɑrted sɑʊθ, əlɔŋ ə dɛsələt roʊd θru ðə fɔrəst. nɑʊ ən ðɛn wi hɝd frɒgz ɪn ðə swɑmps ɑn ðə pənɪnsələ. letɚ ə gus hɒŋkt, ən fɒg roʊld ɪn frəm ðə watɚ. æftɚ θri ɚ fɔr maɪlz, ðə roʊd keɪm ɑʊt ɑntu ə bɛrən sændi strɛtʃ. hɪr ən ðɛr wəz ə bɑrnjɑrd, wɪð ə dɔŋki ɚ ə fju hɔgz. səm ɔrɪndʒ flɑʊɚz gru bisaɪd ðə roʊd. sʌdn̩li ðə reɪn keɪm dɑʊn ɪn tɔrənts, ən ðə rʊf əv ðə kɑr bigæn tə lik. wi wɚ sɑri ðət wi hædn̩ fɪkst ɪt bifɔr livɪŋ hoʊm, bət ɑr plænz əd ɪnvɑlvd so mɛni ˈditeɪlz ðət wi hædn̩t bɑðɚd. ɑr kloʊz əbzɔrbd so mʌtʃ dæmpnəs ðət wi fɛlt koʊld, so wi hɜrid tə ðə nɛkst vɪlɪdʒ. æftɚ livɪŋ ðə kɑr tə bi grist ət ə gərɑdʒ, wi fɑʊnd ə rɛstrənt, hwɛr wi ɔrdɚd kɒfi ən pænkeks wɪð mepəl sɪrəp. wi wetəd fɚ lʌntʃ baɪ ə hjudʒ faɪrples, hwɛr ə tʃɪrfəl lɔg faɪr wəz bɝnɪŋ. ðə wɔlz ən flɔr wɚ meɪd wɪð hɛvi paɪn bɔrdz, hwɪtʃ wɚ blæk wɪð sʊt. wi wɚ sɚpraɪzd tə sii vɛriəs kwɪr θɪŋz ɪn ɑd kɔrnɚz. ðɛr wəz ə glæs kes fɪld wɪð dɑlz, sʌm əv hwɪtʃ wɚ frəm fɔrən lændz. nɛks tə ðə tʃɪmni wəz ə kæləndɚ ðət ædvɚtaɪzd ə lɑndri, ən bijɑnd ɪt wəz ə hɔrəbəl oʊld pɛrət ɑn ə pɝtʃ. wi watʃt ðɪs əbsɝd siin əntɪl ə wetɚ brɒt ɑr lʌntʃ θru ə nɛro sɔrt əv kɔrɪdɚ frəm ðə kɪtʃən. hwaɪl wi et wi traɪd tə sɔlv ə krɒswɝd pʌzəl, bət ɑr hændz wɚ soʊ grisi ðət wi hæd tə waʃ ən rɪns ðəm fɝst. hwɛn wi fɪnɪʃt wi fɑʊnd ðət ðə reɪn əd klɪrd ʌp inʌf tə wɔrənt ɑr goɪŋ ɑn. wi bɑrəd ə klɒθ tə klin ðə kɑr wɪndoz, ən hoʊpt ðət təmɑro wəd brɪŋ gʊd wɛðɚ. ðə rɑʊt nʌmbɚ simd tə kɔrɪspɑnd wɪθ ðə wʌn ɑn ɑr roʊd mæp, ən wi fɑlod ɪt pæst ði ɔrigən stet laɪn. ðæt naɪt wi slɛpt ɪn ə tʊrəst kæbɪn, ən lɪsn̩ tu ə wɪndmɪl hwɪtʃ rivɑlvd sloʊli ən nɔɪzəli ɑʊtsaɪd ɑr dɔr.

**10: Southwest Coastal Area: 93 speakers from southern California, south of the east-west surveyor's line that forms the northern boundaries of San Luis Obispo, Kern, and San Bernardino counties**

wʌn hɔrɪd reɪni deɪ, ræðɚ let ɪn fɛbjuɛri, wi stɑrtəd sɑʊθ, əlɔŋ ə dɛsələt roʊd θru ðə fɔrəst. nɑʊ ən ðɛn wi hɝd frɔgz ɪn ðə swɑmps ɑn ðə pənɪnsələ. letɚ ə gus hɔŋkt, ən fɒg roʊld ɪn frəm ðə wɔtɚ. æftɚ θri ɚ fɔr maɪlz, ðə roʊd keɪm ɑʊt ɑntu ə bɛrən sændi strɛtʃ. hɪr ən ðɛr wəz ə bɑrnjɑrd, wɪð ə dɔŋki ɚ ə fju hɔgz. səm ɔrɪndʒ flɑʊɚz gru bɪsaɪd ðə roʊd. sʌdn̩li ðə reɪn keɪm dɑʊn ɪn tɔrənts, ən ðə rʊf əv ðə kɑr bɪgæn tə lik. wi wɚ sɑri ðət wi hædn̩t fɪkst ɪt bifɔr livɪŋ hoʊm, bət ɑr plænz əd ɪnvɑlvd so mɛni ˈditeɪlz ðət wi hædn̩t baðɚd. ɑr kloʊz əbsɔrbd so mʌtʃ dæmpnəs ðət wi fɛlt koʊld, so wi hɝrid tə ðə nɛkst vɪlɪdʒ. æftɚ livɪŋ ðə kɑr tə bi grist ət ə gərɑdʒ, wi fɑʊnd ə rɛstrənt, hwɛr wi ɔrdɚd kɔfi ən pænkeks wɪð mepəl sɪrəp. wi wetəd fɚ lʌntʃ baɪ ə hjudʒ faɪrples, hwɛr ə tʃɪrfəl lɔg faɪr wəz bɝnɪŋ. ðə wɔlz ən flɔr wɚ meɪd wɪð hɛvi paɪn bɔrdz, hwɪtʃ wɚ blæk wɪð sʊt. wi wɚ səpraɪzd tə si vɛriəs kwɪr θɪŋz ɪn ɑd kɔrnɚz. ðɛr wəz ə glæs kes fɪld wɪð dɑlz, sʌm əv hwɪtʃ wɚ frəm fɔrən lændz. nɛks tə ðə tʃɪmni wəz ə kæləndɚ ðət ædvɚtaɪzd ə lɒndri, ən biand ɪt wəz ə hɔrəbəl oʊld pɛrət ɑn ə pɝtʃ. wi wɑtʃt ðɪs əbsɝd sin əntɪl ə wetɚ brɔt ɑr lʌntʃ θru ə næro sɔrt əv kɔrɪdɚ frəm ðə kɪtʃən. hwaɪl wi et wi traɪd tə sɑlv ə krɔswɝd pʌzəl, bət ɑr hændz wɚ soʊ grisi ðət wi hæd tə wɔʃ ən rɪns ðəm fɝst. hwɛn wi fɪnɪʃt wi fɑʊnd ðət ðə reɪn əd klɪrd ʌp ɪnʌf tə wɔrənt ɑr goɪŋ ɑn. wi bɑrod ə klɒθ tə klin ðə kɑr wɪndəz, ən hoʊpt ðət təmɑro wəd brɪŋ gʊd wɛðɚ. ðə rut nʌmbɚ simd tə kɔrɪspɑnd wɪθ ðə wʌn ɑn ɑr roʊd mæp, ən wi fɑlod ɪt pæst ði oʊld stoʊn kwɔri nɪr ði ɔrɪgən stet laɪn. ðæt naɪt wi slɛpt ɪn ə turəst kæbɪn, ən lɪsn̩d tu ə wɪndmɪl hwɪtʃ rivɑlvd sloʊli ən nɔɪzəli ɑʊtsaɪd ɑr dɔr.

# CHAPTER 24

# Standards of Pronunciation

The use of the term "standard" in the discussion of linguistic questions is perhaps unfortunate. Usually we think of standards as fixed and immutable measurements, and all too often we transfer the abstract concept of immutability over to our linguistic discussions. We ask for the "correct" pronunciation, with the assumption that only one can be correct, and that all others must be incorrect.

But even in more rigidly standardized fields than that of speech there is always a certain amount of unavoidable variation. An inch is more flexible to a carpenter than to a watchmaker. Standards of linear measure, and tolerance of variation, are set for the carpenter and the watchmaker by the nature of the job to be done. Standards of speech are basically set by the job to be done—the act of communication.

Communication requires that certain signals be distinguished from one another, sometimes by circumstances, sometimes by linguistic context, sometimes by phonemic differentiation. If I point to a pen that lies in plain sight on a table and ask for it, the circumstances (pen, table, and gesture) and the linguistic context

("Give me that . . .") make my pronunciation of [pɛn] relatively unimportant. Much of our daily conversation depends on such contextual and circumstantial aids.

But if a pen and a pan lie side by side on the table, I must either make my gesture more specific or my pronunciation of [pɛn] clearly distinct from [pæn]. This is another way of saying that [ɛ] and [æ] are separate English phonemes, and that the basic standard of English requires that they be kept distinct. Other languages have other conventions: the contrast between *pen* and *pan* is meaningless in Italian; the German contrast between *Bruder* and *Brüder* is meaningless in English.

The uniformity required for communication varies greatly. Spelling is more uniform than pronunciation. To avoid the charge of illiteracy I must use only one spelling for *address*, but I have my choice of pronunciations. I have only one way of acceptably spelling *oranges*, but I may expect to hear as many as eighteen different pronunciations of the word.

British and American spelling, though identical for most words, differs in the contrast between British *labour* and *analyse* and American *labor* and *analyze*. British and American terminology, though the same for many items, sometimes differs, especially in the technical terms which have developed in the nineteenth and twentieth centuries since the political tie was cut: British *lorry* and American *truck*, British *valve* for a *wireless* set and American *tube* for a *radio* set.

Within the limits of a single language the phonemic pattern may also vary from place to place. The pronunciation [lɑst] means *last* to a Londoner, but *lost* to a Pittsburgher; [la:f] means *laugh* in Boston, but *life* in Mobile. To the extent that different areas of the English-speaking world have different phonemic patterns, they may be said to have different standards of pronunciation.

Whether consciously or not, the vast majority of the inhabitants of those areas recognize their own basic standard and the social gradations inherent within it. Whether they speak well or badly, they are unconsciously affected by the existence of their own standard. The stranger who speaks according to a different standard will be, at least, noticeable; at most, difficult to understand.

These basic standards are not sets of rules imposed by schoolmasters, social leaders, or dictionary makers; they are part of the social context of each linguistic area. The New Yorker recognizes the Bostonian as a person who speaks differently. The Iowan who converses with an Alabaman is aware of the manner as well as the content of the other's speech. In his own judgment the linguistically naïve person speaks English; the other person speaks a dialect. Such simplicity may be found either among the untutored or among the superficially sophisticated who have cultivated artificial standards.

The truly sophisticated person recognizes that it is normal for the Bostonian, the Iowan, the New Yorker, and the Alabaman to speak each according to his own standard. He makes this observation without developing any undue sense of either superiority or inferiority in his own speech. With a little further acquaintance he may come to the conclusion that some Bostonians, some New Yorkers, some Iowans, and some Alabamans speak better than he does; others, not as well. No one area has a monopoly on "correctness."

On this natural social basis rests the justification for the regional classifications outlined in the three preceding chapters. Eastern New England, New York City, the South, and the North Central area clearly speak according to different conventions, different phonemic patterns, different standards. Although some of the other areas are less clearly defined, and more transitional in nature, each has a subtle unity which binds it together, and a large enough population to give it more than local standing. The New York City area, geographically the smallest, has a population verging on ten million. Most of the other areas have larger populations.

Within each of the regional areas we may distinguish various levels of speech. In civilized countries the basic requirement of efficient communication is not enough; conventions of good breeding develop in speech, as in other aspects of social life. These conventions are, of course, less fundamental than those which serve the needs of basic communication, and which distinguish one area from another. They are accepted more self-consciously and with less approximation to unanimity. Arguments about the differences between Southern and North Central speech can be settled more readily than those about the differences between standard and substandard Southern, or between standard and substandard North Central speech.

In many ways good speech requires slow growth. The person with substandard speech and a substandard social background who attempts to remedy both deficiencies with a veneer of "cultured" speech, or the person who tries to find a shortcut to elegance through some dialect supposedly superior to his own, is likely to create more smiles than admiration.

Most of us are armchair critics of radio and television, and we score points for ourselves when we catch an announcer or master of ceremonies saying, "Ladies and gemmun," or "Congrajulations!" But some of us, carried away by our enthusiasms, go so far as to maintain stoutly that there must be three syllables in each of such words as *history*, *restaurant*, and *chocolate*. The purist may be just as wrong as the sloppy speaker; he's merely wrong in a different way. Good usage suggests the avoidance of both extremes.

## Improve by Listening

What then can the seeker after speech improvement do? First, he must listen. If he lives in his native speech area he will know the regional type on one level or another. His problem then is to bring his speech into conformity with the upper rather than with the lower levels. He must listen to those whose positions in the community seem assured, and who give evidence of breeding and good taste. He must listen to himself, preferably on a recording of some kind, since only on tape or a disc can he hear himself objectively, as others hear him.

If he is a native of some other American speech area he will have to acclimatize himself to the new area before seeking out his models. Or he will have to decide that he is proud to be a Texan or a Vermonter and decide to keep on as he is. Too many people are ashamed of being natives of Portland, Maine, or Portland, Oregon, of North Dakota or North Carolina. Pride in one's native background can be an asset; one does not need to become a faceless figure in a crowd.

If he is a foreigner, even an English-speaking foreigner, he may need help with basic American speech habits before he attempts to acclimatize himself to any particular American area or begins to look for acceptable models. Again his pride of origin may make him wish to keep some trace of the north of England or the south of France in his speech. But if he wishes to Americanize his speech, he must play the sedulous ape to the speech which commands respect around him, not to some vague universal standard which exists only in his own imagination.

## Dictionaries

Secondly, he can make use of dictionaries. Here, however, he must be cautious. He must ask himself the source of the dictionary's authority and the extent of the authority it claims for itself. There are dictionaries and dictionaries. In the best will be found somewhat more modest claims than you might suppose, more modest claims than the advertisements for those dictionaries might sometimes lead you to expect.[1] Dictionaries do not determine usage; they record it. Usage does not acquire its authority from any dictionary. On the contrary, a dictionary is authoritative to the extent that it faithfully and accurately reflects current usage.

Dictionaries differ in scope. For example, Jones's *English Pronouncing Dictionary* records the usage of some of the inhabitants of the south of England and of those who, in other parts of the world, speak according to a similar convention. Jones's dictionary is therefore useful, extremely useful, if we wish to find out what pronunciations are current in the south of England. It is of no use whatever if we wish to find out what pronunciations are current in the north of England, in Ireland, South Africa, Canada, New York, or California. The Kenyon-Knott *Pronouncing Dictionary of American English* records the usage of three

---

[1] See the "Guide to Pronunciation" in *Webster's New International Dictionary* (2d ed.; Springfield, Mass.: G. & C. Merriam Co., 1934; the section on pronunciation in Funk & Wagnall's *New College Standard Dictionary* (New York: Funk & Wagnalls Co., 1947); the preface to John S. Kenyon and Thomas A. Knott, *A Pronouncing Dictionary of American English* (Springfield, Mass.: G. & C. Merriam Co., 1944); the preface to the *Thorndike-Barnhart Comprehensive Desk Dictionary* (Garden City, N. Y.: Doubleday & Co., Inc., 1951); and the preface to Daniel Jones, *Everyman's English Pronouncing Dictionary* (11th ed.; New York: E. P. Dutton & Co., Inc., 1956). See also the section on dictionaries in Albert H. Marckwardt, *Introduction to the English Language* (New York: Oxford University Press, 1942), pp. 69–76; Thomas A. Knott, "How the Dictionary Determines What Pronunciations to Use," *Quarterly Journal of Speech*, XXI (1935), 1–10; George P. Wilson, "American Dictionaries and Pronunciation," *American Speech*, XIII (1938), 243–54; C. K. Thomas, "American Dictionaries and Variant Pronunciations," *American Speech*, XIV (1939), 175–80; and James B. McMillan, "Five College Dictionaries," *College English*, X (1949), 214–21.

American types of speech, but does not always give a clear picture of the types current in New York City or any of the Midland areas.

In short, you must judge the authority of a dictionary by determining what it sets out to do, and by its success in reaching its goal. What it sets out to do can be learned by studying the preface rather than the advertisements. Its success in reaching its goal can be measured by comparison with the speech which you hear around you if the particular dictionary considers that type of speech at all.

Generally speaking, no dictionary should be used as the authority for the pronunciation of common words; the true authority lies in the speech around you. Webster's *New International*, for example, uses different symbols for the vowels of *damp* and *dance*. Do not therefore make the mistake of assuming that if you use the same vowel in *dance* as in *damp* you are speaking "incorrectly". A glance at Webster's "Guide to Pronunciation" will inform you that some people in some areas distinguish the vowel of *dance* from that of *damp*, and that others make no such distinction. The dictionary's function is to keep the categories straight, not to compel you to forsake the established usage of your community.

The naïve American who pronounces *schedule* [ˈʃɛdjul] after looking up the word in Jones's dictionary is merely substituting a fragment of Jones's dialect for a fragment of his own, and has obviously not taken Jones's preface to heart. The American who wishes to know how an educated Londoner might pronounce *schedule*, or *dance*, or the English place-name *Cirencester*, can use the dictionary intelligently and profitably.

For unfamiliar words, on the other hand, the dictionary can be used more freely. It is simpler to look up *campanula* in *Webster's New Collegiate Dictionary* or the *Thorndike-Barnhart*

*Comprehensive Desk Dictionary* than to hunt up a convention of botanists, simpler to look up *lycanthropy* than to hunt up the psychiatrists or the students of folklore. For many unfamiliar words, indeed, we do not know whether to ask the botanists or the psychiatrists, and in any case they may not be handy. The dictionary serves our purpose and, for general information, serves it well. Such unfamiliar words cannot be said to have a common pronunciation, since they are not in common use. The dictionary therefore serves the useful purpose of letting the general public know what the botanist, the psychiatrist, and the boilermaker mean when they use technical terms, as well as how they pronounce them. For the common words which make up all but a minute fraction of our daily discourse, a trained and understanding ear is better than a shelf full of dictionaries.

The acquisition of good speech is part of the individual's adaptation to his social environment. Some types of speech mark the speaker as inferior. Unless he gives unmistakeable evidence of superiority in other respects, some opportunities will be closed to him. The traditional American goal of rising in the world can rarely be achieved by speech improvement alone, but speech improvement often helps. Not all of us will become great public speakers, great actors, or great preachers. But most of us can adapt our speech to what the community accepts as normal, and be accepted as normal by our neighbors.

# Bibliography

ABEL, JAMES W. "The Phonetic Context of [ɔɪ]," *Speech Monographs,* Vol. XX (1953), pp. 247–52.

AHREND, EVELYN R. "Ontario Speech," *American Speech,* IX (1934), 136–39.

AIKEN, JANET R. *Why English Sounds Change.* New York: The Ronald Press Co., 1929.

AIKIN W. A. *The Voice.* (2nd ed.) New York: Longmans, Green & Co., Inc., 1910.

ALEXANDER, HENRY. "American English," *Queen's Quarterly,* XLIV (1937), 169–75.

——. "Soiving the Ersters," *American Speech,* I (1926), 294–95.

AYEARST, MORLEY. "A Note on Canadian Speech," *American Speech,* XIV (1939), 231–33.

AYRES, HARRY MORGAN. "Bermudian English," *American Speech,* VIII (1933), 1–10.

——. "England's English—and America's," *Current History,* XXXVI (1932), 702–6.

BARROWS, SARAH T. "Watch, Water, Wash," *American Speech,* IV (1929), 301–2.

BERREY, LESTER V. "Southern Mountain Dialect," *American Speech,* XV (1940), 45–54.

BLACK, JOHN W., and MOORE, WILBUR E. *Speech: Code, Meaning, and Communication.* New York: McGraw-Hill Book Co., Inc., 1955.

BLOCH, BERNARD, and TRAGER, GEORGE L. *Outline of Linguistic Analysis.* Baltimore: Linguistic Society of America, 1942.

BLOOMFIELD, LEONARD. *Language.* New York, Henry Holt & Co., Inc., 1933.

——. "The Stressed Vowels of American English," *Language,* XI (1935), 97–116.

BRONSTEIN, ARTHUR J. "Nineteenth-Century Attitudes towards Pronunciation," *Quarterly Journal of Speech,* XL (1954), 417–21.

——. "Trends in American Pronunciation." *Quarterly Journal of Speech,* XXVIII (1942), 452–56.

261

262    PHONETICS OF AMERICAN ENGLISH

BRONSTEIN, ARTHUR J. "The Vowels and Diphthongs of the Nineteenth Century." *Speech Monographs*, Vol. XVI (1949), pp. 227–42.

––––––– and SHELDON, ESTHER K. "Derivatives of Middle English ō in Eighteenth- and Nineteenth-Century Dictionaries," *American Speech*, XXVI (1951), 81–89.

BROOKS, CLEANTH. *The Relation of the Alabama-Georgia Dialect to the Provincial Dialect of Great Britain*. Baton Rouge: Louisiana State University Press, 1935.

CAFFEE, NATHANIEL M. "The Phonemic Structure of Unstressed Vowels in English," *American Speech*, XXVI (1951), 103–9.

CARNOY, ALBERT J. "The Real Nature of Dissimilation," *Transactions of the American Philological Association*, Vol. XLIX (1918), pp. 101–13.

CARPENTER, CHARLES. "Variation in the Southern Mountain Dialect," *American Speech*, VIII (1933), 22–25.

CARROLL, JOHN B. *The Study of Language*. Cambridge: Harvard University Press, 1953.

CROWNINGSHIELD, GERALD. "Dialect of Northeastern New York," *American Speech*, VIII (1933), No. 2, 43–45.

CURRY, ROBERT. *The Mechanism of the Human Voice*. New York, Longmans, Green & Co., Inc., 1940.

DAVIS, ALVA L., and McDAVID, RAVEN I. "Northwestern Ohio: A Transition Area," *Language*, XXVI (1950), 264–73.

DeCAMP, L. SPRAGUE. "Scranton Pronunciation," *American Speech*, XV (1940), 368–71.

DODDS, GEORGE, and LICKLEY, J. D. *The Control of the Breath*. Oxford: Oxford University Press, 1925.

ELIASON, NORMAN E. "The Short Vowels in French Loan Words like City." *Anglia*, Vol. 63 (1939), pp. 73–87.

–––––––. *Tarheel Talk*. Chapel Hill: University of North Carolina Press, 1956.

EMSLEY, BERT, THOMAS, CHARLES K., and SIFRITT, CLAUDE. "Phonetics and Pronunciation." *History of Speech Education in America*, ed. Karl R. Wallace. New York: Appleton-Century-Crofts, Inc., 1954

FLETCHER, HARVEY. *Speech and Hearing*. New York, D. Van Nostrand Co., Inc., 1929.

FRIES, CHARLES C. "Implications of Modern Linguistic Science," *Quarterly Journal of Speech*, XXXIII (1947), 321–27.

–––––––. *Teaching and Learning English as a Foreign Language*. Ann Arbor: University of Michigan Press, 1945.

GLEASON, H. A. *An Introduction to Descriptive Linguistics*. New York: Henry Holt and Co., Inc., 1955.

GRAHAM, IAN CHARLES CARGILL. *Colonists from Scotland*. Ithaca: Cornell University Press, 1956.

GRANDGENT, CHARLES H. "From Franklin to Lowell. A Century of New England Pronunciation," *Publications of the Modern Language Association*, XIV (1899), 207.

GRANDGENT, CHARLES H. *Old and New*. Cambridge: Harvard University Press, 1920. The following articles: "The Dog's Letter," "Fashion and the Broad A," "New England Pronunciation."

GREET, W. C. "Delmarva Speech," *American Speech*, VIII (1933), No. 4, 57–63.

———. "A Phonographic Expedition to Williamsburgh, Virginia," *American Speech*, VI (1931), 161–72.

———. "A Record from Lubec, Maine, and Remarks on the Coastal Type," *American Speech*, VI (1931), 397–403.

———. "Southern Speech." *Culture in the South*, ed. W. T. Couch. Chapel Hill: University of North Carolina Press, 1934. Pp. 594–615.

———. "A Standard American Language?" *New Republic*, XCV (1938), 68–70.

HALL, JOSEPH S. "The Phonetics of Great Smoky Mountain Speech," *American Speech*, XVII (1942), Sec. 2 of April issue.

HALL, ROBERT A., JR. *Leave Your Language Alone*. Ithaca: Linguistica, 1950.

HALLE, MORRIS, *et al. For Roman Jakobson*. The Hague: Mouton & Co., 1956.

HANLEY, MILES L. "Observations on the Broad A," *Dialect Notes*, V (1925), 347–50.

———. "The Texas L," *Dialect Notes*, V (1923), 247.

HEFFNER, R-M. S. *General Phonetics*. Madison: University of Wisconsin Press, 1949.

HEMPL, GEORGE. "*Grease* and *Greasy*," *Dialect Notes*, I (1896), 438–44.

———. "Loss of *R* in English through Dissimilation," *Dialect Notes*, I (1893), 279–81.

HOCKETT, CHARLES F. "How to Learn Martian," *Astounding Science Fiction*, LV (1955), 97–106.

———. *A Manual of Phonology*. Bloomington: Department of Anthropology, University of Indiana, 1955.

HOUSEHOLDER, FRED W., JR. "Unreleased ptk in American English." *For Roman Jakobson*, ed. Halle. The Hague: Mouton & Co., 1956. Pp. 235–44.

HUBBELL, ALLAN F. "'Curl' and 'Coil' in New York City," *American Speech*, XV (1940), 372–76.

———. *The Pronunciation of English in New York City*. New York: King's Crown Press, 1950.

IVES, SUMMER. "Pronunciation of 'Can't' in the Eastern States," *American Speech*, XXVIII (1953), 149–57.

JONES, DANIEL. *An English Pronouncing Dictionary*, 11th ed. New York: E. P. Dutton & Co., Inc., 1956.

———. *An Outline of English Phonetics*, 8th ed. New York: E. P. Dutton & Co., Inc., 1956.

———. *The Phoneme: Its Nature and Use*. Cambridge, Eng.: W. Heffer & Sons, Ltd., 1950.

JONES DANIEL. *The Pronunciation of English*, 3d ed. Cambridge, Eng.: Cambridge University Press, 1950.

JOOS, MARTIN. *Acoustic Phonetics*. Language Monograph No. 23. Baltimore: Linguistic Society of America, 1948.

JUDSON L. S., and WEAVER, A. T. *Voice Science*. New York: Appelton-Century Crofts, Inc., 1942.

KEITH, ARTHUR. "The Mechanism of Respiration in Man." *Further Advances in Physiology*, ed. Leonard Hill. New York: Longmans, Green & Co., Inc., 1909.

KENT, ROLAND G. "Assimilation and Dissimilation," *Language*, XII (1936), 245–58.

KENYON, ELMER L. "Action and Control of the Peripheral Organs of Speech," *Journal of the American Medical Association*, XCI (1928), 1341–46.

KENYON, JOHN S. *American Pronunciation*, 10th ed. Ann Arbor: George Wahr, 1950.

———. "Flat A and Broad A," *American Speech*, V (1930), 323–26.

———. "Some Notes on American R," *American Speech*, I (1926), 329–39.

———. "Syllabic Consonants in Dictionaries," *American Speech*, XXXI (1956), 243–51.

——— and KNOTT, THOMAS A. *A Pronouncing Dictionary of American English*. Springfield, mass.: G. C. Merriam Co., 1944.

KNOTT, THOMAS A. "How the Dictionary Determines What Pronunciations to Use," *Quarterly Journal of Speech*, XXI (1935), 1–10.

KÖKERITZ, HELGE. *Shakespeare's Pronunciation*. New Haven: Yale University Press, 1953.

KRAPP, GEORGE PHILIP. *The English Language in America*. New York: The Century Co., 1925.

———. *The Pronunciation of Standard English in America*. New York: Oxford University Press, 1919.

KURATH, HANS. *American Pronunciation* (SPE Tract No. 30). New York: Oxford University Press, 1928.

———. "Dialect Areas, Settlement Areas, and Culture Areas in the United States." *The Cultural Approach to History*, ed. Caroline F. Ware. New York: Columbia University Press, 1940.

———. *Handbook of the Linguistic Geography of New England*. Providence: Brown University, 1939.

———. "The Origin of the Dialectal Differences in Spoken American English," *Modern Philology*, XXV (1928), 385–95.

———. *A Word Geography of the Eastern United States*. Ann Arbor: University of Michigan Press, 1949.

LOTSPEICH, C. M. "The Cause of Long Vowel Changes in English," *Journal of English and Germanic Philology*, XX (1921), 208–12.

LOWMAN, GUY S. "The Treatment of au in Virginia." *Proceedings of the Second International Congress of Phonetic Sciences*, Cambridge, England, 1936. Pp. 122–25.

LUCIANI, LUIGI. *Human Physiology.* 5 vols. London: Macmillan & Co., Ltd., 1911–1921.

MCDAVID, RAVEN I., JR. "Low-Back Vowels in the South Carolina Piedmont," *American Speech*, XV (1940), 144–48.

———. "Postvocalic /–r/ in South Carolina," *American Speech*, XXIII (1948), 194–203.

——— and MCDAVID, VIRGINIA GLENN. "*h* before Semivowels in the Eastern United States," *Language*, XXVIII (1952), 41–62.

MCMILLAN. "Five College Dictionaries," *College English*, X (1949), 214–21.

MARCKWARDT, ALBERT H. "Middle English *ŏ* in American English of the Great Lakes Area." *Papers of the Michigan Academy of Science, Art, and Letters*, Vol. XXVI (1940), pp. 561–71.

———. "Middle English *WA* in the Speech of the Great Lakes Region," *American Speech*, XVII (1942), 226–34.

———. "Phonemic Structure and Aural Perception," *American Speech*, XXI (1946), 106–11.

MATTHEWS, WILLIAM. "Two Notes on Seventeenth Century Pronunciations," *Journal of English and Germanic Philology*, XXXII (1933), 296–300.

MILLER, DAYTON C. *The Science of Musical Sounds.* New York: The Macmillan Co., 1916.

MILLER, VIRGINIA R. "Present-Day Use of the Broad A in Eastern Massachusetts," *Speech Monographs*, Vol. XX (1953), pp. 235–46.

NEGUS, V. E. *The Mechanism of the Larynx.* St. Louis: The C. V. Mosby Co., 1929.

ODUM, HOWARD W., and MOORE, H. E. *American Regionalism.* New York: Henry Holt & Co., Inc., 1938.

ORBECK, ANDERS. *Early New England Pronunciation.* Ann Arbor: George Wahr, 1927.

PENZL, HERBERT. "Der [r]-Einschub nach me. *ă* in Neu-England," *Anglia*, LXI (1937), 81–92.

———. "Relics with 'Broad A' in New England Speech," *American Speech*, XIII (1938), 45–49.

———. "The Vowel in *rather* in New England." *Publications of the Modern Language Association*, LIII (1938), 1186–92.

———. "The Vowel-Phonemes in *Father, Man, Dance* in Dictionaries and New England Speech," *Journal of English and Germanic Philology*, XXXIX (1940), 13–32.

PIKE, KENNETH L. "On the Phonemic Status of English Diphthongs," *Language*, XXIII (1947), 151–59.

———. *Phonemics.* Ann Arbor: University of Michigan Press, 1947.

———. *Phonetics.* Ann Arbor: University of Michigan Press, 1943.

POTTER, RALPH K., KOPP, GEORGE A., and GREEN, HARRIET C. *Visible Speech.* New York: D. Van Nostrand Co., Inc., 1947.

RANDOLPH, VANCE, and INGLEMANN, ANNA A. "Pronunciation in the Ozark Dialect," *American Speech*, III (1928), 401–8.

READ, WILLIAM A. "Some Phases of American Pronunciation," *Journal of English and Germanic Philology*, XXII (1923), 217–44.

———. "The Vowel System of the Southern United States." *Englische Studien*, Vol. XLI, pp. 70–78.

REED, CARROLL E. "The Pronunciation of English in the State of Washington," *American Speech*, XXVII (1952), 186–89.

REED, DAVID W., and SPICER, JOHN L. "Correlation Methods of Comparing Idiolects in a Transition Area," *Language*, XXVIII (1952), 348–59.

ROBERTSON, STUART. *The Development of Modern English.* 2d ed. rev. Frederic G. Cassidy. Englewood Cliffs, N. J.: Prentice-Hall, Inc., 1954.

SAPIR, EDWARD. *Language.* New York: Harcourt, Brace & Co., Inc., 1921.

———. "Notes on Judeo-German Phonology," *Jewish Quarterly Review*, n. s., VI (1915), 231–66.

SHEWMAKE, EDWIN F. *English Pronunciation in Virginia.* Privately printed, 1927.

———. "Laws of Pronunciation in Eastern Virginia," *Modern Language Notes*, XL (1925), 489–92.

STANLEY, OMA. "The Speech of East Texas," *American Speech*, XI (1936), 3–36, 145–66, 232–51, 327–55.

STARLING, E. H. *Principles of Human Physiology.* 2d ed. Philadelphia: Lea & Febiger, 1915.

STRONG, LOIS. "Voyelles et Consonnes de New-York," *Revue de Phonétique*, V (1928), 70–107.

SWADESH, MORRIS. "Phonemic Contrasts," *American Speech*, XI (1936), 298–301.

———. "The Phonemic Interpretation of Long Consonants," *Language*, XIII (1937), 1–10.

———. "The Phonemic Principle," *Language*, X (1934), 117–29.

———. "Some Minimally Different Word-Pairs," *American Speech*, XII (1937), 127.

THOMAS, C. K. "American Dictionaries and Variant Pronunciations," *American Speech*, VII (1932), 321–26.

———. "The Dialectal Significance of the Non-Phonemic Low-Back Vowel Variants before R." *Studies in Speech and Drama in Honor of Alexander M. Drummond.* Ithaca: Cornell University Press, 1944. Pp. 244–54.

———. "The Foreigner's English," *The Speech Teacher*, II (1953), pp. 161–65.

———. "Jewish Dialect and New York Dialect," *American Speech*, VII (1932), 321–26.

———. "Notes on the Pronunciation of 'Hurry'," *American Speech*, XXI (1946), 112–15.

———. "Notes on the Pronunciation of 'On'," *American Speech*, XXII (1947), 104–7.

———. "The Place of New York City in American Linguistic Geography," *Quarterly Journal of Speech*, XXXIII (1947), 314–20.

———. "Pronunciation in Downstate New York," *American Speech*, XVII (1942), 30–41, 149–57.

THOMAS, C. K. "Pronunciation in Upstate New York," *American Speech* X (1935), 107–12, 208–12, 292–97; XI (1936), 68–77, 142–44, 307–13; XII (1937), 122–27.

————. "Recent Discussions of Standardization in American Pronunciation," *Quarterly Journal of Speech*, XIII (1927), 442–57.

————. "The Sound of US1," *Town & Country Magazine*, January, 1955.

————. "You, Too, Speak a Dialect," *Town & Country Magazine*, November, 1955.

TRAGER, GEORGE L. "Pronunciation of 'Short A' in American Standard English," *American Speech*, V (1930), 396–400.

————. "What Conditions Limit Variation of a Phoneme," *American Speech*, IX (1934), 313–15.

———— and BLOCH, BERNARD. "The Syllabic Phonemes of English," *Language*, XVII (1941), 223–46.

———— and SMITH, HENRY LEE. *An Outline of English Structure.* Studies in Linguistics, occasional papers No. 3. Norman, Okla., 1951.

TRESIDDER, ARGUS. "The Sounds of Virginia Speech," *American Speech*, XVIII (1943), 261–72.

————. "The Speech of the Shenandoah Valley," *American Speech*, XII (1937), 284–88.

TWADDELL, W. F. *On Defining the Phoneme.* Language Monograph No. 16. Baltimore: Linguistic Society of America, 1935.

WATSON, F. R. *Sound.* New York: John Wiley & Sons, Inc., 1935.

WHEATLEY, KATHERINE E. "Southern Standards," *American Speech*, IX (1934), 36–45.

WHORF, BENJAMIN L. *Language, Thought, and Reality*, ed. John B. Carroll. Cambridge, Technology Press, and New York, John Wiley & Sons, Inc., 1956.

WISE, C. M. "Southern American Dialect," *American Speech*, VIII (1933), No. 2, 37–43.

# Index

adjectives, 67
affricates, 108–9
Afghans, 70
allophones, 5, 43–44, 51–53, 56, 59,
    61, 63, 72–74, 90, 94, 110, 116–
    18, 120–21
alphabet, 8–9
alveolar consonants, 47–52, 55–57, 59
American English, 38, 47, 49, 51, 57–
    58, 72–75, 89, 91, 93–97, 100,
    115, 118, 120, 126, 148–49, 174,
    195, 206, 213, 222, 254
aspirate, 43, 48, 49, 58, 157
assimilation, 68, 169–80, 185

back vowels, 36, 90–91, 110–12,
    124–29
bilabial consonants, 43–45, 59, 69
British English, 47, 86–89, 111, 115–
    16, 120, 126, 132, 139, 149, 173,
    174, 192, 201–2, 205, 209, 213,
    254
broad *a*, 201–2, 220

central vowels, 36, 63, 94–97
charts, diagrams, figures, maps, 15,
    16, 17, 20, 24, 25, 59, 80, 122,
    128, 140, 153, 158, 159, 188, 232
children, 56, 57, 79, 84
Chinese, 70, 109
classification
    of consonants, 33–35
    of sounds, 32–38
    of vowels, 36–38
clear [l], 51
Cockney, 137, 207
compounds, 149–50

Connecticut valley, 192, 216
consonants
    [b], 34, 44–45, 47, 63, 58, 59
    [ç], 138, 185
    [d], 35, 49, 58, 59, 66–68, 79, 86
    [dʒ], 108–9
    [f], 34, 46, 53, 59, 72
    [g], 58–59, 80–84
    [h], 72, 77, 136–39
    [hj], 138
    [hw], 138–39
    [j], 70–72, 131–34, 213, 214
    [k], 57–58
    [l], 34, 35, 50–52, 63, 101–5, 213
    [ɫ], 51, 53, 213
    [ʟ], 213
    [ʎ], 176–77
    [m], 35, 45–46, 59, 105
    [n], 34, 35, 50, 59, 101–5
    [ŋ], 80–84, 105, 222
    [ɲ], 176–77
    [p], 34, 43–44, 48, 58, 59
    [r], 34, 48, 51, 63, 70, 74, 86–89,
        93–97, 195–201
    [s], 35, 55–57, 68–69, 212–13
    [ʃ], 56, 107–8
    [t], 35, 47–49, 58, 59, 66–68, 77–79,
        86
    [tʃ], 108–9
    [θ], 48–50, 52, 56, 77–80
    [ð], 77–80
    [v], 34, 46–47
    [w], 35, 69–70, 138–39
    [ʍ], 138
    [x], 185
    [z], 57, 68–69, 212–13
    [ʒ], 108

269

manner of formation, 35
metathesis, 184
mid vowels, 36, 63, 72–75, 110–11,
   126–29
Mormon country, 119
mouth, 14, 30–31
muscular tension, 36–37, 60–64, 72,
   74, 90, 94, 110, 124
musical pitch, 5, 107

nasal passages, 14, 28–29, 45, 60, 80
nasal sounds, 45–46, 50, 60, 80–84,
   178
non-distinctive variations, 5, 73, 110–
   11, 125, 131, 139
non-syllabic sounds, 93
North, 75, 194

Ohio valley, 119–20, 192, 194, 208,
   212, 234, 236
orthography, 4
overtones, 25–26

palatal sounds, 70, 131–34, 176–77
Pennsylvania German, 47
pharynx, 14, 28
Philippine languages, 56, 83, 109
phoneme, 5, 13, 32, 34, 37, 42, 56,
   59, 61, 78, 83, 89, 109, 110–11,
   115–17, 121, 139–44, 202, 206–7,
   217, 220, 239, 254
phonemic diphthongs, 139–44
phonetics, 4–5
physics of sound, 22–27
pillars of the fauces, 29
place of articulation, 35–36, 43–52
Polish, 51
Potomac valley, 222

raised allophones, 73, 207, 209, 227,
   228, 231, 239
regional types
   Alabama, 142, 191, 225, 234, 246–
      47, 255
   Arizona, 236, 240

Arkansas, 94, 225, 236
Atlantic City, 62, 212
Baltimore, 120, 193
Boston, 111, 193, 202, 203, 221,
   229, 254, 255
California, 119, 195, 238, 240, 252,
   258
Canada, 51, 119, 141, 144, 173,
   210, 211, 231, 258
Central Midland area, 122, 194,
   199, 201, 204, 206, 209, 210–11,
   225, 235, 236–40, 250
Charleston, S. C., 73, 193, 195,
   207, 222, 225, 227, 228, 231
Cleveland, 230
Connecticut, 96, 204, 219, 229
Dakotas, 117–19, 143, 200, 230,
   238
Delaware, 142, 209, 222, 223
Delmarva peninsula, 224
District of Columbia, 222
Erie, Pa., 230
Florida, 195, 225, 240
Georgia, 94, 225, 234
Hudson, N.Y., 219
Illinois, 229
Indiana, 117
Iowa, 117, 192, 229, 236, 255
Kansas, 250
Kentucky, 234, 235
Los Angeles, 221, 240
Louisiana, 225
Maine, 94, 96, 191, 198, 217–18,
   243–44, 257
Maryland, 67, 94, 142, 209, 212,
   222, 223, 225, 233
Massachusetts, 218, 229
Miami, Fla., 195
Michigan, 73, 117, 125, 141, 143–
   44, 192, 207, 211, 229, 231
Middle Atlantic area, 111, 122,
   143, 193–94, 199–201, 204, 208–
   9, 211, 222–25, 233, 234, 245–46
Midland areas, 120, 141–43, 194,
   198–99, 209, 214, 240, 259